A COMPLETE GUIDE TO EMBROIDERY

INTRODUCTION BY
PAM DAWSON

Marshall Cavendish

Published by Marshall Cavendish Books Limited
58 Old Compton Street
London W1V 5PA

© Marshall Cavendish Limited 1972 — 83

First printed 1976
Reprinted 1977
This printing 1983

Printed in Hong Kong

ISBN (hardback edition) 0 85685 191 4
ISBN (paperback edition) 0 85685 141 8

Picture Credits:
American Museum in Britain   3.
Beta Pictures   30.
Camera Press   5, 8, 9, 23, 27, 36, 116.
Cooper Bridgeman   11.
100 Idees de Marie Claire   12.
PAF International   14, 15, 16.
Transworld   29.

Photographers: Steve Bicknell, John Carter, Alan Duns,
Melvin Grey, Peter Heinz, Tony Horth, Jeany, Peter Kibbles,
Chris Lewis, Sandra Lousada, Dick Millar, Julian Nieman,
Kjell Nilsson, Roger Phillips, Peter Pugh Cook, Iain Reid,
John Ryan, Jill Smyth, Jean Claude Volpeliere, Paul Williams.

CONTENTS

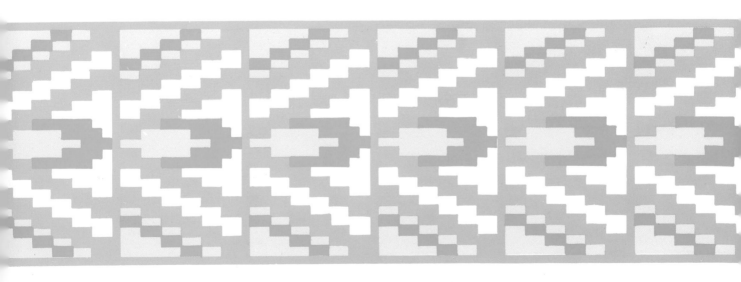

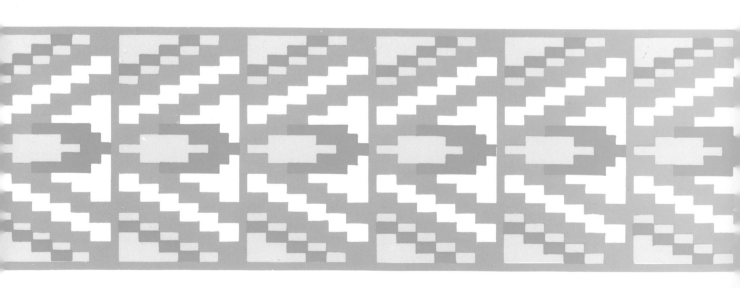

AN INTRODUCTION TO EMBROIDERY

Although I am more generally associated with knitting and crochet and cannot claim to be a specialist in any other field, I have always strongly believed that one must have an overall interest in all crafts, in order to explore the full possibilities of any particular field. The structure and embellishment of different types of fabric may point the way to a new approach in almost any craft, and embroidery, in particular, has many applications in both knitting and crochet. A knowledge of something like herringbone stitch – called casing stitch in knitting terms – is essential for some stages in making up garments, and simple embroidery stitches look most effective when worked on a knitted background.

Before primitive man had even learned to cure skins or weave and knot fabrics, he had already begun the search for some way to distinguish himself from the animal kingdom and proclaim his creative ability. Body painting was, and still is in some remote parts, a form of art which satisfied this need. Once the human race began to clothe itself, this creative urge was so strong that it was not sufficient to make a warm and protective covering, and ways of displaying wealth and individuality had to be devised as a form of decoration.

The art of embroidering with a needle had already reached a high standard in Old Testament days and has since formed a part of the cultural development of almost every nation in the world. Embroidery has evolved into many different forms and the overall names of some of these categories have a ring of grandeur about them. Groups of stitches which comprise Hardanger, Hedebo and Assisi techniques all evoke memories of past glory and history.

Some stitches, such as cross stitch and chain stitch, are so simple that a child can easily master them. Others are so complex that even a small example could eventually become a prized heirloom. The Victorians had a passion for exquisite embroidery and their method of perfecting as many stitches as possible could well be adopted today. A child would be encouraged to begin a sampler of stitches, which would be continued throughout adult life to form a unique and lasting record of achievement. Another popular form of sampler for a child to undertake would be worked entirely in cross stitch, to build up a series of pictures and quotations, mostly biblical, and proudly completed with a signature and date.

Although I have experimented with embroidery in the past, I must class myself as a beginner. Many of the simple stitches, such as lazy-daisy, cross stitches, French knots, smocking and back stitch, all play a part in the formation of knitted and crochet designs, so I am familiar with these. I have also enjoyed simple canvas work and have even tried my hand at drawn thread work. Despite an interest in more advanced techniques, such as quilting and cut work, I have been prevented from exploring these more fully because I have never been able to find a reference book which did not assume that I was already familiar with these methods.

In introducing this book, I have greatly enriched my own knowledge of this craft and I intend to try and develop my meagre skills. I find the clear and concise instructions, and simple illustrations of the working methods, very easy to follow and the text is presented in a logical way, which means you can begin with something quite simple but effective, before progressing to more difficult examples. With the aid of this book, I hope that you and I together can extend our knowledge, and explore the possibilities which this craft has to offer.

Pam Dawson

BASIC SKILLS
EQUIPMENT

The basic tools of the embroideress are simple: a pair of good embroidery scissors with fine points; a pair of paper-cutting scissors or blunt, older scissors for making a design of cut paper shapes – embroidery scissors should never be used to cut paper; a thimble; assorted needles, i.e. crewels, betweens, sharps, tapestry, a large chenille needle or a thick needle such as is used in the making-up of heavy wool garments and called a 'stiletto', used to take heavy threads through to the back of your work by means of a sling for certain embroidery methods. However, the correct needle choice for each method of work is given in the relevant chapter. Other essentials are beeswax for waxing thread, necessary for some methods of embroidery; a piece of tailor's chalk or a white dressmaking pencil for use on darker materials; tacking cotton; pins, embroidery threads; and a frame to hold the fabric firm as you work.

Embroidery fabrics

There are many fabrics for embroidery, providing a constant source of inspiration for both beginner and expert.

Linen is a favourite choice and is woven in many weights and colours and in both even-weave and coarser textures. Suitable cotton materials include dress fabrics, poplin, organdie, gingham, cotton satin and glazed cotton. Woollen fabrics are suitable for many stitches, particularly even-weave wool, flannel and wool tweeds, both in light and heavy weights. There is also silk in all its varying weights. and textures, from thin Chinese silk to wild silk and the heavier silk tweeds. Many man-made furnishing fabrics make excellent backgrounds for stitchery and make the choice for the embroideress even wider. A comprehensive chart to guide you in your choice of fabrics, threads and needles is included later.

Embroidery frames

For a really professional finish in embroidery, a frame is essential. This holds the fabric taut while you are working and helps you to form the stitches evenly and accurately as you go along.

Before starting work, oversew the edges of the fabric. This will prevent the edges fraying once the fabric has been placed in the frame.

Types of embroidery frame

There are two main types of embroidery frame, the round, or tambour, frame which is used for small pieces of work with surface or counted embroidery, and the traditional slate frame which is used for large pieces of embroidery.

Round frames

These are available in different sizes from 7.5cm–30.5cm (3 inch–12 inch) diameter and are usually made from wood, although it is sometimes possible to buy them in aluminium which holds the fabric more securely.

The frame consists of two circular hoops, one over which the fabric is stretched and another hoop, slightly larger, which fits over the first one and holds the fabric in place. This second hoop has a screw which can be adjusted to tighten or slacken the fabric as required.

To prevent the fabric from slipping through the frame when you are mounting it, it is advisable to bind the inner hoop with tape or strips of cotton fabric first. To mount the fabric, stretch the section of embroidery to be worked over the inner hoop, keeping the grain of the fabric square, press down the outer hoop and tighten the screw.

Traditional frames

Embroidery worked in this kind of frame rarely needs pressing before mounting and this is a great advantage when various methods and stitchery have been combined which might react differently to heat and damp.

The frames are available in different sizes from about 46cm–76.5cm (18 inches–30 inches), although it is possible to obtain larger ones still, often combined with a floor stand.

The frame consists of two rollers which form the top and bottom of the rectangle and two flat strips which form the side slats of the frame. The side pieces have a series of holes down their length which enables them to be fitted into the rollers – with wooden pegs or screws – at any point to make a frame of the right size for your embroidery. Each roller has a strip of tape or webbing nailed along the edge

to which the fabric is firmly sewn.

For embroidery which will not be damaged by rolling, such as petit point and some forms of canvas work, it is possible to buy frames with rotating rollers so the work can be rolled up as it progresses.

A less expensive substitute for the rectangular frame is a canvas painting stretcher, obtainable from art suppliers in various sizes. The embroidery fabric is attached to it with drawing pins, but care must be taken to ensure that enough pins are used and that the fabric is firmly pinned under tension so that it is completely taut.

Preparing a traditional frame

Preparing a traditional frame for embroidery is known as dressing the frame.

1 Assemble the frame by inserting the side pieces into the rollers at the required height and secure in place.

2 Mark the centres of the tape or webbing on both rollers with coloured thread.

3 Make a 1.3cm ($\frac{1}{2}$ inch) turning along the top and bottom edges of the fabric and hem them if the fabric is likely to fray. Mark the centre points of the edges.

4 Turn under the side edges of the fabric for 1.3cm ($\frac{1}{2}$ inch), enclosing a length of cord or string to give strength for attaching it to the side slats. Machine stitch in place.

5 Match the centre of the top edge of the fabric to the centre of the roller and pin it in position, working from the centre out to each side. Then overcast it, using strong thread.

6 Repeat on the bottom roller so that the fabric is quite taut between the two rollers.

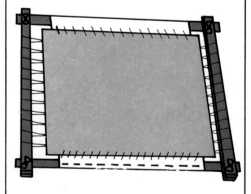

7 To secure the fabric to the side pieces, use very strong thread or fine string and a heavy needle and lace them together using a diagonal movement, placing the stitches about 2.5cm (1 inch) apart. Leave a good length of string at the ends, pull taut, then tie through the last hole at the

top and bottom of the slat.

Attaching fine fabrics

If you are mounting a very fine fabric, such as jap silk or organdie, which is likely to tear if laced, a different method of attaching the edges to the side slats should be used.

1 Using long pieces of 2cm ($\frac{3}{4}$ inch) wide tape, start at the top and pin the tape to the side edge of the fabric, placing the pin about 1.3cm ($\frac{1}{2}$ inch) from the edge.

2 Fold the tape back over the pin (to prevent it from pricking you while you work) and take it over and around the side slat. Pin it to the fabric about 2.5cm (1 inch) further down, then take it over the side slat again. Continue in this way to the bottom of the fabric and then complete the opposite side.

Backing the fabric

If you are using a variety of threads in different weights or beads for the embroidery which might be too heavy for the fabric alone, it is advisable to back the fabric to add strength. The backing can be washed linen, cotton or sheeting – unbleached calico is normally too firmly woven for this purpose.

The embroidery is worked through the double thickness and when it is finished the surplus backing fabric is cut off and trimmed back to the line of embroidery. The method of dressing a frame when using a backing is slightly different.

1 Tack a line down the centre of the backing and of the embroidery fabric. Working on a flat surface, place the fabric on to the backing, matching the centre lines. Pin in position, working out from the centre and with the pins pointing inwards to avoid puckering. Take care not to stretch either layer. Firmly tack the layers together all round the outer edge.

2 Turn under the side edges of the backing for 1.3cm ($\frac{1}{2}$ inch), enclosing a length of cord or string to give strength for attaching it to the side slats. Machine stitch in place.

3 Attach the top and bottom edges to the rollers and lace the sides to the slats as for unbacked fabrics.

Backing small pieces of embroidery

If the embroidery fabric is much smaller than the backing fabric, pin it in position on to the backing using fine pins or needles to avoid leaving marks. Overcast it by taking the needle from the embroidery fabric, and down into the backing fabric 1cm ($\frac{3}{8}$ inch) above the edge of the embroidery fabric. This pulls the fabric completely taut on the backing.

DESIGN TRANSFERS

There are three main methods of transferring embroidery designs to fabric and usually the type of design and fabric decides which method is most suitable. Whichever method you do choose, however, it is normally best to transfer the design before the fabric has been mounted into a frame because it will be difficult to keep the fabric completely flat owing to the bulk of the frame.

For all methods, start by making a tracing of your design – whether it is freely drawn, copied from an illustration or composed of cut paper shapes – using tracing or greaseproof paper and a non-smudge pencil.

Tacking

Use this method for transferring a design on to a fabric with a pile e.g. velvet.
1 Pin the tracing in place on the fabric. Using a contrasting thread and small stitches, tack along the lines of the design.

2 Remove the paper by tearing it away.

Dressmaking carbon

Use this method on fabrics with very fine and even weave, without irregular slub threads. Do not use it if the design contains any fine detail, as the prick and pounce method is the only reliable one.

The carbon paper is available in light colours for use on dark fabrics and vice versa. Simply place the carbon paper under your tracing in the correct position on the fabric and trace over the design with a sharp pencil.

Prick and pounce method

This method is the only reliable one for transferring designs with fine detail or where you are using fabric with irregular slub threads.

Basically, prick holes are made through the tracing paper along the lines of the design and the design is transferred to the fabric underneath by rubbing a mixture of 'pounce' over the paper. When the paper is removed, the design shows up on the fabric as a series of fine dots where the pounce penetrated the prick holes.

'Pounce' was originally a powder made from ground cuttlefish bone used as a wig powder in the 18th century, but nowadays it is made from powdered chalk for dark fabrics and powdered charcoal for light fabrics. A mixture of powdered chalk and charcoal is the most useful and can be obtained from wholesale drapery suppliers; alternatively you can use talcum powder.

To apply the pounce, you need a felt pad which can be made by rolling up several thicknesses of felt and securing the roll with oversewing.
1 Place the tracing paper on to a folded towel or ironing blanket to give a good base for pricking the design.
2 Use a fine needle for smooth fine fabrics or designs with a lot of detail and a larger needle for heavier fabrics. Insert the eye of the needle into a cork to make it easier to handle.
3 Go over the lines of the design, pricking it with holes 0.15cm ($\frac{1}{16}$ inch) apart on fine fabrics and 0.3cm ($\frac{1}{8}$ inch) apart on heavier ones.
4 Pin the tracing in position on the embroidery fabric. It is advisable to weight the edges of the tracing with something heavy to prevent it moving.
5 Using the felt pad, rub the pounce all over the paper. Lift off the paper carefully.
6 Paint in the lines of the design, using a fine brush and white poster paint mixed with a little blue or yellow to make the design clearer on a white or very light fabric. Water colour paint can be used instead of poster paint but it does not give as good an outline and is best for fine transparent fabrics. As you work the embroidery the paint can be flicked off with the point of a needle.

Transferring designs on to sheer fabrics

1 Trace the design on to paper using a hard pencil or waterproof ink. Check whether this shows through the fabric, and if necessary go over the design with white poster paint or a light crayon.
2 Place the fabric over the tracing and weight down to prevent it moving. Paint over the lines of the design, using a fine brush and poster or water colour paint as in the prick and pounce method.

Transferring designs to canvas

For simple designs use the tacking method, or for more complicated designs place the canvas over the tracing and trace the

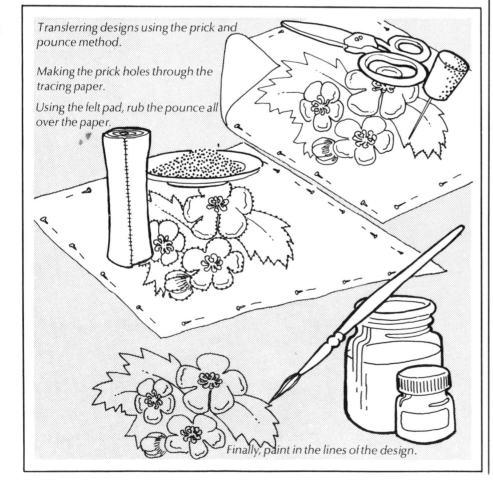

Transferring designs using the prick and pounce method.

Making the prick holes through the tracing paper.

Using the felt pad, rub the pounce all over the paper.

Finally, paint in the lines of the design.

outline with waterproof ink.

Enlarging and reducing designs

Whether you are using your own design or a pattern or illustration you have copied, you will often need to enlarge or reduce it to fit the size you need. This is easy to do if you divide the design into little squares and divide the area where you want it enlarged into the same number of squares: you will find you can easily copy each square individually and so build up the whole design. You can reduce a design in just the same way, but copying on to smaller squares.

To avoid marking the original design, and to save the bother of drawing out lots of little squares, transfer the design on to graph paper. To do this, you can either trace it direct, if the graph paper is thin enough, or use tracing paper.

Trace the design on to tracing paper.

1 Lay this over graph paper. If you can see the squares clearly through the tracing paper, stick it down with clear tape, taking care that the tracing paper lies flat. This way, you can re-use the graph paper.

2 If, however, you cannot see the squares clearly through the tracing, transfer the design to the graph paper either with carbon paper (dressmakers' carbon is fine) or by shading the back of the tracing paper with a soft pencil and drawing firmly over the design with a ballpoint.

3 Draw a rectangle to enclose the design. This will be divided into a certain number of squares by the graph paper. If you are using plain paper you must, at this stage, divide the rectangle up by marking off each side and joining up the marks to make a lot of small squares. It is helpful to number these for reference.

4 Draw, preferably on tracing paper as before, a second rectangle, to the size you want the finished design to be and in the same proportions as the first one. Do this by tracing two adjacent sides of the first rectangle and the diagonal from where they meet. Extend them as much as you need and then draw in the other sides of the second rectangle. Divide this into the same number of squares as the smaller one. A backing sheet of graph paper will make this process easier.

5 Carefully copy the design square by square. If you have to copy a flowing, curved line across several squares, mark the points at which it crosses the squares and then join them up in one flowing movement.

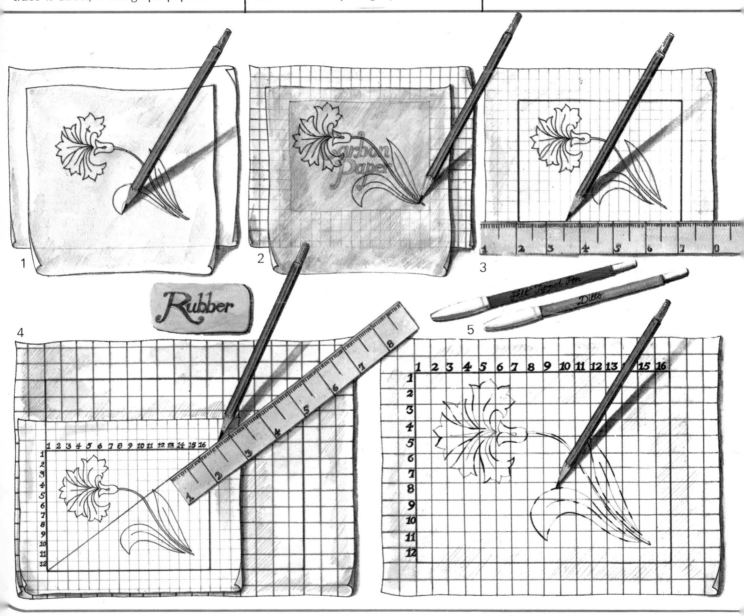

1 *Draw the design carefully onto the tracing paper.*

2 *Lay the tracing paper over the graph paper.*

3 *Draw a rectangle to enclose the design and number the squares in it.*

4 *Draw the second rectangle by tracing two sides and a diagonal from the first.*

Extend as needed.

5 *Transfer the design square by square till it is complete. Try to use one flowing movement for joining curves.*

SIMPLE STITCHES
Line and straight stitches

A knowledge of basic stitchery is the prime factor in the many methods which combine to make embroidery a creative and stimulating hobby, and it is essential if you intend to create your own individual embroideries.

Probably the simplest stitches with which to start are line or straight stitches. These are illustrated below and can be used for any of the designs illustrated using the trace patterns illustrated overleaf. A basic guide to these elementary stitches can be found in the Guide to Basic Stitches (Page 41).

Basic stitches

Running stitch
Make the stitches on the right side the same length as those on the wrong side.

Laced running stitch
This can be effective using either the same or contrasting yarn. Use a tapestry needle and thread it in and out of the running stitches without catching in the cloth. This lacing can be used with other stitches.

Back stitch
Bring the needle through to the right side of the fabric and make a small stitch backwards. Bring the needle through again a little in front of the first stitch and

make another stitch backwards to make a continuous line.

Stem stitch
Make a sloping stitch along the line of the design, and then take the needle back and bring it through again about halfway along the previous stitch.

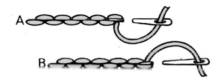

Cable stitch
Work lower stitch A on line of design, as shown; then work upper stitch B in same way with yarn above needle.

Ideas for using the motifs – brightening up a pretty nightdress.

A simple dress in a plain colour is made demurely pretty with a few motifs.

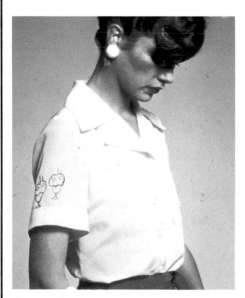

The use of an ice-cream cone motif gives this blouse a distinctive look.

Motifs to use on their own or in groups.
Trace the motifs off the page, transfer
them to the fabric, then embroider them
in pretty colours, using any of the
straight stitches illustrated.

Satin stitches

Although satin stitch is essentially a simple over-and-over stitch, skill is required to produce the beautiful satiny effect that its name implies. It is a surprisingly versatile stitch and, as it imposes no pattern of its own, is invaluable in pictures when stitches of varying lengths and shades produce illusions of distance and depth. There are several variations, one of which is padded and gives the effect of an extra dimension (see the Essential Stitches, later).

Satin stitch flower motif

This simple flower motif is a good example of the stitch when worked with long and short and split stitch. The motif below can be worked in stranded cottons on a table napkin, dress or blouse.

You will need

Stranded cotton (used with three strands in the needle) in six or seven colours. You should allow about one skein of yarn in each colour but the exact amount you use will depend on the fabric used.

The design

1 Work the motif into the corner of the napkin, placing it about 2.5cm (1 inch) from the sides.
2 The flowers of the design are worked in long and short stitch, the four upper leaves in satin stitch and the lowest leaf in split stitch. French knots (page 20) decorate the flower centres.
3 The dotted line on the trace pattern (below) indicates the meeting point for stitches and suggests the position of the leaf vein. Transfer the design by the tissue paper method.
Begin by working the leaves, stitching from the inner line towards the outer edge. Work flower colour 4 first, then colour 6, taking the stitches just into the edge of the leaves. Finally, work flower colour 5. Work each half of each leaf in turn. Make dots with a couple of small satin stitches or French knots at the centres.

▲ A beautiful example of satin stitch worked in silk for picture making.

▼ The motif worked in cotton on a linen napkin.

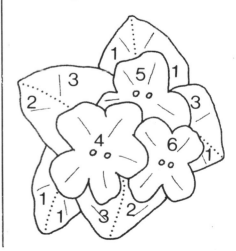

A delightful embroidery design 'Panier de Fleurs' is featured on this cushion. It is worked in wool on canvas and satin stitch is used throughout. Designed by Jean-Yves Rocher for the D.M.C. 'New Tapestry Collection'.

Guatemalan motifs

Reversible satin stitch worked in bright colours in geometric designs is a popular feature of Guatemalan peasant embroidery as shown in the poncho and bag in the photograph. A similar motif can also look effective on the flap of a clutch bag and, because it is reversible, the motif will look equally good when the bag is closed or open.

Making a clutch bag

Make the clutch bag from a rectangle of loosely woven fabric, such as coarse linen. The minimum size of fabric for the motif is 45cm (18 inches) × 23cm (9 inches).

Working the motif

Draw the motif (right) to scale and trace it on to tissue paper. Place the tracing in position on the top third of the rectangle. Tack over the lines indicating the colour areas and then pull away the paper. Start stitching each area, working from the middle outwards.

Making up

Fold up the bottom third of the rectangle with wrong sides together to form the pocket and pin the sides. Trim the edge of the flap to within 1.5cm ($\frac{1}{2}$ inch) of the stitching. Cover the turnings and raw edge of the flap with a continuous length of bias binding machine stitched on both sides

Top: Graph pattern for Guatemalan motif. Work it in bright colours for a bag.

Right: The poncho and bag embroidered with Guatemalan motifs.

Each square=2.5cm (1 in) sq

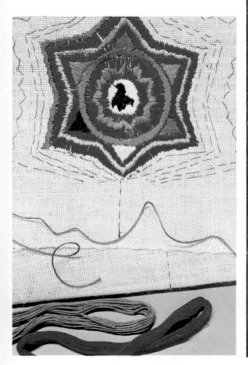

Chain stitches: continuous

Chain stitch has no single origin but can be traced to all parts of the world where ancient fabrics have been found. Chain stitch was found on basket-work from predynastic Egypt (c.350 BC), on the earliest surviving Egyptian textiles, in graves in the Crimea dating from the 4th century BC and on some old textiles in China and Japan worked during the 7th and 8th centuries AD and still extant.

The Chinese worked chain stitch using silk thread on silk in a single line technique, widening or tightening the loop with a thread of uniform thickness to produce an effect of variable depths of colour and shadow. Some of the finest examples worked with chain stitch alone, using silk thread on satin, are 18th– and 19th-century Indian garments from Kutch.

In mediaeval western Europe the grandest embroidery used more elaborate stitches and chain stitch only appeared on more humble objects. In 18th-century England chain stitch was revived and widely used, often under Chinese influence, to decorate silk coats and satin bedspreads. It appears independently in peasant work throughout the world.

Using chain stitch

Chain stitch worked in lines and curves is very versatile. The stitch can be worked large or small to give a fine or a bold outline. For a regular appearance the proportions should remain the same; as a rough guide the width should be two-thirds of the length of the stitch.

Chain stitch adapts well to tight curves and can be worked round and round to partially fill in areas.

Chain stitch

When worked, this stitch makes a chain of loops on the right side of the fabric and a line of back stitches at the back. Bring the needle through on the line of the design, loop the yarn under the point of the needle and draw the needle through. Insert the needle close to where the yarn came out. Bring the needle through a little further along the line of the design, loop the yarn under the point of the needle and draw through (see below). Continue in this way until the required length has been worked.

Suitable yarns

Small stitches worked in a thick yarn give a solid line, while larger stitches in fine yarn give an open stitch. Use these characteristics to their fullest advantage.

▲ *Working a line of chain stitch.*

Using chain stitch to brighten up the back of a plain jacket.

These designs are shown about one-third of their actual size, but they may be enlarged to the size you require.

This pretty butterfly picture would be ideal for a girl's bedspread or embroided on to a dress or apron pocket.

An appropriate design for a beach bag or beach cover-up – a colourful landscape scene with rolling waves.

Brighten up plain table mats with this simple motif. All these designs are worked in Soft Embroidery Cotton.

Any of the finer yarns previously mentioned are suitable for chain stitch but for quickly worked chain stitch use a thick embroidery yarn (such as one of those shown below) on a large weave backing.

2 ply Crewel wool: a twisted, matt wool. Use one or, more usually, several strands.

Tapestry wool: a twisted, matt, separable wool.

Twilley's Lyscordet: a twisted knitting cotton.

Mercer Crochet Cotton: a fine knitting cotton.

Sudan Wool: a twisted, matt, separable wool.

Paton's Turkey Rug Wool: a twisted, matt wool for using on rug canvas.

To work the designs

Choose your fabric – perhaps a T-shirt, cotton jacket or whatever you wish to embroider on. Enlarge the design to the required size. Transfer the design to the material in one of the ways already suggested. If you are using thick yarn you will need a chenille needle.

Follow the lines of the design with closely worked chain stitch until you have covered them.

Flower bed cushion

Fabric required

Single thread even weave linen, 26 threads per 2.5cm (1 inch), 36.5cm × 36.5cm (14 inches × 14 inches).

You will also need

☐ Soft Embroidery Cotton, 3 skeins purple, 4 skeins red, 4 skeins mauve, 5 skeins lilac, 6 skeins light green, 6 skeins dark green, 6 skeins orange.

☐ Fabric for back of cushion 36.5cm × 36.5cm (14 inches × 14 inches).

☐ Square cushion pad 35cm × 35cm (14 inches × 14 inches).

The design

1 Transfer the pattern on facing page centrally to the linen.

2 Lightly mark a square 2cm (¾ inch) in from outer edges with a transfer pencil.

3 Work the design in fairly small chain stitch, working over 2 or 3 threads to make stitches uniform in length.

4 Work around the edge of the square in chain stitch and work two more squares of chain just inside the first.

5 Make up into a cushion stitching 1.25cm (½ inch) seams.

This flower bed design is set off well by a natural-coloured background.

Trace pattern for flower bed cushion

Detached chain stitch

Although chain stitches can be used continuously this stitch can also be used individually and arranged to form flower or leaf shapes. This is known as daisy or detached chain stitch. The stitches may be worked in any size you require, but remember, if the stitches are very long they will catch easily and so are not suitable for working on articles that are used every day.

Cotton mesh

This is an embroidery fabric woven in blocks of cotton strands separated by holes through which the needle is drawn. The number of holes per centimetre (inch) vary: 6 holes per 2.5cm (6 holes per inch) have been used here and embroidery on this scale grows quickly. Penelope Binca and Panama cotton mesh are examples of this type of embroidery fabric. Cotton mesh is also available in small sizes for finer work. This fabric may be used for making cushions, table linen, chairbacks or stool tops.

After care

Wash in warm water and pure soap. Squeeze the fabric gently in the soapy water. Rinse thoroughly in warm water and squeeze gently by hand to remove excess water. Leave the fabric on a towel, lying flat, until it is half-dry. Press on the wrong side, using a moderately hot iron, working from the centre outwards until the fabric is completely dry. Alternatively the fabric may be dry cleaned.

Basic stitches

Detached chain stitch

Make a chain stitch and instead of re-inserting the needle inside the loop, make a tiny stitch over the loop to hold it in place (A). Leave a space and bring the needle out again to begin the next stitch. Work daisy stitches in the same way as for detached chain but position the stitches to form a flower shape (B).

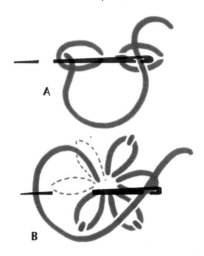

Daisy stitch cushion

The flowers are meant to be worked in a random fashion, so embroider the largest flowers first, spacing them out, and then fill the spaces in between with the smaller flowers. In the remaining spaces work the tiny four-petalled flowers and either bunches of, or single, leaves.

Fabric required

35cm (14 inch) square of cotton mesh, 6 holes per 2.5cm (1 inch)

You will also need

☐ 11 skeins of embroidery wool in 11 different colours
☐ Tapestry needle No. 18
☐ Material for back of cushion-cover, 35cm (14 inches) square
☐ Cushion pad, 32cm (13 inches) square

Working the design

1 Work the required number of flowers over the fabric leaving a 2.5cm (1 inch) border unworked. To give the edge of the cushion definition, work a border of leaves 2.5cm (1 inch) in from the edge. Vary the height of the leaves so that they frame the flowers.
Note While working with the wool it is important to twist it to the right to keep the ply tightly twisted. This gives a clean line to shapes. Work the larger flowers one at a time.
2 Leave the ends on the wrong side and sew them in neatly at the back of the work.

This colourful cushion displays a random pattern of flowers in detached chain stitch. Fabric: Penelope Binca.

3 The detached chain stitches are held in place in two ways; either by bringing the yarn over the loop through the same hole (see below) or by bringing the yarn over the

Compact detached chain stitch.

loop, over one block and through the next hole to form a stem (below).

Detached chain stitch with a stem.

To make up

1 Fold the edges of the fabric to the wrong side so that the border of leaves is right on the edge, and pin. Fold the back of the cover to the same size and shape and pin the edges to secure them. Pin the back and front together, wrong sides facing as below. Slip stitch around three edges,

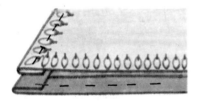

Pin with wrong sides together.

insert cushion pad and slip stitch along the fourth side. The cushion is now complete.

2 The motifs show the variety of shapes that can be worked over a similar number of squares. Each square represents the number of blocks worked over – ie, if the 'petal' covers three squares there are two holes missed between inserting and drawing out the needle. Work out the position of the motifs to form a pleasing design on the fabric.

Bright and pale colours show up well against either dark brown or cream backgrounds. The motifs may be arranged to make a pattern the same as, or similar to, the one opposite. The motifs given are only a few of the many you can work.

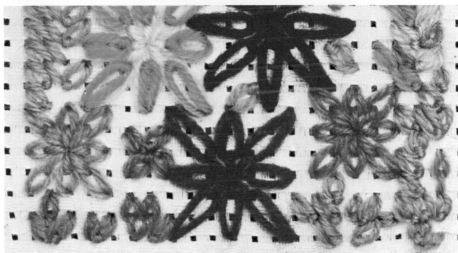

Chain stitch as a filling stitch

When using chain stitch as a filling stitch it is easiest to start off with shapes which are fairly round. With these shapes it is easier to work round and round and keep the lines of stitches close together. Once you have completed a few such shapes you will be able to tackle irregular ones.

When working a design which is filled in with closely packed stitches, choose a medium-weight dress or furnishing fabric which is comparable to the weight of the stitching. Also, to obtain the most successful results, choose a colour and texture which is suited to the design.

When filling in a shape, work the stitches around the outline of the shape, then, as you return to the starting point, bring the needle point just inside the first round of stitches so that the start of the second round is hardly visible when the work is completed (see below). Keep working round and round, completely covering the background, until the centre is reached, then bring the needle over the last loop and draw the yarn through to the back. Fasten off.

Filled chain stitch can be made to look almost three-dimensional if you start along the outline with larger chain stitches and gradually make them smaller and smaller as you progress towards the centre.

However, if you want the surface of the fabric to be completely covered with embroidery, it will be necessary to fill in the centre of the outer chain stitches with detached chain stitches.

Yarn

To use chain stitch as a filling stitch it is important to select a yarn of proportionate thickness to the weight of the fabric, which is why 6-stranded cotton is often the most appropriate. Before you start the embroidery, work a few stitches to find out how many strands you need to achieve a stitch size which is completely filled in with the yarn.

Pressing and stretching

When stitches are worked very close together the fabric sometimes becomes puckered because the tension of the stitching is too tight. Always try to maintain the same even tension.

All embroidery should be pressed on the wrong side with a warm iron to give it a finished appearance, but if the fabric is distorted it must be pressed and stretched to make it smooth.

To press the embroidery

Pad a large surface with a blanket and ironing cloth or use a well-padded ironing board. Place the fabric on the ironing cloth, wrong side uppermost, and press with a damp cloth.

To stretch the fabric

Pad a board with clean, damp blotting paper or, if blotting paper is not available, lay the fabric over several thicknesses of damp, white cotton fabric. Place the fabric on the blotting paper, right side uppermost. Fix one edge of the fabric to the board with drawing pins, aligning the horizontal strands with the edge of the board. Repeat on the opposite edge and at the sides, aligning the vertical strands with the edge of the board.

If the sides of the board are not at right angles, use graph paper or lined blotting paper to obtain accurate stretching. If using graph paper place it under the blotting paper.

To work the iris design

The contrast between the nubbly, dull linen background and the lustrous stranded cotton makes the textural effect more exciting. Note, too, how the narrow spacing between the random, horizontal lines integrates the background cloth with the embroidery; without these lines the embroidery would appear superimposed.

Size

The design enlarged to 17cm × 21.5cm ($6\frac{3}{4}$ inches × $8\frac{1}{8}$ inches).

Fabric required

A piece of natural coloured linen-look fabric, 25.5cm × 27cm (10 inches × $10\frac{1}{2}$ inches).

You will also need

☐ Stranded cotton; for flowers, 2 skeins of peacock blue and 2 skeins of natural; for leaves, 1 skein dark grey, 1 skein chestnut; for horizontal background lines, 1 skein beige; for buds, 1 skein cinnamon.
☐ 1 crewel needle.

The stitches are all worked with two strands of the stranded cotton. While working it is important to remove any kinks from the strands so that they lie side by side to give a smooth appearance.

The design as a picture

Fray the top and bottom edges of the fabric and oversew very neatly to prevent further fraying. The sides may be either frayed and oversewn or turned under and hemmed. Mount the fabric on a coloured cardboard background, leaving about 2.5cm (1 inch) border all round and set in a picture frame.

The design as a cushion

Centre the design on a piece of cloth about 32cm × 40cm (13 inches × 16 inches) and make up into a cushion 30cm × 38cm (12 inches × 15 inches).

The design on a dress

Work the design directly on to the front of a plain woollen dress.

This beautiful piece of embroidery is made up entirely of very small chain stitches, some worked round and round to make up the iris flowers and buds, others in lines to represent the leaves and the background. Yarn: Anchor Stranded Cotton. Designed by Shifrah Fram.

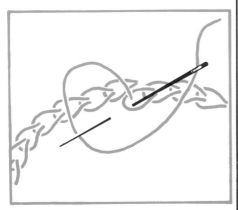

Bring the needle through just inside the first line of embroidery.

French knots and other stitches

For picture making choose a theme with bold and simple shapes. Break down the composition into stitch areas, fitting an appropriate stitch to the type of texture which will best express each part. As you gain experience, more detailed subjects may be attempted with the texture provided by a greater variety of stitches, and you will probably be able to add some invented by yourself.

Background

To start with, choose a finely woven, natural-coloured fabric. When you have become more confident you can use backgrounds which will play a part in the composition of the design with textures of the fabric as well as the stitching becoming an integral part of the picture.

Borders

If you wish to embroider a frame around a picture, choose one that is in keeping with the subject – a rose-festooned one as shown here – or a geometric border for a more modern picture. Of course, many pictures look their best when set in a plain picture frame.

Yarn quantities

For a small picture, such as the one shown, one skein of each colour is usually more than enough. However, if one colour predominates or if the stitches are very closely or thickly worked, two skeins may be needed.

Apple blossom picture

The apple blossom on the tree in the picture is superbly suggested by the use of French knots. These are also used on the girl's dress and hair band and this holds the picture together. Bold straight stitches which lie flat are used for the trellis in front of the bushes. These add a little perspective and contrast in texture.

The colours used are light to medium tones and give the whole picture a pretty, country air.

Trace the design on to tissue paper, being careful not to tear it. Lay the tissue paper over the fabric. Using sewing or tacking cotton and a fine needle, sew through the tissue paper and fabric with back or small running stitches round the outline or indicate the position of the areas to be embroidered. Tear the tissue paper away.

The stitches not hidden by the embroidery are removed when the embroidery is complete.

Fabric required

Piece of fabric 38cm (15 inches) × 30cm (12 inches)

You will also need

- ☐ 1 skein each of stranded cotton in the following colours: brown, pale pink, rose pink, light green, mid green, sage green, golden brown, white
- ☐ 1 ball pearl cotton No. 5 in two shades of brown and pale blue
- ☐ Small amount of gold lurex yarn for trellis

The design

1 Enlarge the picture to measure 33cm (13 inches) × 25cm (10 inches) – see Enlarging designs, earlier.
2 Using pearl cotton, work as follows: The girl's dress, chain stitch and stem stitch. Bark of tree and branches, stem stitch.
3 Using all strands of 6-stranded cotton, work as follows:
apple blossom, flowers under tree, girl's hairband and part of girl's dress: closely worked, loose French knots. Place some knots over the branches of the tree.
Grass and flower leaves, random straight stitches.
Background bush, feather stitch.
Foreground bush, herringbone stitch outlined with stem stitch.
Girl's hair and feet, stem stitch.
Girl's hairband, French knots.
Girl's arms, backstitch.

The trellis

Use all strands of cotton and work a lattice, couching it with the gold lurex yarn. In front of the trellis work the flowers in French knots and leaves in detached chain stitch.

The border

The border consists of herringbone in stranded cotton with stem stitch in pearl cotton on either side.
Work the rosettes in stem stitch from the outside towards the centre, and add one or two French knots at the centre. Work leaves in detached chain stitch.
To press the picture, lay it right side downwards on a well-padded ironing board, cover with a damp cloth and press it lightly. When dry mount the picture.

Basic stitches

French knots (Figure 1)

Bring the thread out at the required position, hold the thread down with the left thumb and encircle it twice with the needle as in A. Still holding the thread firmly, twist the needle back to the starting point and insert it as close as possible to where the thread first emerged. Pull the thread through to the wrong side and secure if you are working a single knot or pass to the next.

Couched lattice (Figure 2)

Lay threads along the lines of the design and, with another thread, secure the intersections down by taking a small stitch into the fabric.

Feather stitch (Figure 3)

Work in a vertical line. Bring the needle through to the right of the centre line of the design and take a small vertical stitch to the right as shown, catching the thread under the point of the needle. Continue making a series of stitches to the left and right of the design line, catching the thread under the needle.

Herringbone stitch (Figure 4)

Work from left to right. Bring the needle through above the centre line of the design and insert it below this line to the right, taking a small stitch to the left, keeping the thread above the needle. Then insert the needle on the upper line a little to the right, taking a small stitch to the left with the thread below the needle. Continue working these two movements alternately.

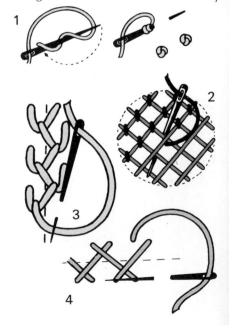

Texture is created in this pretty picture by the use of French knots for blossom and couching for the trellis.

Cross stitch

Cross stitch is one of the simplest and most ancient of all embroidery stitches. It dates back to the Coptic period and has been a form of peasant art for many centuries, appearing in one form or another throughout the world.

The best examples of this work come from the Slavonic countries of Eastern Europe where it has been used to adorn national dress.

Cross stitch can be exciting and absorbing to work and in Victorian times in Britain it was a popular pastime to make cross stitch pictures, often mis-named 'samplers' (true samplers should consist of several stitches).

Many of these pictures were made by small girls and consisted of the alphabet, a text, their age and the date of working, all in minute cross stitch.

How to use cross stitch

Cross stitch can be used for exciting designs on clothes, such as smocks, blouses, and dresses; for accessories, to decorate bags, belts and slippers; and for the home for rugs, table linen, cushions and curtains.

Whether it is worked in an all-over design or simply in a border pattern depends on the size of the item and the background fabric.

The design

Because of the geometrical nature of the stitch, it looks its best when the design is formal and has a repeating pattern, such as shown on the border in the photograph. The shape of the spaces between the areas is as important as those areas filled with the stitch. Often main areas are left unworked and the spaces suggest detail – a technique known as voiding – which is the main characteristic of another form of cross stitch, Assisi work (see Assisi work, later).

The colours

Cross stitch is usually worked in colours – often very bright – which contrast with the background fabric, and the interplay of the colours you choose is all-important. It is often more effective to use several tones of one colour rather than introducing completely different colours.

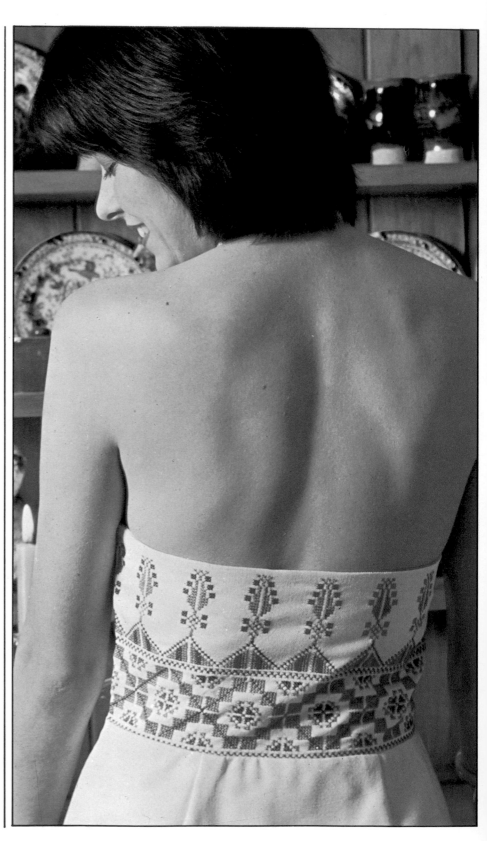

Planning your design

Although it is possible to buy transfers of cross stitch patterns to print on to fabric, it is much more satisfying to use an even-weave fabric and make up your own designs.

To plan your design, draw it first on to graph paper, using different coloured pencils or symbols to represent each colour, with one square representing one stitch or unit. When working from the graph each square or unit may be considered as consisting of one or more threads, which remains standard throughout the work.

A unit of three threads usually makes a good average size cross, each stitch being made by counting three threads along the fabric and then three threads up.

By reducing or increasing the number of threads in the units – or by using fabric with fewer or more threads to the centimetre (inch) – a design may be made smaller or larger accordingly.

An essential point in working cross stitch is that the counting of both stitches and threads must be accurate, and if you are using a transfer it is important to ensure that the lines of the crosses lie on the weave of the fabric.

The fabric

Even-weave fabrics with threads which are easy to count are obviously the best to use for cross stitch and as well as the traditional embroidery linens you can also use hessian, hopsack, 'Hardanger' cotton, Binca and many synthetic furnishing fabrics. Checked fabrics can also be used even if the weave is uneven as the size of the crosses can be determined by the size of the checks.

The threads

Any threads – cotton, silk, linen and wool – can be used provided that they are suitable in weight to the background fabric. A coarse fabric needs a thread of heavier weight while a fine fabric needs lighter threads. Variety can be introduced by using threads of different textures.

The stitches

Cross stitch is formed by two oblique stitches, crossing in the centre. There are two basic methods in which it can be worked, either by making one complete stitch at a time or by making a line of single oblique stitches in one direction, then completing the stitch on the return journey.

It is important that the upper half of the stitch should lie in the same direction if an even and regular effect is to be achieved. Traditionally the upper stitch should slope from bottom left to top right.

Combining cross stitch

While there are numerous variations of cross stitch which are used in other methods of embroidery, the stitch which is most often allied to regular cross stitch is Holbein or double running. This is a small line stitch which is used to break up a mass of cross stitch pattern and lighten it. It produces a light filigree effect and is always worked in two journeys.

The first journey is worked along the required outline in running stitches which are of equal length to the spaces left between them. The work is turned for the return journey when the spaces left between the first stitches are filled in, thus making a solid line. To keep the second line of stitches straight and even, bring the needle out of the fabric immediately below the stitch that was made on the first journey, but still using the same hole of the fabric.

Working the design

The design shown in the photographs here is made up of two simple repeat motifs and it can easily be adjusted to make borders for other garments or to decorate soft furnishings for the home (see diagram below).

The top motif is 5cm (2 inches) wide × 8.5cm (3¼ inches) high. The border motif is 7cm (2¾ inches) wide × 8cm (3⅛ inches) high.

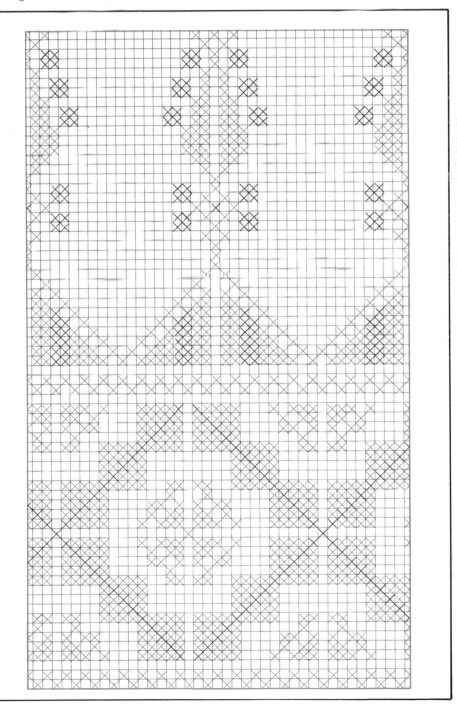

Cross stitch motif

The photograph opposite shows a charming example of the kind of pictorial 'sampler' worked by Victorian children. Notice how the spaces between stitches are used to suggest features. If you do not wish to make a complete item from even-weave fabric, you could work the embroidery only on it, cut round leaving a margin of about 5cm (½ inch) and apply it as a patch on to the finished item.

Fabric required

The motifs, shown worked individually, were done in stranded cotton on linen fabric. Alternatively, you could work in wool to brighten up a favourite cardigan or sweater.

You will also need

☐ Remnants of stranded cotton or knitting wool in various colours. Try to match the weight of the yarn to the background using six strands of cotton or a double-knitting wool on a heavy background.

The design

1 Working over two or three threads of the fabric, work the stitches in the appropriate shades as shown in the charts. Darn all ends neatly through the backs of the stitches on the wrong side.

2 The size of the motif will of course vary according to the weave of the background.

3 On a fabric with 19 threads per 2.5cm (1 inch) for example, the cow motif would be about 11cm (4½ inches) by 5cm (2 inches) when each stitch is worked over two threads.

On a knitted background, work over a unit of one or two knitted stitches counted vertically and horizontally.

Basic cross stitch

To work cross stitch in two journeys, bring the needle through on the lower right line of the cross and insert at the top left line of the cross. Take a straight stitch along the wrong side of the fabric and bring the needle through on the lower right line

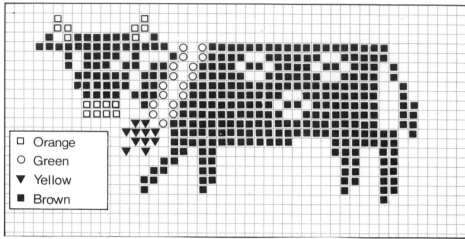

The cow worked on linen with 19 threads per 2.5cm (1 inch); each stitch = two threads.

Working chart for the cow. Each square represents one cross stitch.

□ Orange
○ Green
▼ Yellow
■ Brown

of the next stitch. Continue to the end of the row in this way (Figure 1a). To complete the stitch, work left to right in a similar way (Figure 1b).

Outlines and single stitches

To work cross stitch individually, start as for the two-stage stitch but complete the

cross each time before beginning the next stitch. Pass the thread on the wrong side of the fabric to the lower right line of the position of the next and subsequent stitches.

Double running stitch

Working from right to left, work a row of running stitch, making the stitches and spaces the same length as the crosses. To complete the stitch, work from right to left, filling in the spaces left in the first row.

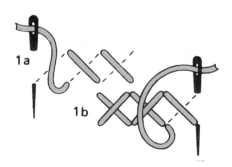

Two-stage stitch

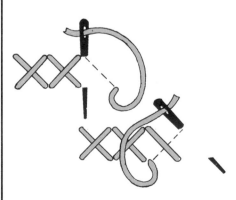

Individually worked stitches

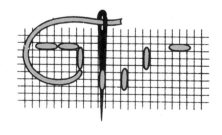

Completing double running stitch

Work this charming cross stitch picture for a nursery or use the motifs individually.

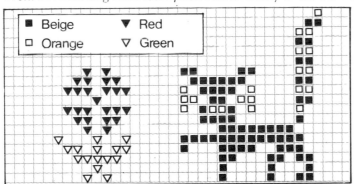

- ■ Beige
- ▼ Red
- □ Orange
- ▽ Green

Working chart for the flower and cat

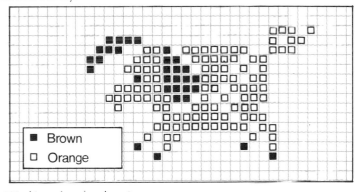

- ■ Brown
- □ Orange

Working chart for the pig

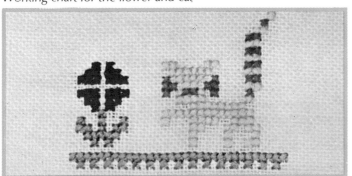

The cat worked on linen as above

The pig worked on linen as above

Cross stitch alphabet

Cross stitch has long been a favourite for embroidered lettering and monograms because it is quick and easy to work. No preliminary outline or transfer is needed when an evenweave fabric is used for the background because the fabric threads can be counted to form each letter.

Although cross stitch designs based on counting threads are necessarily geometric in formation, they still leave plenty of opportunity for embellishment, as shown by the alphabet in the photograph. These letters have been worked in a modern version of the popular Victorian sampler, but you can easily extract the appropriate letters from the chart and use them individually to give a personal finish to your table linen or sheets, or you could combine them to form a monogram to decorate the pocket of a dress or the flap of a bag.

Working the alphabet

1 The alphabet in the photograph is worked on an even-weave cotton with 7 threads to 1cm (*18 threads to 1 inch*) in stranded embroidery cotton, using three strands throughout.

2 Each stitch is worked over one thread of the fabric and the letters are about 3cm (*1¼ inches*) high.

Enlarging the letters

If you simply want to double the size of the letters – and this means increasing their width too – you can work the stitches over two threads of the fabric.

Alternatively, work four stitches for every one stitch indicated on the chart. If you do not want the increase to be so great, you can work the stitches over two threads but on a finer fabric.

Reducing the letters

The only method of reducing the size of the letters is to use a fine fabric.

Monograms

Composite intertwined initials are fun to plan and work. The initials may be arranged so that the base lines are level or you could place them diagonally (see below).

Sketch out your monogram on graph paper before you start work so that you can see how the initials link and where they will have stitches in common.

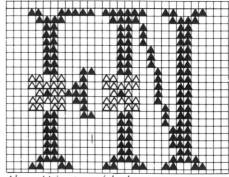

Above Using two of the letters as a monogram.
Left Trace patterns for some of the more complex letters.

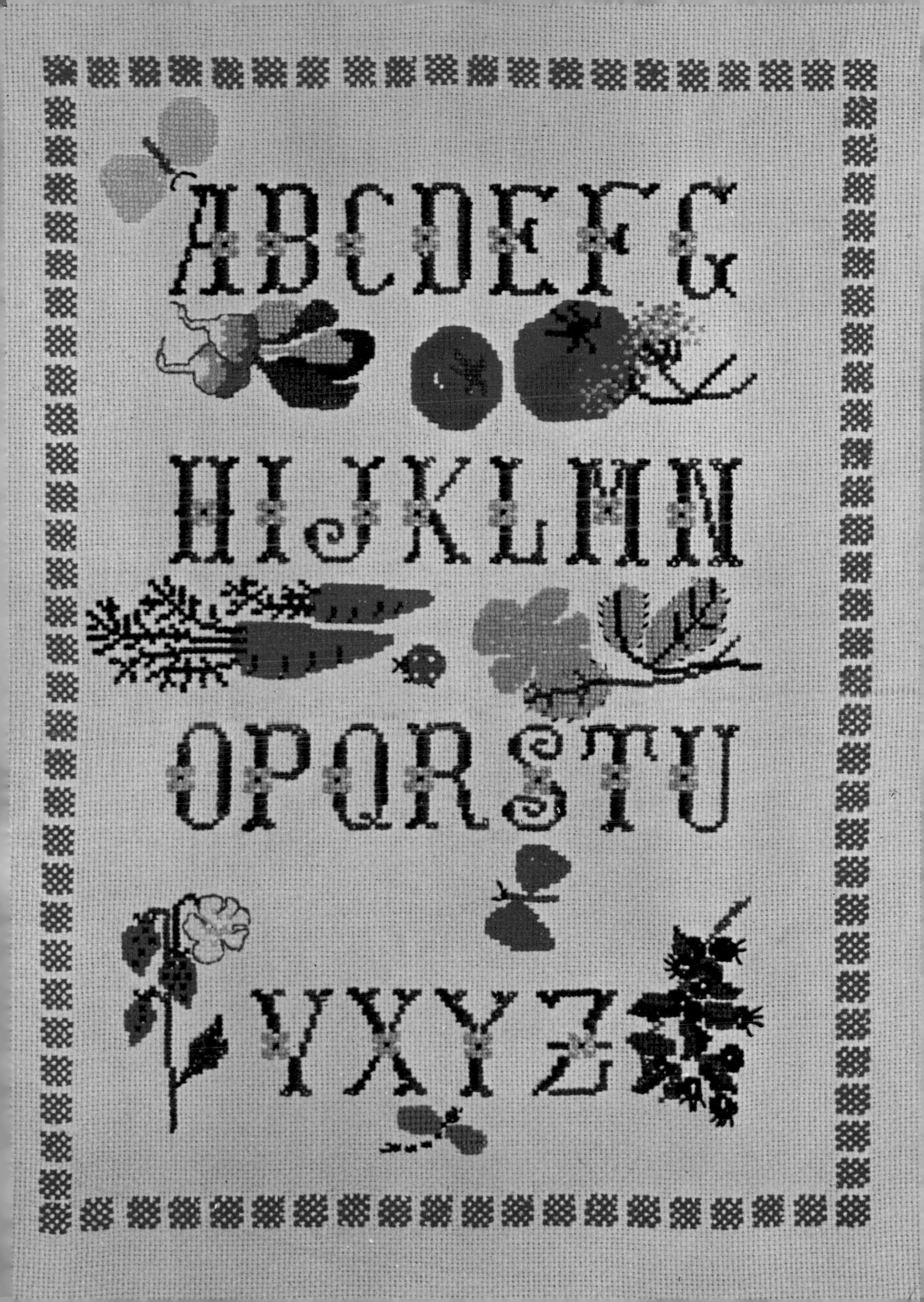
ABCDEFG
HIJKLMN
OPQRSTU
VXYZ

FIRST PROJECTS
Simple peasant design

This beautiful embroidery design is worked with the simplest of stitches. The beginner will be able to work the design after following the previous few chapters – and the experienced embroiderer will have no difficulty at all. The design is suitable for a garment with yoke and sleeves.

To work the embroidery
Materials required
☐ Clark's Anchor Stranded Cotton: 3 skeins each of 047 turkey red, 052 rose pink, 0100 violet, 0130 cobalt blue, 0218 forest green, 0264 moss green, 0304 amber gold
☐ 1 each crewel needle Nos.5 and 7

Placing the motifs
The trace pattern gives half the design used on the yoke with the broken lines indicating the fold. The section within the dotted outline gives half the design used on the sleeve.

Mark centre-front of blouse yoke with a line of tacking stitches.

Placing fold line to centre-front trace motif on to right hand side of yoke. Reverse and trace on to the left hand side. Trace section given within dotted outline on to sleeves, approximately 12.7cm (5 inches) from cuff. Repeat in reverse to complete the design as shown.

Method of working
Following diagram 1 and number key, work the embroidery. Use 6 strands of cotton and No.7 needle for the French knots and 3 strands with No.5 needle for the remainder.

Most of the design is worked in simple satin stitch, stem stitch and French knots, with the centres of flowers in spider's web filling stitch. Work this as shown below. Work nine straight stitches on each side of the fly stitch tail, into the centre of the circle. This divides the circle into nine equal sections and the spokes form the foundation of the web. Weave over and under the spokes until the circle is filled.

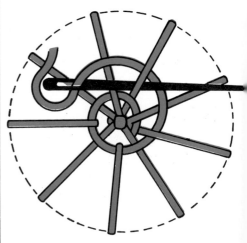

Spider's web filling stitch

KEY TO DIAGRAM

1 — 047
2 — 052
3 — 0100
4 — 0130   Satin Stitch
5 — 0218
6 — 0264
7 — 0304

8 — 0100
9 — 0218   Stem Stitch
10 — 0264
11 — 0304

12 — 0304   Spider's Web Filling Stitch

13 — 0304   French knots

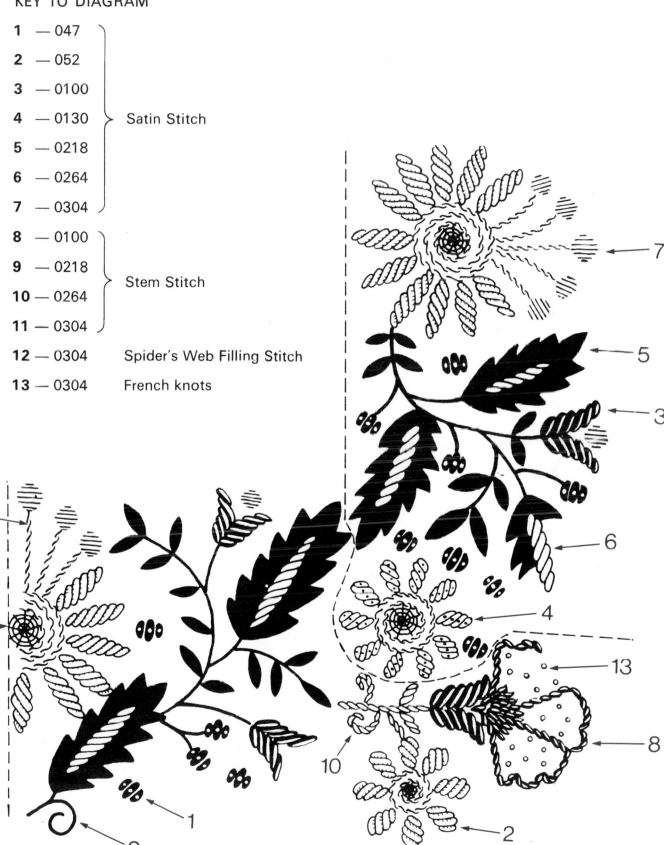

A magnificent dragon

You will also need

☐ Anchor Stranded Cotton in the following colours and quantities: 2 skeins each 0187 jade and 0307 amber gold; 1 skein each 0132 cobalt blue; 0185 and 0189 jade; 0242 and 0245 grass green; 0297 buttercup; 0300 gorse yellow; 0305 and 0309 amber gold; 0335 flame

☐ Alternative thread: Anchor Pearl Cotton No. 8 (10grm ball), 1 ball each: 0132 cobalt blue; 0185, 0187 and 0189 jade; 0243 and 0245 grass green; 0297 buttercup; 0300 gorse yellow; 0306, 0307 and 0309 amber gold; 0335 flame

☐ McCalls kimono pattern No. 3738

☐ Milward 'Gold Seal' crewel needle No. 8

The design

1 Lay out the pattern pieces on the fabric as directed in the pattern. Do not cut out the back and pocket pieces, but mark the cutting line on the fabric with either small tacking stitches or with a tracing wheel and dressmakers' carbon paper. This is because the embroidery may pull and distort the fabric slightly.

2 Enlarge the design on to graph paper and transfer on to the fabric. To do this either use an embroidery transfer pencil or trace the design on to tissue paper and sew it to the fabric with small tacking stitches along the lines of the design, tearing the paper away afterwards.

3 Position the dragon on the back of the kimono 7.5cm (3 inches) from the neck edge. The bat and pearl should be placed centrally on the pocket.

To work the embroidery

4 Use two strands of Stranded Cotton in the needle throughout. Follow the diagram and stitch key to work the embroidery. All parts similar to the numbered parts are worked in the same colour and stitch.

5 To complete the dragon work a French knot in the centre of each eye on top of the satin stitch.

To make up the kimono

6 Press the embroidery on the wrong side under a damp cloth.

7 Lay the pattern pieces on the embroidered back and pocket pieces. Check that the outlines of the pattern on the fabric have not been distorted by the embroidery. Adjust if necessary. Make up the kimono as directed by the pattern.

In China the dragon is regarded as the lord of all animals, a rain bringer and symbol of the highest intelligence. This magnificent dragon, embroidered on the back of an emerald green kimono, is chasing a flaming pearl, another popular Chinese symbol which represents the spring moon, herald of the fertile rainy season. A bat, symbol of happiness, is worked on the pocket.

Fabric required

Length of emerald green fabric

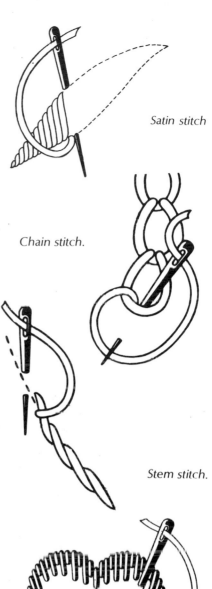

Satin stitch

Chain stitch.

Stem stitch.

Long and short stitch.

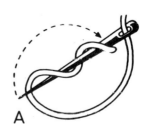

A

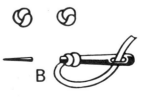

B

French knot.

Graph pattern for dragon design

each square = 2.5 cm (1 in) sq

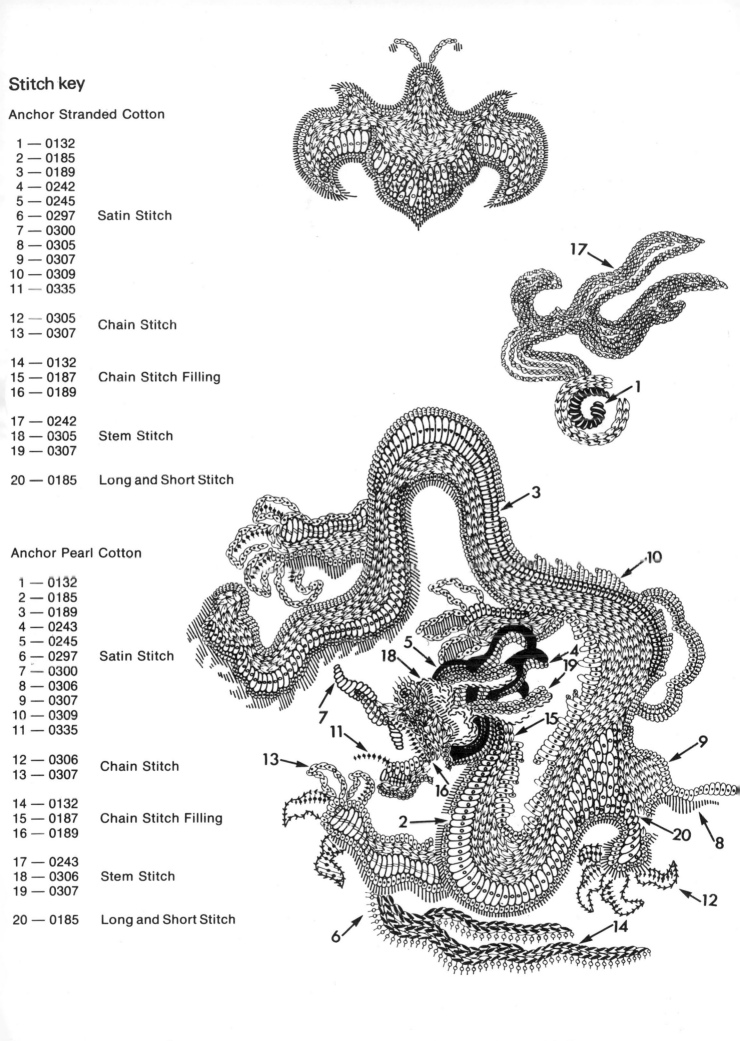

Stitch key

Anchor Stranded Cotton

1 — 0132		
2 — 0185		
3 — 0189		
4 — 0242		
5 — 0245		
6 — 0297	Satin Stitch	
7 — 0300		
8 — 0305		
9 — 0307		
10 — 0309		
11 — 0335		
12 — 0305	Chain Stitch	
13 — 0307		
14 — 0132		
15 — 0187	Chain Stitch Filling	
16 — 0189		
17 — 0242		
18 — 0305	Stem Stitch	
19 — 0307		
20 — 0185	Long and Short Stitch	

Anchor Pearl Cotton

1 — 0132		
2 — 0185		
3 — 0189		
4 — 0243		
5 — 0245		
6 — 0297	Satin Stitch	
7 — 0300		
8 — 0306		
9 — 0307		
10 — 0309		
11 — 0335		
12 — 0306	Chain Stitch	
13 — 0307		
14 — 0132		
15 — 0187	Chain Stitch Filling	
16 — 0189		
17 — 0243		
18 — 0306	Stem Stitch	
19 — 0307		
20 — 0185	Long and Short Stitch	

Circles and spirals

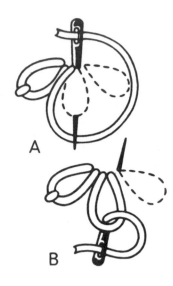

Detached chain stitch

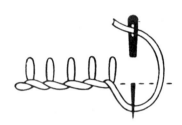

Buttonhole stitch

The colourful design on this cushion is based on a theme of circles. A vibrant range of colours and a few simple stitches combined to give this effect. A more striking finish could be achieved by matching one embroidered cushion with others in plain fabrics, chosen to pick up the embroidery thread colours.

Fabric required
2 × 43cm (17 inch) squares of furnishing cotton

You will also need
- ☐ 1 × 40.5cm (16 inches) square cushion pad
- ☐ Crewel needles, No. 6 and No. 7
- ☐ Contrast bias binding
- ☐ Coats Anchor Stranded Cotton in the following colours and quantities: 1 skein each 0125 indigo; 061 magenta; 097 violet; 0889 bark; 0122 delphinium; 0853 tawny beige; 0893 muted pink; 0117 periwinkle; 0164 kingfisher

The design
Work the chain stitch flowers with three strands of cotton. Stitch in a spiral from the outer edge to the centre. The violet flowers are worked in a long detached chain stitch angled towards the centre point. Work a smaller second stitch within each petal. The florets in the delphinium are made with closely stitched buttonhole wheels. Use four strands in the needle.

To make up the cushion
Press the embroidery face down over a thick pad. Decorate the edges with a bias binding piping. Match it to one of the colours in the embroidery. Pin the two cushion pieces, right sides together, with the folded bias binding sandwiched between the two layers. The fold of the binding faces into the centre. Stitch three sides together through all layers. On the fourth side, the binding is stitched to the seam line of the embroidered square. Turn

Chain stitch

to the right side and press. Insert the cushion pad and close with oversewing, with a zip, or with press studs.

Trace pattern for cushion

Colour key
1 0125 indigo
2 061   magenta
3 097   violet
4 0889 bark
5 0122 delphinium
6 0853 tawny beige
7 0893 muted pink
8 0117 periwinkle
9 0164 kingfisher

Continue outer leaf pattern
to match opposite side

37

Working a family tree

One of the best ways of using stitches recently learned and to put them into practice is to make up a sampler. This family tree uses four simple stitches illustrated in the previous pages and will make a beautiful and personal addition to your home.

This adaptable embroidered version of a family tree was worked by Mrs Mary Pilcher for her grandson Robin (at the top of the tree), who is the fifth generation of Pilchers shown.

This family tree was worked as a present for Robin's second birthday, but a family tree for your own family would make an equally appropriate wedding or christening gift. The number of branches and sprigs will, of course, vary with the size of the family represented and also with the degree of lineage shown.

Choose your own fabric and colours, remembering that the more personal the choice, the more your embroidered family tree will mean to you and to those who will, in time, inherit it.

Be sure to date your tree too, as Mrs Pilcher has done, because one day some member of a future generation will regard it with pride as a family heirloom.

To make the family tree
Size
25.5cm (*10 inches*) by 40cm (*15¾ inches*) dimensions of mounting board as frame: 33cm (*13 inches*) by 47.5cm (*18¾ inches*)

Fabric required
☐ 46cm (*½ yard*) ivory linen
☐ 46cm (*½ yard*) textured linen or similar fabric in contrasting colour.

You will also need
☐ Anchor Stranded Cotton in the following colours: 0258 medium moss green, 0269 dark moss green, 0280 medium muscat green, 0281 dark muscat green, 0308 amber gold, 0358 medium peat brown, 0359 dark peat brown, 0326 dark orange, 0332 flame
☐ Shelf paper or similar and grease-proof or tracing paper, each sheet measuring approximately 25.5cm (*10 inches*) by 35.5cm (*14 inches*)
☐ Two pieces heavy card for mounting, measuring 25.5cm (*10 inches*) by 40cm (*15¾ inches*) and 33cm (*13 inches*) by 47.5cm (*18¾ inches*)
☐ 1.83m (*2 yards*) ricrac trim
☐ Rubber adhesive
☐ 2.3m (*2½ yards*) gum strip.

The design
Planning the design
1 Use the design given as a basic pattern for your own family tree, altering it as required.

Each square=2·5cm (1in) sq

The design for the family tree shown here reduced by half.
Alter the design to accommodate a larger or smaller family.

Work out these alterations on a sheet of shelf paper, doing this preliminary work in pencil so that changes can be easily made.
2 Fold the sheet of shelf paper in half length-ways, making a sharp crease. Open it out and use the centre, vertical fold as a guide line for the tree trunk. Draw in the tree trunk with a pencil. Make a list of the baby's relations or member of the family to be included, and decide how many branches the tree will need. If working the tree for a baby, the names of his parents and grandparents will be embroidered down the main trunk of the tree and great aunts, uncles and cousins on the side branches. Additional side branches can be worked in if necessary and a strategically placed flower or leaf will balance the design if it becomes asymmetrical. After adjusting the design of the tree, outline it in ink. Underline the names to be worked in ink, but omit the names on this pattern.

Transferring the design
1 Fold the greaseproof or tracing paper vertically as above, open it out and place over the design, matching the centre folds. Trace all the lines you will need for the embroidery.
2 Fold the background material in half length-ways, making certain the fold is along the straight grain of the fabric. Put a few pins along the centre fold as a guide-line. Place the tracing of the design over the material, matching the folds; then pin and tack them together.
3 With small tacking stitches tack along all the lines for embroidery, being careful to start and finish securely so that the tacking threads won't pull out. Tear away the paper, leaving the tacked design on the background fabric. The tacking stitches are removed as the embroidery progresses: snip the thread and pull out a short length at a time.

Working the embroidery
Follow the working chart and key for stitches and colours to be used in the design. The key also indicates the number of strands to be used in each area.

Mounting the embroidery
1 Use two pieces of heavy card to mount the embroidered panel and 'frame' it. The smaller piece measures 25.5cm (*10 inches*) by 40cm (*15¾ inches*) and the larger, 33cm (*13 inches*) by 47.5cm (*18¾ inches*).
2 Place the smaller piece of card on a table so that one side projects over the edge by a few inches. Lay the embroidery over it, right side up, centring the work as carefully as possible. Starting at the centre of one side, feel the edge of the card through

KEY TO DESIGN FOR FAMILY TREE

Grass	outer row	chain stitch	2 strands	0268 med. moss green
	middle row	stem stitch	1 strand	0281 dk. muscat green
	inner rows (two)	stem stitch	1 strand	0280 med. muscat green
Tree trunk	outer row	stem stitch	3 strands	0359 dk. peat brown
	inner row	stem stitch	2 strands	0358 med. peat brown
	inner row	stem stitch	1 strand	0308 amber gold
Roots		stem stitch	3 strands	0359 dk. peat brown
		stem stitch	2 strands	0358 med. peat brown
		stem stitch	2 strands	0281 dk. muscat green
Flowers		detached chain stitch	2 strands	0332 flame
			2 strands	0326 dk. orange
Sun	centre	stem stitch	1 strand	0308 amber gold
		stem stitch	1 strand	0332 flame
		stem stitch	1 strand	0326 dk. orange
	rays	open Cretan stitch	1 strand	0326 dk. orange
Leaves	outer row	stem stitch	3 strands	0269 dk. moss green
	centre	open Cretan stitch	3 strands	0268 med. moss green
		open Cretan stitch	3 strands	0280 med. muscat green
		open Cretan stitch	3 strands	0281 dk. muscat green
Lettering		stem stitch	1 strand	0359 dk. peat brown
Underlining		stem stitch	1 strand	0326 dk. orange
Butterflies		stem stitch	3 strands	0308 amber gold
		French knots	3 strands	0308 amber gold

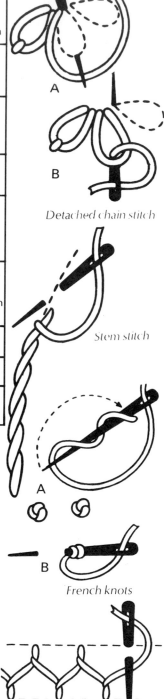

Detached chain stitch

Stem stitch

French knots

Open Cretan stitch

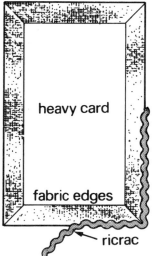

Ricrac is stuck down along the back edge of the panel to add a decorative trim.

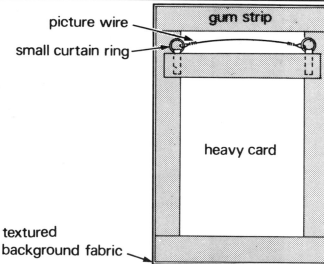

Finish off the back of the completed panel with gum strip and curtain rings for hanging

the material with your left thumb and pin at 2.5cm (1 inch) intervals. Stick the pins straight through the edge of the card, perpendicular to it. Turn the card round and pin along the opposite edge, pulling as tight as possible. Check to see that the embroidery is centred on the card and that the grain of the fabric is straight in both directions; take the pins out and adjust accordingly. Then pin the third side and the fourth, so that the fabric is very tight but the embroidery not distorted.

3 When you are quite certain that the em-

broidery is positioned correctly, turn the card over and stick down the edges with rubber adhesive. Leave the pins in place until the ahesive is dry; then remove them and trim the corners.

4 Cover the larger piece of card with the textured background fabric in the same way. Spread a small amount of rubber adhesive in the centre of the material to join the two panels.

5 If ricrac trim is to be used, stick it down along the back edge of the smaller panel before joining the two panels. Start stick-

ing down the ricrac half way down one side of the panel, adjusting as necessary from the front. Make certain that a loop appears at each corner, stretching or easing the ricrac to make this possible.

If you prefer not to frame the finished panel, cover the raw edges of the material on the back with gum strip. Slip a short length of tape through each of two small curtain rings and fix in place with gum strip. A length of picture wire can be extended between the two rings, and the panel hung by this wire.

THE ESSENTIAL STITCHES

Stitches can be divided into six main groups, according to their general method of construction, and as you become more expert you will see how they can be adapted to add interest and individuality. In cases where you pass the needle under the stitches without penetrating the fabric it is easier to do so if you reverse the needle and lead with the head.

Line stitches
Stem stitch
This stitch is used principally as a line or outline stitch. Work from left to right taking small slanting stitches along the line of the design. The thread should always emerge on the left-hand side of the previous stitch.

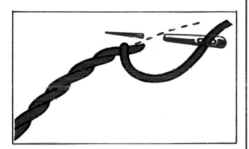

Back stitch
Work from right to left. Bring the thread through the stitch line, take a small stitch back into fabric and bring out the needle the same distance in front of the first stitch. To repeat, insert the needle into the fabric at the point of the first stitch.

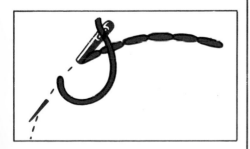

Split stitch
This can be used as a line stitch and a filling stitch when worked closely together. Work from left to right. Bring the thread through the stitch line and make a small stitch with the needle pointing backwards.

Bring the needle up piercing the working thread and splitting it.

Running stitch
Work from right to left. Insert the needle into the fabric making stitches of equal length above and below the fabric so that on both sides the stitches and spaces are of equal length.

Pekinese stitch
Work a row of back stitch, then interlace it with a different, preferably heavier thread, for contrast. The bottom part of the interlacing should lie flat, leaving a looped edge on the upper side of the back stitch.

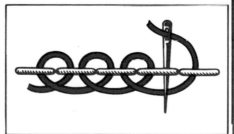

Flat or filling stitches
Satin stitch
This is a close straight stitch which is usually used as a filling stitch. The stitches

should lie flat and even on the right side of the work.

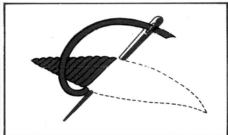

Herringbone stitch
Work from bottom left to upper right. Bring the needle out on the lower line at left and insert at top right, making a small stitch to the left and keeping the thread below the needle. Repeat, making a small stitch at bottom and top as you progress. The stitch can be laced in a variety of ways with ribbon or thread and can be as narrow or as wide as required.

Encroaching satin stitch
This is another useful way of shading. Work the tops of the stitches in the second and subsequent rows in between the bases of the stitches in the row above.

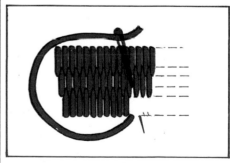

Padded satin stitch
For small surfaces in a design and to give additional texture, some parts may be padded with rows of small running stitch before the satin stitch is worked. To make a neat contour you can outline the edge

first with split stitch and then work satin stitch over the whole shape.

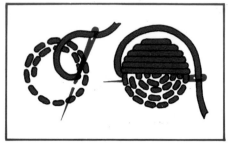

Raised satin stitch

This is effective for small parts of pictures where you want a three-dimensional effect, Start in the same way as for padded satin stitch across the shape. Then work a second layer at right angles to the first one.

Chevron stitch

Work from bottom left to top right and from top right to bottom left alternately making small back stitches. Bring out the needle halfway along each back stitch, keeping the thread alternately above and below the needle as the stitch progresses.

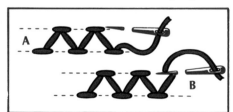

Fishbone stitch

This is a useful filling stitch which should be kept even and compact. Note the small straight stitch at the beginning which is not repeated. Bring the thread through at A and make a small straight stitch along the centre line of the shape. Bring the thread through again at B and make a sloping stitch across the centre line at the base of the first stitch. Bring the thread through at C and make a similar sloping

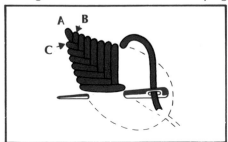

stitch to overlap the previous stitch. Continue working alternately on each side until the shape is filled.

Looped stitches

This group of stitches shows only some of the many which are formed by looping thread round a needle.

Buttonhole stitch

Work from left to right, starting on the bottom line. Insert the needle into the fabric above the line at required distance, take a straight downward stitch, and bring out the needle with the thread under it. Pull up the stitch to form a loop and repeat the process. Once the basic method of working the stitch is mastered, the variations such as closed, up and down and knotted buttonhole stitch are not difficult.

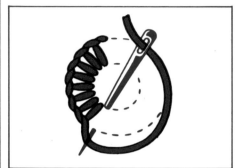

Vandyke stitch

This stitch closely worked will form a thick plaited line but it can also be used as a filling stitch. It must be worked very evenly to form a good plait. Bring the thread through at A. Take a small horizontal stitch at B and insert the needle at C. Bring the thread through at D. Without piercing the fabric, pass the needle under the crossed threads at B and insert at E. Do not pull the stitches too tightly or the regularity of the centre plait will be lost.

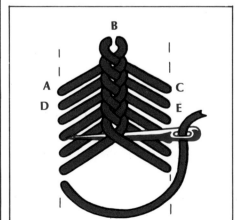

Cretan stitch

A most useful and versatile stitch with a number of uses when worked closely or

openly and irregularly. Work from left to right. Bring the needle through on the left-hand side, take a small stitch on lower line with the needle pointing upwards and the thread behind it. Take a stitch on the upper line with the thread under the needle. Repeat movements.

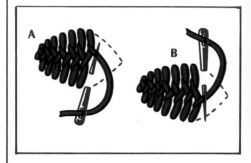

Loop stitch

This is similar to Vandyke stitch but its effect is not so heavy and the two should not be confused. Work from right to left. Start at centre of the stitching line, take the thread through at A and insert at B, bring through at C immediately below B. Keep the thread to the left and under the needle, pass the needle under the first stitch without entering the fabric.

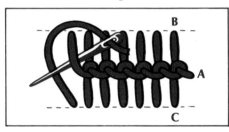

Feather stitch

This stitch is seen at its best in the traditional forms of Dorset feather stitchery but is not so often used today. The stitch gives a feathery effect but must be worked very evenly to prevent it becoming straggly. Bring out the needle at top centre, hold the thread down with the left thumb, insert the needle a little to the right on the same level and take a small stitch down to the centre, keeping the thread under the needle point. Insert the needle a little to the left on the same level and take a stitch to centre, keeping the thread under the needle. Work these two movements alternately.

Fly stitch

This can be worked closely as a line and either regularly or sparsely as a filling. Work from the left when using it horizontally and from the top when working on a vertical line. Bring the thread through at top left, hold it down with the left thumb, insert the needle to the right on the same level and take a small stitch down to the centre with the thread below the needle. Pull through and insert the needle below the centre stitch to hold the loop and bring it through in position to begin the next stitch.

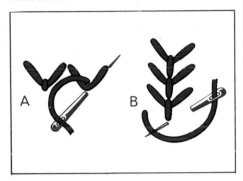

Chained stitches

There are at least nine varieties of chain stitch and the simpler versions, such as ordinary chain, twisted chain and open chain, can be whipped, overcast or threaded.

Chain stitch

This is usually worked from top to bottom vertically and from right to left horizontally. Start by bringing the thread through at the top and inserting the needle again at the same place, forming a loop. (If you are working in the hand, you may find it easier to hold the loop down with your left thumb.) Take a small stitch forward, bringing the needle up through the loop, keeping the thread under the needle. Repeat the stitch, varying its length as required.

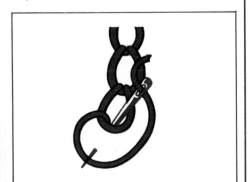

Twisted chain stitch

This is a most useful stitch which should be worked closely and evenly to produce a firm twisted line. Work as for ordinary

chain stitch but insert the needle just outside the last loop and at a slight angle to the stitching line with the thread below the point of the needle, as shown.

Open chain stitch

This must be worked evenly to prevent it from becoming very loose and untidy. Bring the needle through at A, hold down the thread and insert the needle at B, the required width of the stitch. Bring the needle through at C, the required depth of the stitch, leaving the loop thus formed slightly loose. Insert the needle at D and, with the thread under the needle, bring it through for the next stitch. Secure the last loop with a small stitch at each side.

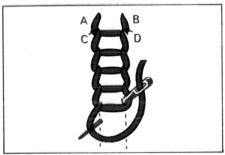

Heavy chain stitch

This makes a very firm close line. Start at the top and work down. Bring out the thread at point A and make a small vertical stitch. Bring the thread through at B and pass the needle under the vertical stitch without penetrating the fabric (use the head of the needle, rather than the point, as this is easier). Insert the needle again at B and bring it out at C. Pass the needle under the vertical stitch and insert again at C. Continue forming stitches in this way, passing the needle under the two preceding loops.

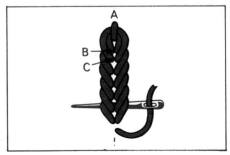

Rosette chain

For this stitch to be effective with either thick or thin threads it must be worked evenly and closely, with no loose top edge. Work from right to left and bring the thread through at the right end of the upper line, pass it to the left and hold down with the left thumb. Insert the needle into the upper line a short distance from where it first emerged and bring it out on the lower line with the thread under the needle point. Draw the needle through the loop and, using the head of the needle, pass it under the top edge of the stitch.

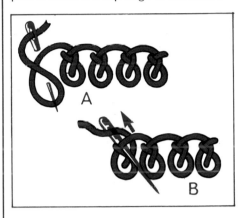

Wheatear

This is a simple stitch which combines straight stitches and a chain stitch. Work two straight stitches at A and B. Bring the thread through below these at C and pass the thread under the two straight stitches without penetrating the fabric. Insert the needle again at C, bring it through at D and repeat.

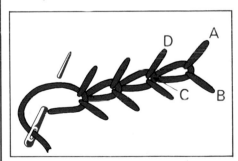

Knotted stitches

Some of the stitches in this group, such as French knots and bullion, are intended to be worked as single stitches while others are more suitable for use as line stitches.

French knots

Bring out the needle at the required position, hold the thread down with the left thumb and encircle the thread with the needle two or three times (depending on the thickness of the thread and the size of knot required). Still holding the thread firmly, return the needle to the starting point and insert *very close* to where the thread emerged. Pull the thread through to the wrong side of the fabric and secure if working a single stitch or pass on to the position of the next stitch if you are working a group. It is a common error to insert the needle too far from the point where the stitch was started, making a loose, untidy knot.

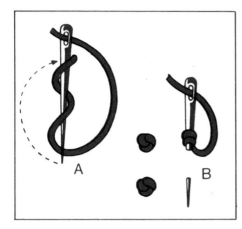

Bullion stitch

The second part of this stitch is taken back over the first part so it is this first part which dictates the finished length of the stitch. Pick up a back stitch of the required length, bringing the needle point out where it first emerged from the fabric. Coil the thread round the needle point as many times as required to equal the space of the back stitch, hold the coiled thread down with your left thumb and pull the needle through. Still holding the coil, return the needle to where it was first inserted (see arrow) and pull through until the stitch lies flat.

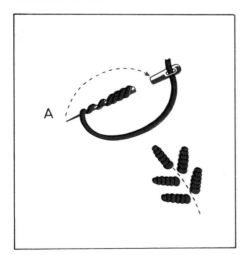

Coral stitch or knot

This is best worked as a firm line as it becomes weak and straggling if the knots are too far apart. Work from right to left or from top to bottom. Bring the thread out at the starting point and lay it along the line to be worked, holding it down with the left thumb. Take a small stitch under

the line where the knot is to be spaced (the thread lies on top of the needle as it enters the fabric) and pull through, taking the needle over the lower loop to form the knot.

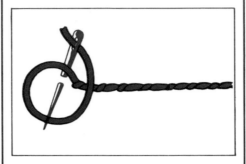

Double knot

This is a slightly more complicated knot stitch. The knots should be spaced evenly and closely to obtain a beaded effect. Bring the thread through at A and take a small stitch across the line to be worked at B. Pass the needle downwards under the stitch just made without penetrating the fabric as at C. With the thread under the needle, pass it under the first stitch again as at D. Pull the thread through to form a knot.

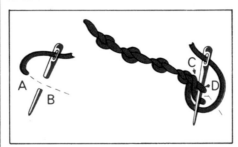

Knotted cable chain

Work from right to left. Bring the thread through at A and place it along the line to be worked. With the thread under the needle, take a stitch at B (which is a coral knot). Pass the needle under the stitch between A and B without penetrating the fabric, as shown at C. With the thread under the needle, take a slanting stitch across the line of stitching at D, close to the coral knot. Pull the thread through to form a chain stitch.

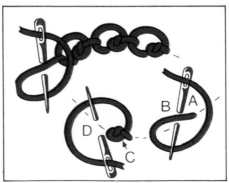

Composite stitches

These form a group which are usually worked on a foundation of satin stitch bars and they can be used as filling or line stitches. The satin stitch bars can be lengthened or shortened as required.

Portuguese border stitch

Work the required number of horizontal straight stitches (satin stitch bars). Working from the bottom upwards, bring the thread through at the centre and below the first bar (point A). Keeping the thread to the left of the needle take the thread over and under the first two bars, over the first two bars again and then under the second bar only without penetrating the fabric. With the thread now at B, work the second pair of stitches in a similar way and continue upwards to the top of the row. Return to point A and work the second row of stitches up the foundation bars, keeping the thread to the right of the needle. Do not pull the surface stitches too tightly.

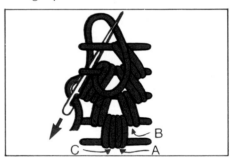

Raised chain band

If worked as a heavy line stitch it is advisable to use a finer thread for the foundation bar, but this should be of suitable weight to carry the chain stitch which can be in a heavier thread (for example Anchor Stranded for the bars and Anchor Soft for the chain stitches). Work the required number of satin stitch bars. Starting at the top and working down, bring the needle through at A in the centre of the first bar. Pass the needle up to the left and down to the right under the foundation bar, as shown, then through the chain loop thus formed. Repeat for the following stitches.

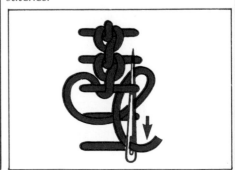

Raised stem band

This is worked in a similar way as for raised chain band but substituting stem stitch for chain stitch. The stem stitch can be worked from top to bottom but the effect is more even if worked from the bottom up.

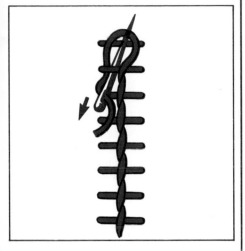

Woven band

This stitch is worked on evenly spaced foundation bars from the top down. You will require two needles with contrasting thread and you will obtain a better effect if one is shiny and the other dull in the same colour, rather than with two contrasting colours. Bring both threads through at the top of the foundation bars with the lighter or silky thread to the left. Pass the light thread under the first bar and leave it lying. Take the darker or dull thread over the first bar, under the second bar and under the light thread. Leave the dark thread lying and pass the light thread over the second bar, under the third bar and under the dark thread. Continue in this way to the end of the band. Begin each following row at the top. By altering the sequence of the contrasting thread, various patterns can be achieved.

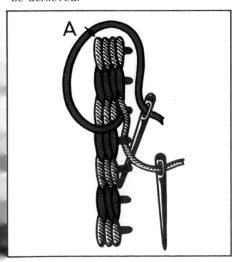

Interlaced band

This stitch is composed of two rows of back stitch with an interlacing band. The distance between the back stitch rows depends on the thickness of the interlacing thread, and should be greater when using a thick thread. For the back stitch, the centre of the stitches in the bottom row should be directly in line with the end of the stitches in the top row so that the interlacing can be worked evenly. Bring the lacing thread through at A and interlace through every stitch as shown.

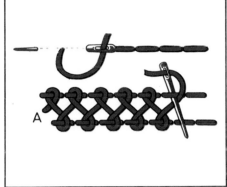

Spider's web

This is a useful and decorative stitch of which there are two varieties.

Back-stitched spider's web Work an even number of equal or unequal length stitches radiating from a centre point – six or eight stitches is the usual number. Bring the needle through the centre. Working from right to left as you progress round the spokes of the web, work a back stitch over each spoke. Pass the needle under the next thread before working the back stitch over it. To finish off, take the thread down into the fabric immediately under a spoke and fasten off underneath. The spokes of the web can be completely filled in but a better effect is made by leaving some unworked with the spokes showing.

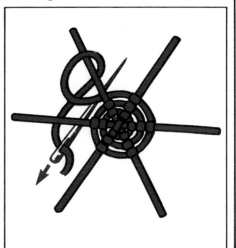

Woven spider's web or woven wheel

Work an uneven number of stitches radiating from a centre point. Bring the needle up in the centre and weave the thread over and under the spokes. This can be worked from left to right or vice versa. Finish off as for the back-stitched web.

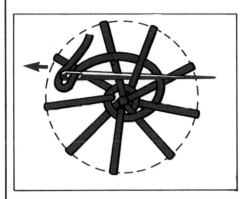

Couching

Couching a line means to lay a line of thread (heavy, light, thick or thin) on the fabric on the line of the design and stitch it down at regular intervals with another thread which may be contrasting. The stitching must be evenly spaced.

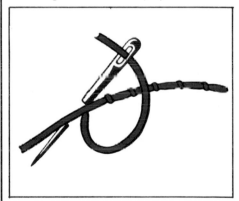

Sheaf stitch

This is a useful stitch which can be used as a filling or as an isolated stitch. It can be worked at spaced intervals or closely grouped. It consists of three vertical satin stitches which are overcast with two horizontal satin stitches, worked with the head of the needle without penetrating the fabric.

ADVANCED STITCHERY
ASSISI WORK

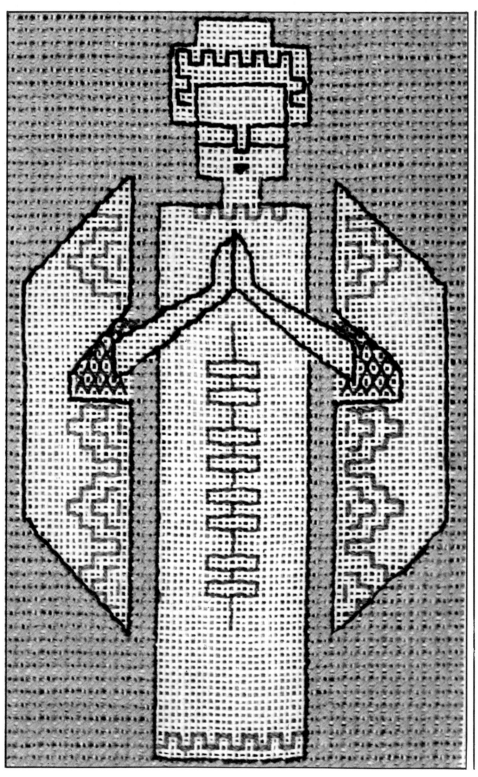

Assisi work is basically a form of cross stitch embroidery although the principle of the work is reversed and the stitches form the background of the design while the basic shapes are left unworked. (This technique is known as 'voiding'.)

As its name suggests, Assisi work originated in Italy. For centuries it has been used to decorate ecclesiastical linen and vestments as well as peasant clothing and household linen. Today it can be used to decorate cushions, place mats and tray cloths or it can form an unusual embroidery on a child's dress or on an accessory such as a bag or belt.

The designs

Traditionally the designs for Assisi work were formal and generally naturalistic; representing animals, birds or flowers in a stylised manner.

Contemporary Assisi work can be inspired by designs from many sources; mosaics, carvings, wrought iron work, screen walling, architectural details, geometric patterns and lettering.

Abstract shapes or stylised reversed initials can also look effective in a border or on the pocket of a dress.

Making your own design

The simplest way is to draw the design on to a graph starting by outlining the motif in straight lines following the lines on the graph and then filling in the background so that you can get an idea of the effect.

As with cross stitch, (see earlier) each square on the graph should represent a unit or stitch. The basic stitch is then worked over three or four threads of an even weave fabric to form a regular and stylised pattern.

The colours

The traditional colours for the embroidery fabric in Assisi work were either white or natural linen with the stitches worked in two colours — usually browns, blues or dark reds, outlined either in a darker tone of the same colour or in black.

A contemporary colour scheme could be dark blue or navy threads worked on a

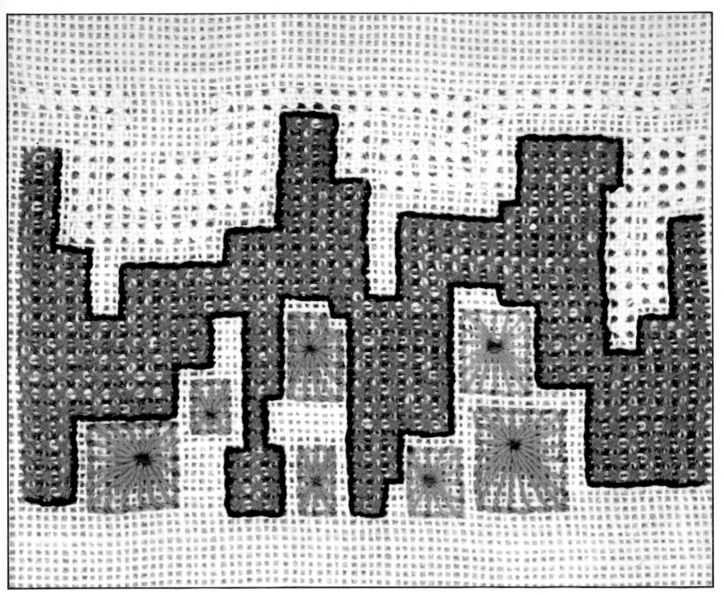

paler blue fabric or orange on yellow, but it is best not to mix colours for the stitchery.

Fabrics
Because all the stitches are worked over a specific number of threads, an even-weave fabric is essential, whether linen, cotton, wool or a synthetic furnishing fabric.

Threads
Pearl cotton, coton a broder and linen threads of a suitable weight for the fabric can all be used for Assisi work.

Needles
Use tapestry needles of a suitable size for the fabric and thread.

Method
There are only two stitches used for this type of embroidery – cross stitch for the background and Holbein (or double running) for the outlining of the motif. The

design illustrated above also used Algerian eye stitch as a filling to give variety to the design.

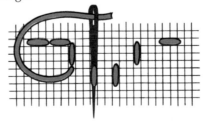

Start by working the Holbein stitch round the outline, counting the threads carefully. Make the stitches about three threads long, with equal spaces. Work round any offshoots of the design, carrying the thread out to the end of the line and back again to the main outline.

On the completion of the first journey the design may look rather disjointed and muddled, but on the second journey the stitch gaps are filled in and the design begins to take form. When all the outlining is complete the background can be

filled in with cross stitch. Either of the two methods of cross stitch given earlier can be used. For large embroidered areas you may find it quicker to work it in two stages. Make sure that the upper stitch in each cross lies in the same direction and that you take the stitches right up to the outline or the character of the work could be lost.

Adding a border
When the background is complete the embroidery should have a very solid appearance and quite often needs a small border to soften it slightly. This can be a small geometric repeating pattern in Holbein worked either side of the design.

Finishing the edges
Final hems should be narrow and un-obtrusive in order not to detract from the work. On table linen a hemstitched hem is usually sufficient, while on a dress, pocket or belt the work can be finished with an invisible hem.

Assisi work tablecloth

The design in Assisi work is achieved by working over counted threads on an even-weave fabric, with a yarn which should be of a similar thickness to the warp and weft threads of the fabric. The finer the weave, the more attractive the design will be.

The actual motifs are formed by outlining them first in Holbein (double running) stitch and then filling in the background area with cross stitch. The fabric is thus left showing through the shape of the motifs. As the embroidery is worked over counted threads, the design has a stylised geometric look, and curves can only be indicated by stepped stitches or by diagonal stitches.

If you wish to make up or adapt your own design, it is best to work it out on graph paper first (10 squares to 2.5cm (1 inch) is suitable). Each square on the graph paper should represent one stitch and then, according to the fabric used, you can decide how many threads to work each stitch over. Most designs are repetitive and can be varied to suit the size required. Figures 1 and 2 show two simple treatments of a flower form and figure 3 shows a bird form.

Assisi work table cloth
Size
1.12m (44 inches) square

Fabric required
1.2m (1⅓ yards) × 140cm (54 inches) wide cream evenweave fabric, 30 threads to 2.5cm (1 inch)

You will also need
- ☐ Anchor Pearl Cotton No. 8 in the following colours and quantities: 3 balls 0132 blue; 1 ball 0403 black
- ☐ Milward 'Gold Seal' tapestry needle No. 24
- ☐ Embroidery ring frame

The design
1 Trim the fabric to an exact square with 117cm (46 inch) sides, cutting along the grain lines. Find the centre by folding the fabric in half both horizontally and vertically and tacking along the creases with a contrast thread, following the grain. The point of intersection marks the centre of the cloth.

2 Turn under 0.6cm (¼ inch) all round the edges and tack to prevent the fabric from fraying while you are working.

3 The chart gives just over half of one side of the square design in the centre of the cloth. Each square represents one stitch worked over three threads of evenweave fabric. The centre is indicated by the white arrow which should coincide with one of the lines of tacking stitches. Commence the Holbein stitch outline at the small black arrow, 213 threads down from the crossed tacking stitches, and follow the pattern as shown on the chart.

4 The design is repeated as a mirror image on the other half of the first side. Work the remaining three sides to correspond.

Working the outline
Work all the embroidery in a ring frame. Embroider the entire outline of the bird and flower design first in Holbein stitch, using black Pearl Cotton. Holbein stitch is worked in two stages. The first row is formed by working running stitch over and under three threads of fabric, following the shape of the design. When this is completed, work back in the opposite direction, filling in the spaces left in the first row. The diagonal stitches are formed by counting three across and three down (or up as required) and inserting the needle at this point. Work the lines of the pattern inside the motifs, for example the bird's eye, at the same time as working the outline.

Working the background
When the black outline is completed, fill in the background with horizontal lines of cross stitch, using blue Pearl Cotton. It is important to work all the stitches with the top stitch facing the same way.

1 Continue each row as far as it will go and fill in any separate areas later. As the back of the cloth should look as perfect as the front, the thread should not be carried over any of the unworked motifs.

2 Where the outline takes a diagonal direction, it may be necessary to use half a cross stitch only in filling in the background. Finally, work the inner and outer borders in Holbein and cross stitch as indicated on the chart, using blue Pearl Cotton.

Finishing off
Press the embroidery on the wrong side. Turn under a 2cm (¾ inch) hem all round, mitring the corners as shown in the diagram, and slip stitch in place. A more decorative hem can be worked if desired by withdrawing one or two threads around the edges of the cloth and finishing off with hem stitch. Finally, repeat the Holbein and cross stitch border about 7.5cm (3 inches) from the edge of the cloth.

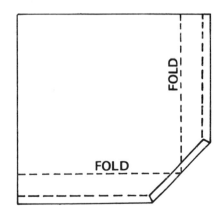

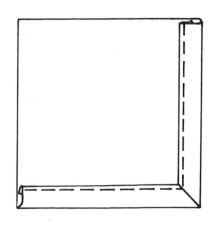

Stitch chart for
Assisi work cloth

Figs 1, 2 Two simple treatments of a flower motif.

Fig 3 A basic bird motif is reversed and a simple
outline added to create an effective design.

The Holbein stitch outline is worked in black Pearl
Cotton and the cross stitch background and the
borders in blue Pearl Cotton ►

centre
of design ⇨

A

B

Cross stitch

Holbein or double running stitch

Each square represents one stitch worked over three threads of fabric

BLACKWORK

Blackwork is a monochrome method of embroidery, and relies for effect on the contrasting tone values produced by varying the density of the pattern fillings and the weight of yarn used.

Blackwork became fashionable in England during the reign of Henry VIII when it was used mainly for the decoration of garments. Later it was also used to decorate household articles and soft furnishings.

Although its name derived from the method of working a geometric pattern in black silk or cotton threads on a white or cream background, any combination which gives a good contrast between dark thread and lighter fabric can be used. In the Tudor period it was frequently worked with a dark red silk on a cream fabric.

The fabric

Blackwork is a counted thread method of embroidery, so choose a fabric which is evenly woven and where the threads can be easily counted.

You could also use a heavy slubbed even-weave linen or cotton which will give a slightly uneven but attractive variation to the stitchery.

The threads and needles

You will need a selection of threads of all weights to provide the depth of tone and contrast in the stitchery. Machine Embroidery cotton No. 30, pure sewing silk, stranded cotton, pearl cotton Nos. 5 and 8, coton à broder and Anchor soft (on a heavier fabric) are all suitable and some of the various types of lurex and metal threads can also be incorporated. You will need tapestry needles in a variety of sizes to suit the fabric and threads.

The stitches

The stitches are simple and mostly variations, of backstitch. Holbein or double running stitch can also be used for building up a border pattern incorporating blackwork filling stitches.

The patterns

The basis of all blackwork patterns is a simple geometric shape which can be adapted to the depth of tone required either by using a heavier or lighter thread or by adding and subtracting additional straight stitches. The spacing of the pattern will also enable a lighter or darker tone to be achieved.

The traditional method of working blackwork was to use the patterns as fillings for shapes of flowers, birds or animals, with the shape outlined with a heavier thread. Nowadays these heavy outlines are usually omitted.

If you are experimenting with blackwork, start by using one basic pattern, working it first over four threads of fabric and then altering the tone or size of the pattern by adding or subtracting part of it. Alternatively, work the pattern over a different number of threads.

The pattern shown below can be made to appear darker, for example, by working a small cross stitch in the centre of each shape. It would appear lighter in tone if each alternate small cross was omitted.

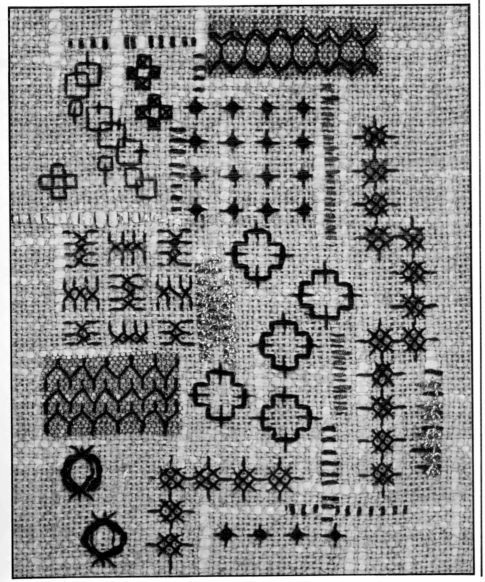

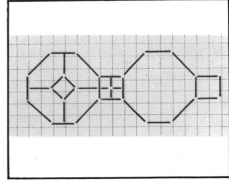

Embroidered chessboard

The chessboard (illustrated overleaf) is in fact a blackwork sampler, showing a variety of filling patterns. By working the patterns in alternate squares with blank squares in between, the sampler becomes an attractive chessboard as well as a permanent reference for the various patterns. The sampler was stretched over plywood, covered in glass to keep it clean and give a good playing surface for chess, and then framed. The materials given below are for a chess-board 40cm (*16 inches*) square, excluding the border, with 5cm (*2 inch*) individual squares.

Fabric required

Evenweave embroidery fabric, 60cm (24

Right A simple design in blackwork ideal to form a border.
Below A complex arrangement of blackwork stitches used to create an abstract design for a wallhanging or picture.

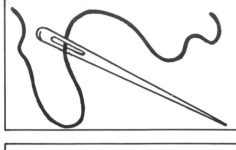

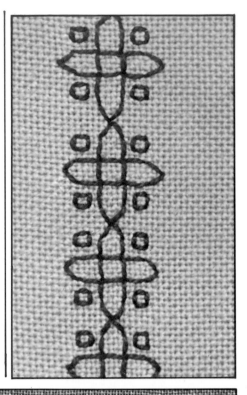

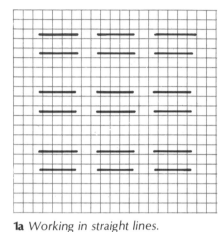

1a *Working in straight lines.*

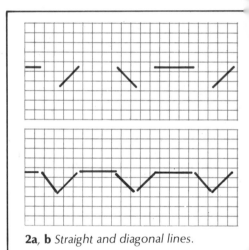

2a, b *Straight and diagonal lines.*

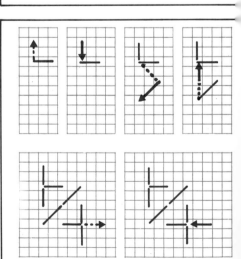

3a–o *Step by step to building up individual units by working in circular movements. This pattern could have bee*

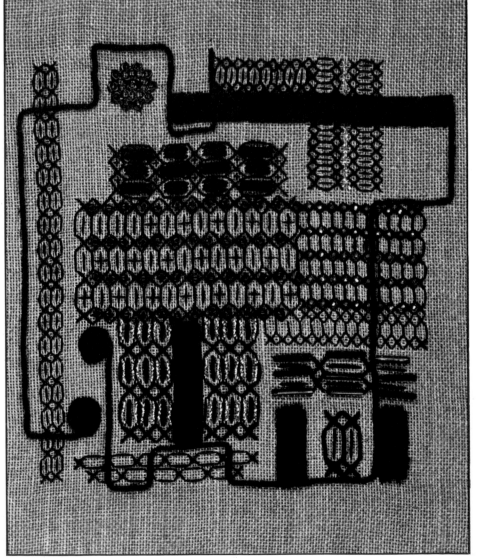

Creating blackwork patterns

All you need to create your blackwork patterns are graph paper, a ruler and a sharp pointed pencil. Work on the basis of one line on the graph equalling one thread of fabric and draw the patterns using basic geometric shapes from which you can develop intricate and interesting patterns. In order to stitch continuously round the design, so that you do not waste thread, you can work straight lines to form a plain grid or straight lines including diagonals or you can move in continuous circles for complicated patterns.

⊞	Threads of fabric
——	New stitch on right side
- - - -	New stitch on wrong side
→	Direction of stitch
⋙⋙	Back stitch
⊘	Detached chain stitch
——	Stitch already worked

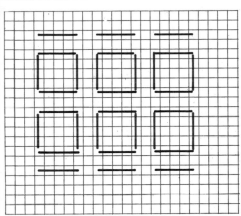

1b *Completing the basic grid.*

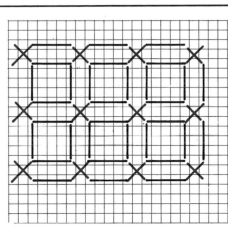

1c *Filling in with cross stitch*

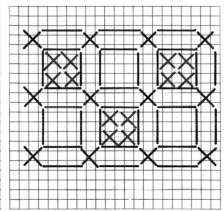

1d *The complete pattern.*

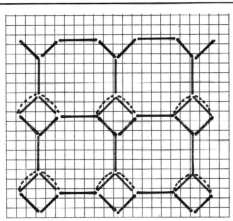

2c *Completing the basic grid.*

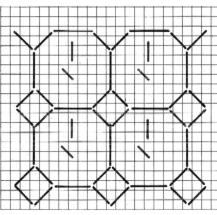

2d *Starting the inner grid.*

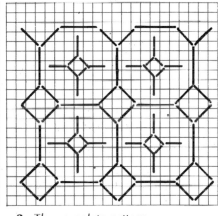

2e *The complete pattern.*

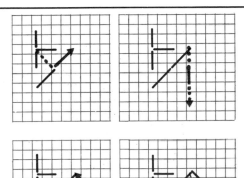

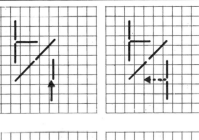

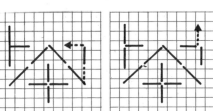

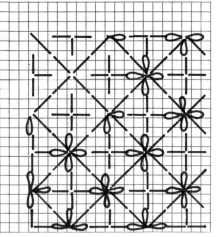

worked in lines to form the grid although it would need long stitches on the wrong side, but by stitching complicated patterns in circular movements you can work more quickly, and use less thread.

The plain grid (top left) with the pattern completed by rosettes of detached chain stitch.

53

inches) square, with 18 threads per 2.5cm (1 inch)

You will also need
☐ Threads, pearl cotton, one 10grm ball No. 5 and two 10 grm balls No. 8 in black, seven reels twisted silk.
☐ Tapestry needles, No. 26 for silk thread and No. 22 for pearl cotton.
☐ Plywood 50cm (20 inches) square (this can be larger if you want a wide frame)
☐ Staples and staple gun
☐ Glass and framing materials

The design
1 Check that the fabric is cut on the straight grain or straighten if necessary.
Find the centre of each side of the fabric by folding it in half and marking the fold at each end with a few tacking stitches. Open out the fabric, refold the other way and mark the fold again.
2 Starting at the centre, and 10cm (4 inches) in from the edge on one side, start by outlining the shape of the board in back stitch, using the No. 5 pearl cotton and working each stitch over three threads of the fabric. At 5cm (2 inch) intervals all the way round on the back-stitch border, work a single stitch of the same size at right angles and facing inwards to indicate the grid for the squares (if you do this there will be no need to recount the threads). Complete the grid by joining up the single stitches in lines across the board.
3 Work the patterns of your choice using different threads to give variety. Work the border to the size you require.

Making up
4 Press the embroidery on the wrong side. Stretch over the plywood and secure on the wrong side with staples. Cover with glass and frame.

This town scene, designed by Pauline Liu, is a clever example of how blackwork gives contrasting tone values by varying the density of the stitchery.

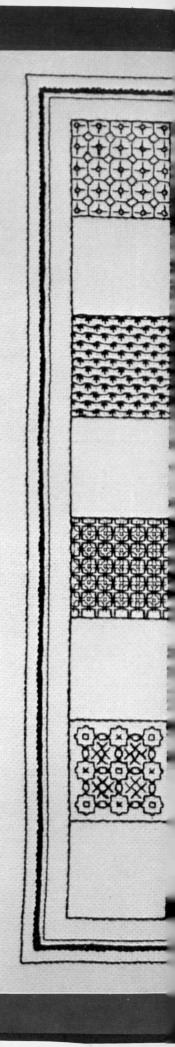

One way of keeping a permanent record of blackwork patterns is to work a sampler, such as this one designed as a chessboard by Pamela Tubby.

DRAWN AND PULLED THREAD WORK
Drawn thread work

Drawn thread work is a method of embroidery which creates a lacy fabric from a plain, closely woven one. It is primarily used for decorative borders for table linen where threads parallel to the edge of the fabric are withdrawn and the remaining threads in the border (those at right angles to the edge) are grouped together by simple stitchery.

The fabric

When choosing a fabric for drawn thread work the most important considerations are that it should be even-weave (with an equal number of warp and weft threads) and the threads should be easily counted and withdrawn.

Linen is the traditional choice for drawn thread work (not least because of its durability for table linen), and it is available in an even-weave with a thread count which varies from very fine to the coarser heavier variety.

There are many other suitable even-weave fabrics, including some synthetics, which do not need ironing and are very practical for place mats, tray cloths, table cloths, etc. To decide whether a fabric is even-weave, cut a hole 2.5cm (1 inch) square in a piece of card, hold it over the fabric and count the threads enclosed in the 'window' – there should be the same number in both directions.

The threads

Threads for this type of embroidery need to be strong and hard wearing. It is usually best to choose a matching thread which is slightly heavier than the threads of the fabric for the decorative stitching and a finer one for hem stitching and buttonholing. On a medium-weight linen, for example, a Sylko perlé thread No.12 is suitable for hem-stitching and buttonholing, with a No.8 thread for the additional stitchery. However, it is worth trying out the thread on a spare piece of fabric as it might be suitable and effective to use one thread throughout.

The needles

Tapestry needles of appropriate size should always be used because their blunt points separate the threads of the fabric which a regular sewing needle would split.

The stitches

The simplest form of drawn thread work is hem-stitching, in which the outer edge of the border is level with the inner edge of the hem so that the stitching can be worked alternately to secure the hem

Cafe curtains, given a neat but delicate border by the use of drawn thread work.

and group the threads in the border. There are numerous ways in which the threads of the border can be stitched, twisted or knotted together decoratively. Some of the most commonly used stitches are ladder stitch, coral knot, double knot and herringbone stitch.

Hem-stitched borders

Before starting a major project, it is advisable to work a simple hem-stitched border for a tray cloth, place mat or napkin.

1 Decide on the finished depth of the hem and measure in double this amount plus the depth of the first turning.

2 Using the point of a tapestry needle, pull out the thread immediately above the total depth of the hem and withdraw it across the width of the fabric.

3 Continue to pull out threads of fabric until the border is the required depth.

4 Turn up the hem to the edge of the border and tack in place.

5 To work the hem-stitching, first knot the end of the thread and run it along the hem so that the knot is securely inside.

6 Starting at the edge of the fabric, wrap the working thread round the first two threads of the border, make a hem stitch into the fold of the hem as for regular hemming, then overcast the next two threads of the border. Continue in this way, overcasting the threads of the border and hemming the fold alternately for the length of the border, always picking up the same number of threads each time.

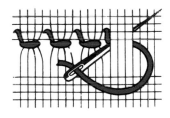

7 To strengthen the opposite edge of the border, work along it in a similar way, overcasting the same pairs of threads and

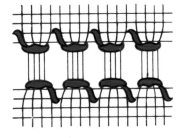

overcasting the edge of the fabric to match the hemmed side.

Four sided borders

When working a border round all four sides of a cloth, the threads are withdrawn in a slightly different way.

1 Calculate the total depth of the hem as for a simple border. Measure in this amount from both directions in each corner and mark the point where they meet with a pin or coloured tack to indicate the outer corners of the border. *Threads must not be withdrawn beyond this point.*

2 Cut the first thread of the border 2.5cm (1 inch) away from the marked point at both ends. Pull out the cut ends as far as the point and leave them hanging. Pull out the remaining portion of thread from the middle completely.

3 Continue to withdraw threads in this way all round the border for the required depth.

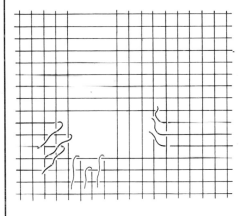

4 The strongest and tidiest way of securing the loose threads at the corners is to turn them back into the hem and enclose them when the hem is stitched. Alternatively, on a very fine and firmly woven linen the threads can be cut close to the edge and secured by buttonhole stitch.

5 Turn up the hem, mitring the corners, and slip stitch the diagonal fold neatly.

6 Work the hem stitching as for a simple border.

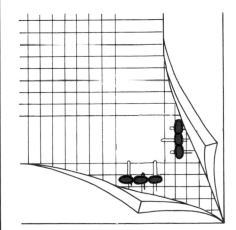

Drawn thread insertions and borders

These insertions can all be used for table linen, to decorate the hems of curtains and, if worked in a heavier thread, for garments. Most drawn thread insertions are first hem stitched along both edges, thus securing the hem if the insertions are used as a border, strengthening the edges when used as plain insertions, and also tying the threads together for the final decorative stitches.

Twisted border

In this insertion, the tied threads are twisted together into bunches of two or three. For wide insertions, two or three rows of twisting can be worked. Beads can also be picked up on the needle between each twisting to make an attractive variation.

1 Using a heavier or contrasting thread to the one used for hemstitching, anchor it to the middle of the outside edge of the corner square of the border.

2 Pass the needle over the space to form one spoke of the spider's web filling to be completed later (see below).

3 Take the needle over the first two tied groups of threads, then back under the second group and over the first group. Pull the thread taut so that the groups twist.

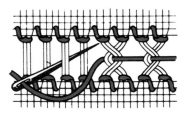

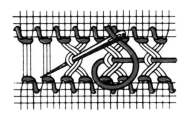

4 Repeat this process along the whole border, take the thread across to the opposite side of the corner space and fasten off on the wrong side.

5 Continue like this on each side of the border.

6 Add four extra crossing threads to the four already formed on each corner space and complete the wheel or web as shown in an earlier chapter.

Coral stitch twisted border

This is worked in a similar way, but coral stitch is used to tie the groups together.

Lattice border

The groups of threads are drawn together with a binding stitch, by taking the thread alternately above and below the groups.

1 Pass the needle over the first two groups, bring the needle round the second group, pass it over the second and third group, round the third group and over the third and fourth group.

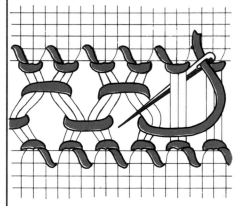

2 Continue in this way, binding the bunches above and below as shown, passing the needle behind the bars from right to left and keeping the working thread above the needle for the upper bars and below the needle for the lower bars.

Needleweaving border

This can be very effective when worked on a heavy slubbed linen with toning and/or contrasting threads.

1 Work the hem-stitching along each edge, tying the threads into bunches of four.

2 Run the working thread into the hem or edge above the starting point, leaving about 2.5cm (1 inch) to be darned in when the needle weaving is finished.

3 Bring the needle through the hem or edge and pass it over the first four threads to the right, bring the needle up again at the starting point and pass it over and under the first two threads to the left.

4 Working on these four threads, weave over and under until you are halfway down the block of withdrawn threads.

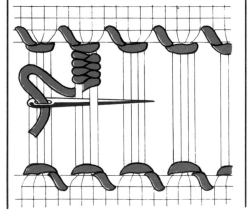

5 Pass the needle to the next four threads to the right and continue weaving over this block until you reach the opposite edge of the insertion.

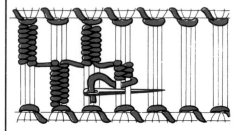

6 Carry the working thread inside this completed block of weaving until you reach the starting point of the block in the middle of the border.

7 Start weaving upwards on the next group of four threads to the right to the top of the border.

8 Continue to weave upwards and downwards on the groups, carrying the needle through the woven blocks to the next position.

9 When you reach the end of the insertion, return to the beginning and weave on the remaining threads in each block to complete the insertion. Fasten the thread securely and thread it back through the last block of weaving to neaten the work. The weaving should be as neat on the back as on the front of the work.

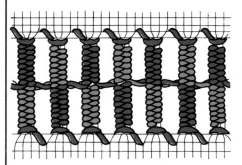

Finishing the corners

Where the withdrawn threads meet at the corners of a border a small square space is formed which should be strengthened and filled with stitchery, such as a woven spider's web. This should be worked after the hem stitching and additional stitchery is worked.

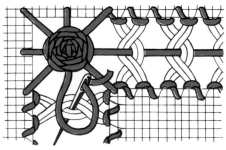

Pulled thread work

Pulled thread work is a method of creating a pattern of holes, spaces or shapes on an even-weave fabric with embroidery stitches which are pulled tightly.

This type of embroidery is ideal for making all kinds of table linen and for lampshades, borders on garments, curtains, bedspreads and cushions.

Sometimes known as drawn fabric work, it is of European peasant origin and developed through the use of embroidery on loosely woven muslins and calicos. To prevent the thread from lying loosely over the fabric the stitches were pulled tightly and it was discovered that this could create attractive patterns.

Pulled thread work should not be confused with drawn thread work, in which the pattern is created by actually withdrawing threads from the fabric and stitching on those remaining.

The fabric

Pulled thread work is a form of counted thread embroidery where the stitches are worked over a specific number of threads. For this reason the fabric should be of an even-weave (one with an equal number of warp and weft threads to the same measurement) and the threads should be large enough to count easily.

Several kinds of fabric are suitable: linen in various weights, from heavy furnishing linen to linen scrim as used for window cleaning; cotton in many weights and colours; even-weave wools; Moygashel dress fabrics and synthetic furnishing fabrics.

The thread

Generally the thread used for the stitchery should be of equal thickness to a withdrawn thread of the fabric, with the addition of thicker or thinner threads to vary the texture and pattern. If the fabric is a good one and will unravel easily, it is possible to remove threads from an unused end and work the embroidery in these.

Other suitable threads include Perlé cotton and crochet cottons in all weights, coton à broder, which is available in a good range of colours, linen threads and lace threads, available from bobbin lace suppliers.

Stranded embroidery cottons and mercerized sewing cottons are not suitable for this type of work as they tend to fray

and break. Pure silk buttonhole thread can be used where you need a fine thread of silky texture. Traditionally the embroidery was worked in thread of the same colour as the fabric, but nowadays a contrasting colour is often used.

Needles

Always use a tapestry needle for pulled thread work as this will not split the threads of the fabric. Normally the needle should be of a suitable weight for the fabric so it passes between the threads easily. But when you are working a border or edging in a progressive stitch such as three-sided or four-sided stitch, you may find it easier to use a larger needle than for the rest of the work.

Frames

Always use a frame for this type of work as it will keep it at an even tension, prevent the fabric from pulling out of shape and enable the threads to be counted easily. The only exception to this rule should be when working an edging.

The stitches

The stitches used in pulled thread embroidery are some of the easiest to work and many are based on satin stitch, worked in lines or blocks at an even tension or pulled tightly. When these two methods are combined, a pattern is produced which can be varied at will. A combination of only two stitches, such as four-sided stitch and satin stitch, can produce a number of patterns when the tension and stitch order are varied. Honeycomb stitch and three-sided stitch are other stitches used. (Border stitches are covered in the next chapter).

Before you start a project, it is advisable to practise some of the stitches, working each separately and then in combinations, using both thin and thick threads (such as a fine crochet cotton and a heavier Perlé cotton).

To begin stitching do not use a knot but bring the thread through the fabric some distance away from the stitching point and make a small back stitch to anchor it. Continue until the thread is finished then return to the starting point and darn in the surplus thread through the stitching line. Alternatively, hold the end of the thread under the stitching line for a short way and work over it.

To finish stitching darn in the end of the thread to the stitchery on the back of the work, making a small back stitch to secure it. Pulled thread work should be as neat on the back of the fabric as on the front, particularly for table linen and lampshades.

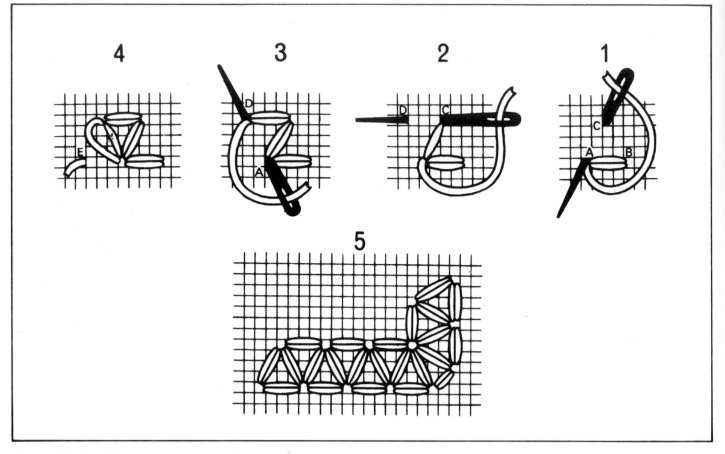

Three-sided stitch

This stitch is worked from right to left. Figure 1. Bring the thread through at A and make two stitches from A to B over four threads of fabric. Bring the needle through at A and take two stitches to C. Figure 2. Bring the needle through at D and take two stitches from D to C. Figure 3. Take two stitches from D to A. Figure 4. Bring the needle through at E. Figure 5. Turning a corner.

Honeycomb filling stitch

This stitch is worked from the top down. Figure 1. Bring the needle through at the arrow and insert at A. Bring through at B and insert at A. Bring through at B and insert at C. Bring through at D, insert again at C and bring through at D. Continue in this way for the row. Figure 2. Where rows connect, the vertical stitches are worked into the same holes.

Four-sided stitch

This stitch is worked from right to left. Figure 1. Bring the thread through at the arrow, insert it at A and bring it through at B.
Figure 2. Insert at the arrow and bring out at C.
Figure 3. Insert at A and bring out at B. Continue like this for a row or close the end for a single stitch.

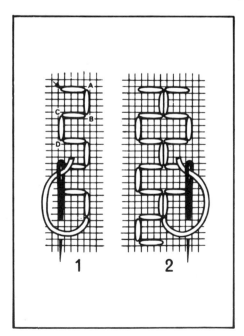

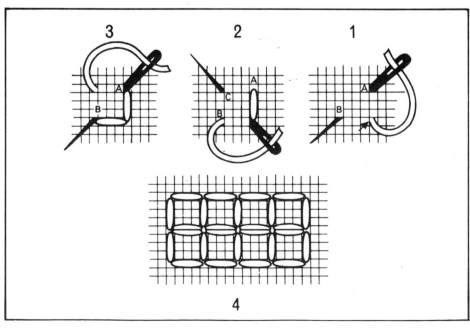

Edgings and borders

One of the most attractive uses for the techniques of pulled thread work is to combine them to form simple yet decorative borders on household linens and tableware.

Four-sided and satin stitch border

This border is suitable for table linen or to decorate the panels of a lampshade. It combines a repeating pattern of seven satin stitches worked over eight threads with a block of four four-sided stitches worked over four threads. The satin stitch is pulled tightly and the four-sided stitch is worked at normal tension.

1 Using a thread similar in weight to the fabric, work seven satin stitches over eight threads of the fabric. Follow this by four four-sided stitches worked over the centre four threads of the eight. Repeat to the end of the row.

2 Repeat this row two or three times to form a border of the required width (you will normally need a wider border for a lampshade than for a place mat, for example).

3 Start the next row with four four-sided stitches worked over the centre four threads of a block of eight. Continue with seven satin stitches over all the eight threads. Repeat to the end of the row.

4 Repeat this row until you have the same number of rows as the first pattern. The satin stitches should alternate with the four-sided stitches every two or three rows, depending on the width of the pattern required. The pattern can be varied further by changing the stitch sequence in alternate rows.

Honeycomb and satin stitch border

This border can be worked vertically as shown in the previous chapter to decorate the panels of a lampshade, or it can be worked horizontally for table linen. Follow the diagram for honeycomb stitch, but incorporate eight satin stitches pulled tightly, followed by one back stitch and eight more satin stitches from each back stitch section of honeycomb stitch.

1 Bring the needle through at the arrow.

2 Insert the needle four threads to the right.

3 Bring the needle through four threads down at B.

4 Insert the needle again at A and bring through two threads below.

5 Work eight satin stitches pulled tightly over these two threads.

6 Work one back stitch pulled tightly over four threads and bring the needle through two threads below the first row of satin stitches.

7 Work eight satin stitches pulled tightly below the first row.

8 Proceed to the next honeycomb stitch and repeat as before.

9 When the line of stitching is the required length, turn the work and repeat the honeycomb and satin stitch combination until the border is complete.

Incorporating beads into the work

The honeycomb and satin stitch border can be made more decorative by adding a pearl or china bead of the right size in the centre space which is formed between the two rows of honeycomb stitching. Use a strong thread and secure the bead with two stitches before passing on to the next space. Carry the thread from space to space along the back of the work and finish off with a secure overcasting stitch on the back of the work.

Eyelets

These are also simple to work and effective, either singly or in groups. They consist of a number of straight stitches worked into a central hole, usually over a square of eight threads of fabric. They can be arranged in groups to form a pattern, or worked singly as squares or rectangles. Some of the most useful are square eyelet, single cross eyelet and back-stitched eyelet. These can all be worked as rectangles instead of squares, and they can also be grouped irregularly together, leaving part of the eyelet unworked.

Square eyelet

This is worked over a square of eight threads.

1 Begin in the centre of one side and take a straight stitch over four threads into the centre hole.

2 Bring the needle up in the next space to the right and take a straight stitch over four threads into the centre hole. Repeat round the square until the eyelet is complete.

Single cross eyelet

Work in a similar way over eight threads as for the square eyelet, but leave one

thread between each quarter.

Back stitched eyelet

This is also worked over eight threads.

1 Begin in the centre of one side and work one straight stitch over four threads into the centre hole.

2 Bring the needle out two threads beyond the straight stitch and make a back stitch into it, then work one straight stitch over four threads into the centre hole. Continue round the sides of the square until the eyelet is complete.

Pulled fabric edgings

One of the features of pulled thread embroidery is that it can be worked round the edge of the fabric and incorporate the hem. The three following edgings are all suitable for most types of table linen.

Edging 1

This is a very simple edging and consists of two rows of four-sided stitch, one of which is worked through a fold or double thickness of fabric.

1 On the right side of the fabric count 10 or 12 threads up from the raw edge and work one row of four-sided stitch over four threads for the required distance.

2 Fold the fabric to the wrong side so that the fold is level with the outer edge of the stitching. Tack in place.

3 On the right side of the fabric work the second row of four-sided stitch through the double thickness of fabric.

4 Remove the tacking and trim the surplus edge back to the line of stitching.

Edging 2

This is worked in the same way as the first edging with the addition of two rows of buttonhole stitch. Work the buttonhole stitch in a fine and firmly twisted thread to produce a hard-wearing edging and use a slightly larger tapestry needle than usual for the four-sided stitch to make the buttonhole stitch easier to work.

1 Count 10 or 12 threads in from the raw edge and work one row of four-sided stitch over four threads as before.

2 Turn the raw edge on to the wrong side and work the second row of four-sided stitch through the double fabric.

3 Using a small tapestry needle, on the right side of the fabric and over the folded

edge, work five buttonhole stitches into each hole made by the first row of four-sided stitch.

4 Work a second row of buttonhole stitch into the holes formed by the second row of four-sided stitch.

5 For a deeper border, the rows of four-sided stitch can be increased. The edging will be further defined if you work the buttonholing in a thread of a slightly darker tone.

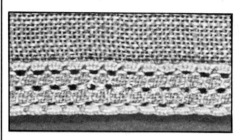

Edging 3

This combines four-sided, three-sided and buttonhole stitch.

1 Count 10 threads in from the raw edge of the fabric and fold the fabric over to the wrong side along this thread. Tack in place.

2 Count three threads in from the fold and work a row of three-sided stitch over the next four threads on the right side of the fabric.

3 Work one row of four-sided stitch above the three-sided stitch.

4 Cut the surplus fabric back to the second line of stitching.

5 Work five buttonhole stitches into each stitch hole formed by the four-sided stitch.

6 To finish the edging, work five buttonhole stitches over the three threads along the folded edge and into the holes formed by the three-sided stitch.

Turning corners

To turn a corner using four-sided stitch, count the threads and check that the number is divisible by four.

To turn a corner using three-sided stitch, count the threads as you near the corner and adjust the fold of the hem so that the stitch can be worked over four threads across the corner.

The corner can also be turned by working one-third of three-sided stitch, known as eyelet filling stitch. The base of the three-sided stitch used for this should come across the corner to be turned.

Pulled fabric runner

This elegant pulled fabric table runner will fit in with any decor, traditional or modern. The three stitches used, satin stitch, ringed back stitch and honeycomb filling are simple to work. Make the runner longer or shorter if you wish, to fit your own furniture.

Size

90cm (35 inches) by 31cm (12 inches)

Fabric required

0.35m (⅜ yard) off-white evenweave fabric, 21 threads to 2.5cm (1 inch), 150cm (59 inches) wide

☐ Anchor Stranded Cotton, 15 skeins 0375 snuff brown.

The design

1 Cut a piece from the fabric measuring 34.5cm (13½ inches) by 95cm (37½ inches). Mark the centre of the fabric lengthwise with a line of tacking stitches. This acts as a guide when placing the design. The working chart shows a section of the design, with the centre marked by a blank arrow which should coincide with the line of tacking stitches.

2 Each stitch must be pulled firmly, except the satin stitch triangles which are worked with normal tension.

3 Use six strands of thread for satin stitch and three strands for the rest of the embroidery.

4 With the long side of the fabric facing, begin working the design with ringed back stitch, 5cm (1¾ inches) from the narrow edge of the fabric. Continue until the embroidery measures 86.5cm (34 inches). Work the rest of the embroidery outwards from this central band. Repeat the three outer lines of satin stitch 7.5cm (3 inches) from the central band of embroidery.

Ringed back stitch

This stitch is worked from right to left and can be used as a border or as a filling. It is worked in two stages as shown in the diagrams. Figure 1: bring the thread through at the arrow; insert the needle at A (2 threads down), bring it through at B (4 threads up and 2 threads to the left); insert at arrow, bring it through at C (2 threads up and 4 threads to the left); insert the needle at B, bring it through at D (2 threads down and 4 to the left); insert it at C, bring it through at E (4 threads down and 2 to the left). Continue making half rings of back stitch for the required length. Figure 2: turn the fabric

63

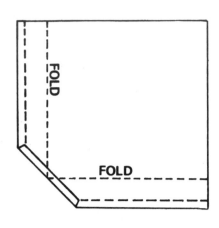

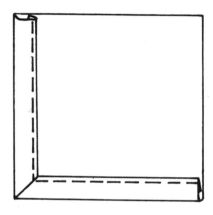

Mitring the corners

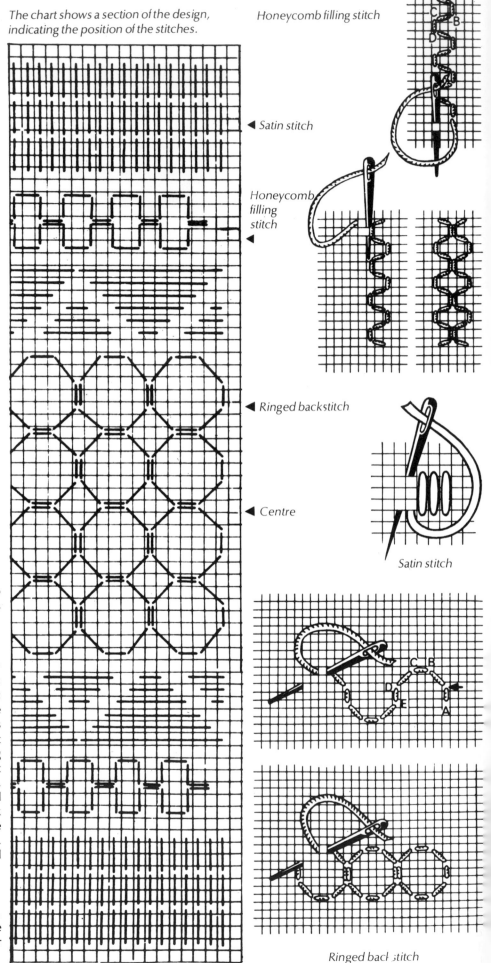

The chart shows a section of the design, indicating the position of the stitches.

◄ *Satin stitch*

Honeycomb filling stitch ◄

◄ *Ringed backstitch*

◄ *Centre*

Honeycomb filling stitch

Satin stitch

Ringed backstitch

round and work back in the same way to complete the rings. All connecting stitches are worked in the same holes.

Honeycomb filling stitch

This stitch is worked from the top downwards, again in two stages. Figure 1: bring the thread through at the arrow; insert the needle at A (2 threads to the right), bring it through at B (2 threads down); insert again at A, bring through at B; insert at C (2 threads to the left), bring through at D (2 threads down); insert again at C and bring through at D. Continue in this way for the required length. Turn the fabric round and work back in the same way. Figure 2 shows the work turned ready for the second row. Figure 3 shows the completed stitch. Pull each stitch firmly.

Finishing off

Press the embroidery on the wrong side. Turn back 1.5cm ($\frac{1}{2}$ *inch*) hems. Mitre the corners and slip stitch. Press the runner again on the wrong side.

HARDANGER WORK

Hardanger work, sometimes called Norwegian embroidery, originated from a district of the same name in western Norway where the local inhabitants were famous for their fine work.

It is a form of drawn thread work which is quick and easy. It is geometric in design with an overall heavy openwork appearance, and is popular in Scandinavia for adorning traditional dress and household linens.

The main characteristic of this type of embroidery is the rectangular grouping of satin stitch, known as kloster blocks, arranged to outline the spaces and build up the basic portion of the design.

Fabric and threads

Hardanger embroidery requires a fabric with a very regular weave in which the warp and weft threads are equal, or special Hardanger linen or canvas which is woven with double warp and weft threads so that it is extremely strong and does not fray in cutting.

This embroidery is traditionally worked on white or natural linen with self-coloured threads but the work can be very effective if a dark thread is used on a light ground and vice versa.

The working threads should be slightly coarser than the threads of the fabric for the satin stitch blocks which form the basis of the design, and slightly finer for the fillings of the open work spaces. Coton à broder and pearl cotton are both suitable for more traditional work.

However, provided the fabrics are of suitable weight and even weave, you could break with tradition and use synthetic or wool fabrics and threads to create your own exciting and contemporary designs for wall hangings, lampshades, cushion covers, dress insertions and accessories. The tools required are tapestry needles and a pair of very sharp pointed embroidery scissors.

The design

By its very nature the design has to be geometrical in form, with squares, triangles, diamonds or oblongs.

The main outlines of the design should be kept as simple as possible and the basic shapes and their relationship to each other in forming a pattern can easily be worked out on graph paper. The design can be developed by building up small shapes around and within the larger shapes, and adding surface stitchery.

Working the design

It is essential throughout the work that both the threads and stitches are counted with great accuracy and that the fabric is carefully cut because any irregularity would spoil the general effect. It is much easier to achieve this and to keep the embroidery at an even tension if a frame is used.

There are four stages in working Hardanger embroidery.

1 Outlining the spaces and design with Kloster blocks.

2 Working any surface embroidery.

3 Cutting and drawing the threads for the open spaces.

4 Decorating the bars of the larger spaces and adding the lace stitch fillings.

Kloster blocks

A kloster block is made up of an irregular number of stitches enclosing a regular number of fabric threads. Five stitches to a block is the usual size, but this can vary from nine stitches enclosing eight threads to three stitches enclosing two. The blocks may be grouped vertically or horizontally to outline the space.

To make a vertical line across the fabric to outline a diamond or triangle the blocks should be worked in steps following the weave of the fabric. If you wish to accentuate certain shapes the blocks may be varied in height as well as length. The head of the stitch should always face the cut space to protect the ends of the fabric and prevent them from fraying.

Surface stitchery

In addition to the outlining blocks, decorative surface stitchery is added to create interest and enrich the design. It should correspond to the general pattern and principle of following the weave of fabric and a variety of stitches can be used, such as back-stitch, star-stitch, herringbone, eyelets, back-stitched or woven wheels, four-sided and interlacing stitches.

Cutting the threads

In Hardanger work the embroidery is half complete before the work is cut, unlike other drawn thread work where the threads are removed first and then the decorative stitchery applied.

Using very sharp scissors, cut the threads in the spaces enclosed by the blocks close to the stitches. Complete one motif at a time, removing either all the horizontal threads or the vertical threads, but do not mix these two stages.

When the cutting is complete it will have created an open mesh of geometric shapes within the outline of the blocks. These now need to be strengthened and decorated.

Decorating the bars

The bars of the threads left in the spaces can be strengthened by overcasting or needleweaving, but it is advisable not to mix the two methods.

At this stage decide if you want to incorporate lace stitch fillings to add to the delicacy of the work as these are made as a series of twists or loops while the bars are being covered.

On articles not subject to wear, you could leave the bars without weaving or overcasting and just add a filling or interlocking lace stitch. An attractive filling for a larger space can be a back-stitched or woven wheel, worked over an even number of anchoring threads.

1 Work the overcasting diagonally across a group of threads, making each stitch firm and covering each bar completely. When one bar is complete, carry the thread behind the work to the next bar, leaving a small square of fabric visible between the bars at the intersections.

2 Work the needleweaving over the bars, following the method given in the section on page 65. At this stage if you are not adding a lace stitch filling, you could incorporate small picots.

3 Place the picots on each side of the bar in the middle, twisting the thread round the needle to make the picot on one side and then moving to the other side and repeating the process.

Hardanger work tablecloth

Size

127cm (50 inches) square

Fabric required

1.40 metres (1½ yards) of 132cm (52 inch) wide medium weight linen with 29 threads to 2.5cm (1 inch)

You will also need

☐ Clark's Anchor Pearl cotton No.5 (10 grm ball): 3 balls white 0402

☐ Clark's Anchor Pearl cotton No.8 (10grm ball): 1 ball white 0402

☐ Tapestry needles, 1 each No.20 and No.24

Preparing the fabric

Trim the fabric so that it is an exact square. Mark the centre in both directions with lines of tacking.

The design

This tablecloth uses the techniques of Hardanger embroidery.

The layout diagram shows the placing of the design for one quarter of the cloth and this is repeated on the remaining three-quarters. The broken lines correspond to the tacked lines across the centre of the fabric, the numerals indicate the number of threads, and the shaded area is the section given in figure 1.

Figure 1 shows the stitches in a section of the design and how they are arranged on the threads. Follow figure 1 and the number key for the actual embroidery, and the layout diagram for the placing of the design. Work all parts similar to the numbered parts in the same stitch.

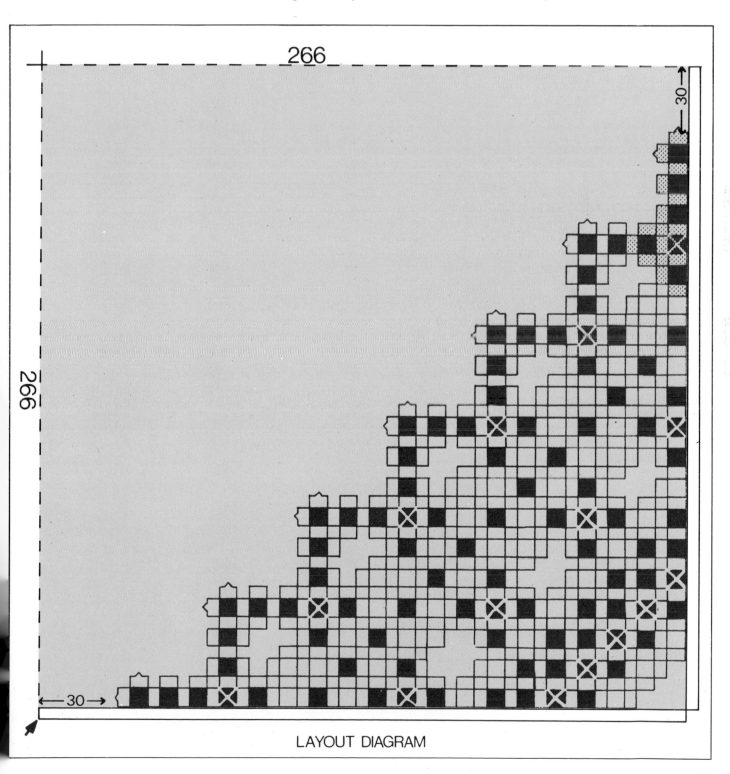

LAYOUT DIAGRAM

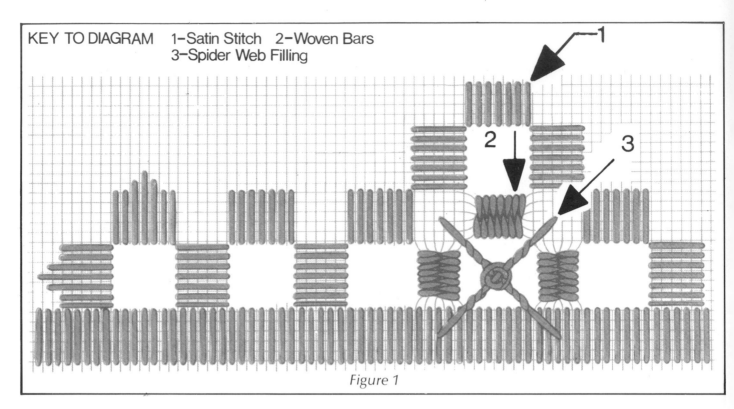

KEY TO DIAGRAM   1–Satin Stitch   2–Woven Bars
3–Spider Web Filling

Figure 1

Working the embroidery

1 Using the No.5 Pearl cotton and the No.20 tapestry needle, start the embroidery at the black arrow shown in the layout diagram, 266 threads down from the crossed tacking threads. Work the section given.

2 When all the satin stitch blocks are complete, cut away the threads shown in the black squares on the layout diagram and blank on figure 1.

3 Using the No.8 Pearl cotton and No.24 tapestry needle, work the woven bars and fillings (see below) and then complete the remaining sections of the cloth in the same way.

Woven bars

Withdraw an even number of threads from the areas shown in figure 1 and separate the remaining threads into bars with three threads in each by weaving over and under them until the threads are completely covered.

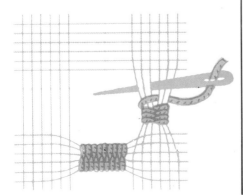

Spider's web filling

1 Work one twisted bar by carrying the thread diagonally across the space. Enter the fabric as shown, twist the thread over the first thread and return to the starting point.

2 Work another twisted bar in the opposite direction but twist the thread back to the centre only.

3 Pass the thread over and under the crossed bars twice and then under and over twice. Complete the twisting of the second bar.

Finishing off

Press the embroidery on the wrong side. Make 2.5cm (*1 inch*) hems all round, mitring the corners.

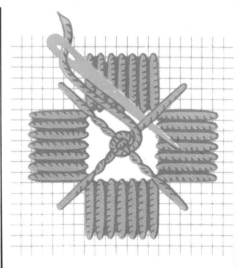

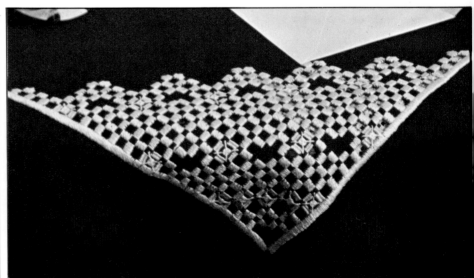

NEEDLEWEAVING

Needleweaving is an ancient craft dating back over three thousand years. Most of the early examples are Coptic and they are known today as loom embroideries as it is thought they were incorporated in the main weaving process of the fabric. Needleweaving is a form of drawn thread work and consists of a decorative pattern worked in weaving or darning stitch upon warp or weft threads after some of the crosswise threads have been withdrawn.

The fabric
Needleweaving is usually worked on a foundation of evenly woven fabric from which threads can be easily removed. Hessians, heavy linens, cottons, woollens and tweeds as well as some acrylic curtain fabrics are all suitable.

The threads
The choice of threads is limitless provided that they are of a similar weight or slightly heavier than the withdrawn threads of the fabric. If the threads supporting the weaving are sufficiently open and strong, you can incorporate a variety of threads, such as carpet thrums, chenille, raffia, heavy nubbly wools and even string, leather thongs, ribbon and thin strips of nylon. Beads, rings and metal washers can all be added as the weaving progresses to add interest and texture.

Needles
You will need an assortment of heavy tapestry needles in various sizes to take the threads you are using. If you are planning to incorporate fine ribbon or thonging an elastic threader or bodkin is also useful.

The design
If you want a fairly free design, the simplest way is to choose a fabric and some interesting threads and begin work without spending time on working out the design first – some of the most exciting results with needleweaving can be created spontaneously.

If the needleweaving is for a specific purpose, such as a border with a geometric pattern or in the form of repeating motifs arranged symmetrically to fill a given space, you should first chart out the design on graph paper showing how the motifs are linked and the colours to be used.

Preparing the fabric
If the needleweaving is for a border, prepare the fabric by withdrawing the threads in the same way as for drawn thread work (see the chapter on drawn thread work). If you weave a simple repeating pattern it can be helpful to hem-stitch the threads into even groups of threads at the top and bottom of the border as this helps in the counting of threads during the weaving process. If you are working on a heavy, loosely woven fabric where the threads are easily counted, this step is not necessary.

The stitch
Weaving or darning stitch is worked by passing the needle over one thread, under the next thread and so on. If you prefer, you can divide the threads into blocks of two, three or four and pass the needle over and under each block.

To start weaving, insert the needle about 2.5cm (1 inch) above the first block of weaving and pull through leaving a length of thread to be darned in later. Begin weaving between the first and second group of threads, working from left to right. Continue weaving between the threads for the required amount, making sure that each row of stitches lies closely to the preceding one and is not pulled too tightly.

To pass to the next block of threads, slip your needle up the side of the block to the top and then work over the next block. You can also pass from one block of weaving to the next by darning the working thread through the back of the work. If you are using several different types of thread, take care to maintain an even tension.

More open effects

You can vary the solid effect of needleweaving with single bars of overcasting with satin stitch. Work needleweaving over the first block of threads for four or six rows, return to the beginning of the block and overcast with satin stitch the first two threads. Slip the needle up the side of the overcast threads and start to weave over the next block. If you wish, the overcast bars can be woven over in the middle of the border.

Needlewoven belt

This belt can be made in wool as shown in the photograph or you could make it in an evenweave cotton or linen, using soft embroidery or stranded cotton threads.

Size

7.5cm (3 inches) wide, to fit any waist size

Fabric required

0.25cm ($\frac{1}{4}$ yard) fabric × the length of belt required + 5cm (2 inches), with approximately 14 threads to 2.5cm (1 inch)

You will also need

☐ Coats Anchor Tapisserie wool: 4 skeins black (0403); 3 skeins each chestnut 0347, 0348; 1 skein chestnut 0351
☐ 7.5cm (3 inches) × the length of belt of non-woven interfacing
☐ Buckle
☐ Tapestry needle No.18

The design

The design is a repeating pattern which can be adjusted to make a belt to your own measurements. The diagram below gives a section of the design with the colours used for each area.

Preparing the fabric

With one long side of the fabric facing you, withdraw 26 lengthwise threads centrally to within 5cm (2 inches) from each end. Darn in the ends neatly.

Working the needleweaving

1 With one long side facing, start the needleweaving at the left-hand edge and work the section given following diagram 1 and the letter key for the colours. Diagram 2 shows how the needleweaving is worked over four threads of fabric and how the connecting stitch is worked over and under the start of a new block.

2 Repeat the section until all the loose threads are woven.

Making up the belt

1 Trim the fabric to within 6.5cm (2½ inches) on the long sides of the belt and to within 2cm (¾ inch) on the short ends.

2 Sew the interfacing lightly in place centrally on the wrong side of the embroidery.

3 Fold one long side of fabric over the interfacing and tack. Turn under the seam allowance of 1.3cm (½ inch) on the other side and hem in place along the centre of the wrong side of the belt. Turn under the seam allowance at each short end and sew. Sew the buckle to one short end of the belt.

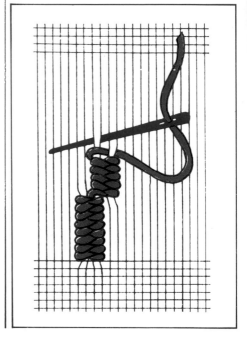

0347   0348   0351   0403

CUT WORK
Simple techniques

Cut work is the name given to open-work methods of embroidery where portions of the background are cut away and, in the more elaborate forms, re-embroidered. Cut work is basically the link between embroidery and needlemade lace and should not be confused with the counted thread methods, Hardanger and Hedebo.

Types of cut work

There are four main types of cut work, varying from simple cut spaces to larger and more elaborately filled spaces
In simple cut work (see below), the cut spaces are quite small. In Renaissance work they grow larger, while in Richelieu work the addition of bars and picots gives a more decorative appearance. Reticella work has the largest cut spaces with intricate fillings, giving a lace-like quality to the embroidery. These more elaborate and highly decorative methods are covered in later chapters.

Uses of cut work

Cut work is suitable for all types of household linen and can also be successfully used as dress decoration, provided the design is planned as an integral part of the dress and is not just added as an afterthought.

Fabric and threads

As the main interest of cut work lies in the variation of texture produced by the cut spaces – either as open shapes or decorated with bars, picots, spider's web or woven wheels and needlepoint fillings – colour is of secondary importance. Most of the charm of cut work lies in it being self-coloured although colour used tonally with simple cut work can be effective. It is important to avoid colour contrasts with the more elaborate forms.
Only a firm, evenly woven linen or very strong cotton should be used for cut work because other fabrics fray when the spaces are cut. Choose a linen or fine pearl cotton or coton à broder in a weight to suit the fabric. Linen lace thread may also be used, although this is available in creamy shades only. Do not use stranded cotton because the strands are not strong enough when divided and would not withstand friction through wear and washing.

Needles

Fine crewel needles are suitable for simple cut work although sharps are normally best for working the lace-like fillings of the other forms of cut work. Choose the size according to the weight of the thread being used. You may also need tapestry needles in various sizes to work the hems and finish the edges.
You should also have a pair of very sharp, finely pointed embroidery scissors.

Designs for cut work

Traditional cut work designs are nearly always floral and the more intricate fillings of Reticella work are similar to old lace patterns.
Simple cut work has no bars or picots and consists solely of a design of simple shapes worked in buttonhole stitch and the background area around the motif cut away, thus throwing the main part of the design into relief.
All cut work, however elaborate, may be designed initially by arranging cut paper shapes, either as a repetitive border or as a single motif or design, to fit a given shape. Whatever the function, the pattern of the cut shapes should balance with the more solid parts of the design.
When planning or adapting a design, check that all the shapes tie up at vital points of the structure or they will hang loosely when the background is cut away. Draw all the main outlines of the design in double lines to act as a guide for the running stitch which is worked within them to act as padding for the buttonhole stitch. A design of curved or circular shapes is much easier to work in this method than a geometric design with sharp angles.
Transfer the design to the fabric using dressmaker's carbon or the prick and pounce method (see the chapter on Transferring designs).

The stitches

1 Start by working several rows of running stitch round the motifs inside the double lines. These form a foundation for the buttonholing and enable a firm edge to be worked. The running stitches should lie very evenly in the fabric – if pulled too tightly the work will pucker.
2 Work the buttonholing close together with the looped edge of the stitches facing the space which is to be cut away.

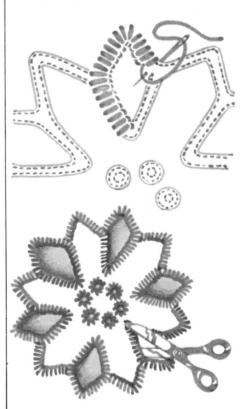

3 Using very sharp scissors, cut away the fabric close to the buttonholing. Cut cleanly, using the points of the scissors so that the edge will not fluff.
Do not be tempted to cut away part of the work before all the stitching is complete or the work will pull out of shape.

Renaissance and Richelieu cut work

Renaissance and Richelieu cut work are more complicated than the simple cut work illustrated in the previous chapter because the cut spaces are larger and need the addition of bars across the spaces to strengthen and hold together the main parts of the design.

The design

As the bars are the most decorative feature of Renaissance cut work, their symmetrical placing is most important. Where there are larger cut spaces than can be adequately filled with a single straight bar, the bar may be branched. These branched bars show to best advantage if they balance the solid parts of the work, but the cut spaces should not be too large and clumsy. Where a number of bars intersect they can be further enriched by a spider's web filling or woven wheel or by a buttonhole ring.

Fabric and threads

Use the same kinds of fabric and thread as for simple cut work and prepare the embroidery in a similar way.

Working the embroidery

1 When the design has been traced or painted on to the fabric, start the embroidery by working the outer row of the padding running stitches. When you reach the position of the first bar, take the thread across the space and make a tiny stitch within the double lines on that side. Return the thread to the starting point of

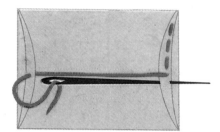

the bar and take another small stitch, go across the space again.

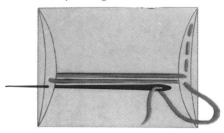

2 Cover the three threads of the bar with close buttonholing, keeping the bar firm and taking care not to let the needle penetrate the fabric below.

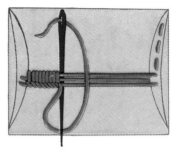

3 Continue with the running stitches around the shape until you reach the next bar and work it in the same way. When all the bars have been worked, complete the second row of padding running stitch.
4 Finish the shape by working close buttonholing over the padding as for simple cut work. Take care not to cut the bars when cutting away the background fabric.

Branched bars

1 Carry the threads across the space in the same way as for a single bar.
2 Work buttonholing over the threads to the point where the bar branches. From this point work the second bar, laying three threads across the space to the point where it joins the double lines. Work the buttonholing over the threads of the second bar back to where it branched from the first bar and then continue working the remaining part of the first bar.

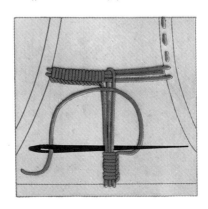

A three or four-branch bar is worked in the same way.

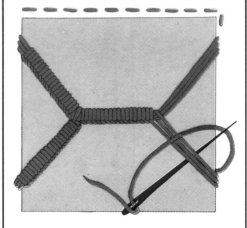

Spider's web filling

If you are filling a large cut space which needs more than a few branched bars, a spider's web filling makes a good alternative. The filling can be placed in the centre or deliberately off-centre by altering the angle at which the twists are made.
1 Carry a single thread across the shape from top to bottom, take a tiny stitch between the double lines and take the thread back to the centre of the space, twisting the thread around the needle.
2 From the centre, take another thread across to the side, twist back to the centre and so on, until you have divided the shape into five sections. Before completing the final twist (over the last half of the first thread worked), work a woven wheel or spider's web by weaving under and over the five threads. Keep the web or wheel fairly small so that it does not detract from the twisted spokes.

Back-stitched wheel

If the space is large enough, six twists can be worked across it, either at regular or irregular intervals, and then a back-stitched wheel worked over them.

Buttonhole ring

This is another decorative filling for a larger cut shape.
1 Wind a fine thread five or six times round a small pencil. Slip the ring off the pencil

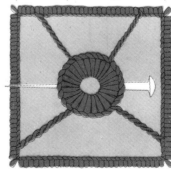

and cover it closely all round with buttonholing.
2 Break off the thread and pin the ring in position on the fabric. To secure the ring to the space, work four or five twisted bars at intervals from the ring to the double lines of the design. To carry the thread to the next twist, work a few running stitches along the double lines to avoid spoiling the ring itself.

Richelieu cut work

This is similar to Renaissance cut work although the cut spaces are a little larger and the bars are decorated with picots.
Looped picots. Work the buttonholing over the bar to the centre from left to right. Insert a pin into the fabric beneath the bar and pass the working thread under the head of the pin from left to right, then up over the bar and out under the bar to the right of the pin. Pass the needle through the loop on the pin and the thread beyond it. Pull the working thread tightly to make the picot and continue buttonholing to the end of the bar.

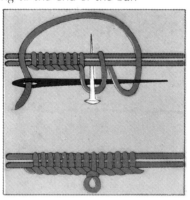

Bullion picots. These are worked on the same principle although they are a little more elaborate. Work close buttonholing to the centre of the bar, make a bullion stitch from the looped edge of the last stitch by twisting the thread four or five times round the needle and pulling the thread through the twists to make a firm twisted loop. To secure the picot, work the next buttonhole stitch close to the previous stitch.

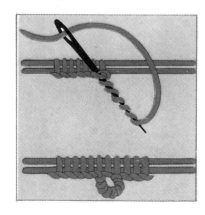

Reticella cut work

This is the most elaborate and lacy form of cut work and bears a strong resemblance to reticella lace. The types of fabric and working threads are the same as for the simple cut work forms and Renaissance and Richelieu work.

The design

The main part of the design for reticella cut work is formed by the stitchery worked within cut squares or geometric shapes. The various fillings are based on a buttonholing or weaving stitch.

While few people today have the time to make large pieces of reticella cut work, small motifs can be made and used to decorate table linen and various types of dress. These motifs can look most effective but do not require the heavy surface stitchery which traditional examples often contained.

A modern pattern or design can be built up by arranging a series of small squares,

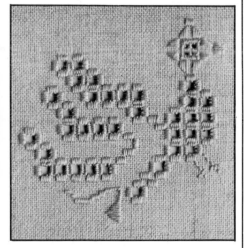

each containing a different filling. The squares can be cut out completely or a number of threads may be left for a basis on which to work the filling stitchery.

Preparing the squares

1 Start by marking the position of the squares accurately and outlining them with several rows of running stitch to strengthen the cut area. If you are planning to leave threads within the square, count them and check that there is an even number. Leave the threads in pairs both horizontally and vertically. It often helps to tack a piece of firm white paper behind the squares as this gives a firmer foundation than the fabric alone, although the stitches are not worked into the paper.
2 Cut the threads to be removed to within three threads of the running stitch. On fine and firm fabrics, turn the cut edges onto the back of the work, overcast the edge and cut away the surplus. On heavier fabrics, work buttonholing over the edge to prevent the filling stitches from pulling away.

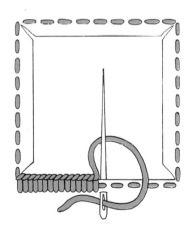

Filling open squares

The fillings on an open square are used to build up small solid shapes, such as triangles, arcs and semi-circles, within a framework of bars worked in buttonholing.
1 Start at the widest part of the shape and take a double thread across from one corner of the square to the other. Work a row of buttonholing on this double thread.
2 Work each following row into the looped edge of the previous row, reducing the number of stitches to form the shape which is anchored to the fabric on the opposite side.

Filling other squares

1 To strengthen the threads left in squares, either cover them with weaving or close

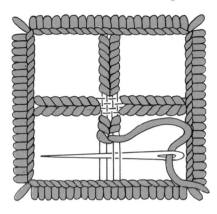

buttonhole stitch. If you add further decoration with picots, check that these do not come at a point where you will be working further bars.
2 To work diagonal lines, take a long stitch from the centre to the corner of the square and back again, and fasten off at the back of the centre. Cover the diagonal threads by overcasting or buttonholing to the position of the first bar or arc.
3 To form the bar or arc, take a double thread across for the foundation, cover it with overcasting or buttonholing and then complete the diagonal line to the centre of the square. The bars or arcs can be decorated with picots.

4 Alternatively a solid triangular shape can be worked in detached buttonhole stitch from the bar which dissects the diagonal line.
5 On fine fabrics the centre of the square can be decorated by working a small back-stitched spider's web over the junction of the threads.

Finishing off

Finish off with a simple hem-stitched border. For something more elaborate, work several rows of hemstitching and twist the threads into bundles (see bead weaving later).

Broderie anglaise

Broderie anglaise is a form of embroidery which consists of eyelets of different shapes and sizes, additional surface embroidery and scalloped edging.

During the 18th and 19th centuries when broderie anglaise was worked in its original form (Ayrshire work) it was composed of much elaborate, floral surface stitchery, eyelets and larger cut spaces with needle-made lace or drawn thread fillings.

The intricacy of the work gave it a very delicate appearance which was ideal for the beautiful christening robes and bonnets made in that period. Traditionally it was worked in white thread on white fabric such as cambric, cotton or fine linen, lawn and muslin.

Later the method became simpler, using less surface stitchery with more emphasis on eyelets and cut shapes and it became known as broderie anglaise or 'Madeira work', after the island where it became a cottage industry. It was used to decorate dress, lingerie, baby wear and household linen, as it still is today.

The design

Broderie anglaise need not be confined to white embroidery, but if colour is chosen it is best to use matching or toning threads rather than contrasting ones. Traditional broderie anglaise was always elaborately floral in design. A contemporary design may be made for a simple border by using a geometric arrangement of circles and ovals of various sizes with a little surface stitchery and scalloping. Both floor and wall tiles can give ideas for this type of design.

The fabrics and threads

Although much broderie anglaise is made by machine nowadays, it is still worth making your own by hand for the beautiful delicate results which can be achieved and the range of fabrics, threads and designs which can be used.

Choose a firm and fine fabric which will not fray with washing, and match the working thread in quality, texture and colour (it can be a different tone). On cotton or linen, use a cotton or fine linen mercerized thread and on silk fabrics, a fine twisted silk.

Stitches and equipment

Only four basic stitches are used in broderie anglaise – running, overcasting, button-holing and satin stitch.

To make the eyelets you will need a pair of really sharp embroidery scissors and a stiletto or steel knitting needle.

Making eyelets

1 To make round eyelets, outline the circle with small running stitches.

2 If the circles are less than 0.6cm ($\frac{1}{4}$ inch) in diameter, pierce the centre with the stiletto or knitting needle and then cover the edge with fine overcasting.

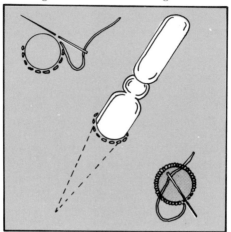

3 For larger circles snip from the centre, vertically and horizontally, out to the running stitch. Turn the points of fabric under to the back of the work with the needle and overcast the edge taking the stitches over the folded edge and the running stitch. Cut away the surplus fabric close to the stitching.

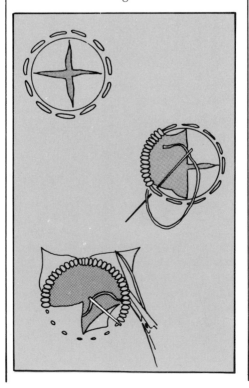

4 If several eyelets run close together, so that they almost touch, work the running stitch along the lower edge of the first hole, cross to the top of the second hole and so on alternately and complete the circles on the return journey. This helps to prevent the work from tearing during working and in wear later on.

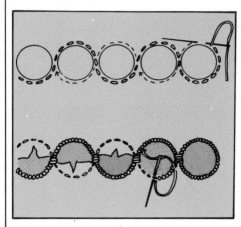

5 To give a heavier effect, or to make the circles thicker on one side, work several rows of running stitch to pad the area and raise it. Then overcast all round the eyelet, grading the length of the overcasting over the padded area.

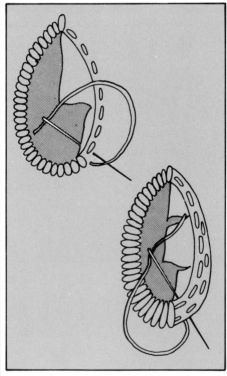

6 To make oval and triangular eyelets, work in the same way as for round ones, taking care that the shapes are kept accurate and do not become distorted.

7 When making a slot for ribbon, mark the slot and work around it before cutting the opening in order to avoid pulling it into a shapeless hole during working.

The surface embroidery

This is usually worked in satin or stem stitch. If you want solid padded shapes to give emphasis or detail to the design, they should be padded by working horizontal satin stitch across the shape just inside the outline, with vertical satin stitch to cover the padding stitches.

Scalloping

This is one of the main features of broderie anglaise and is used to decorate and finish the work.

1 To make a simple scalloped edge, draw the shapes round a coin or small saucer 1.3cm ($\frac{1}{2}$ inch) from the raw edge, or more if the fabric frays badly.

2 Pad the edge by working several rows of running stitch along the outline, graduating the distance between the stitches in the points of the scallops.

For a more solid or raised effect, use chain stitch for the padding instead of running stitch.

3 Cover the padding with closely worked buttonholing, working from left to right and with the looped edge of the stitch to the outside. Keep the stitches as even in tension as possible and do not pull the working thread too tight or the work will pucker. Make the stitches quite small in the points of the scallops, increasing in size round the curves to emphasise their symmetry.

4 To finish off a length of thread, take a few running stitches through the padding on the unworked section and fasten off. Join on the new length in a similar way, bringing the needle up through the loop of the last buttonhole stitch.

5 When all the buttonholing is worked, cut away the surplus fabric close to the stitches with very sharp scissors.

6 To make a more elaborate scalloped edge, draw a pattern of the shape, including about three repeats and then cut it out of cardboard. You can then use this as a template to draw the shapes along the entire edge.

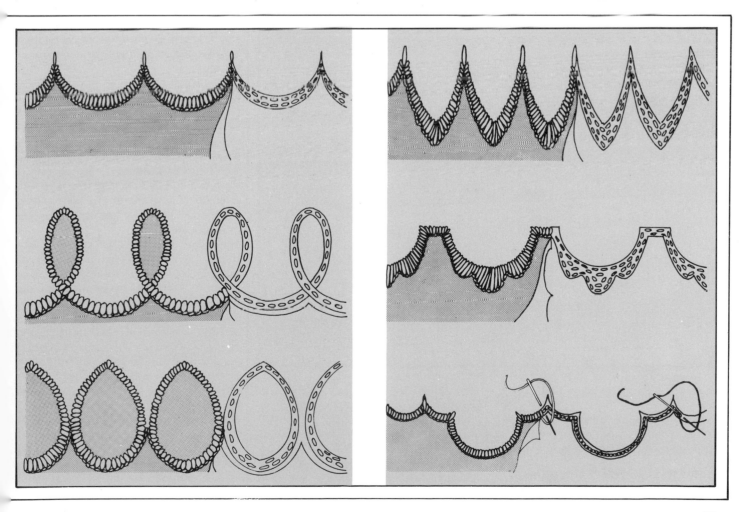

HEDEBO

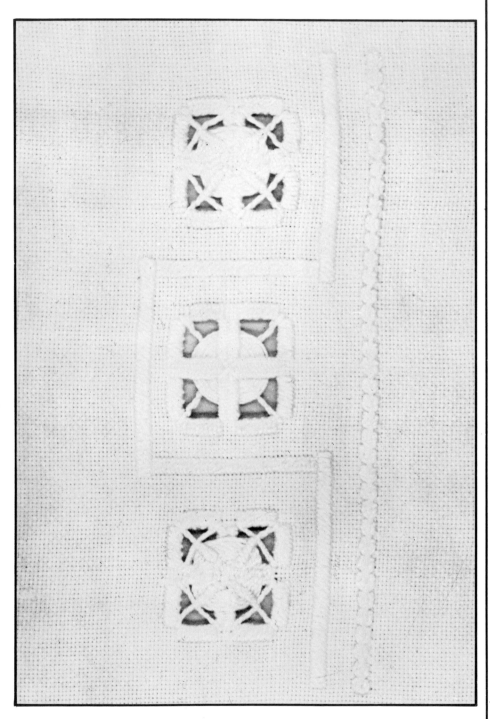

The second type of Hedebo evolved around 1840 when the original floral shapes and cut work were somewhat restrained and the embroidery lost some of its original character. Further cut and drawn thread work was added, usually in squares, making the whole design more formal and geometric.

The third type of Hedebo dates from about 1850 when it became quite popular and gradually lost its peasant-like quality. In modern Hedebo shapes became more conventional and the spaces were cut instead of drawn and cut, and they were filled with more elaborate lace stitchery.

Designs for old Hedebo

Old Hedebo is traditionally worked on a close handwoven linen in a medium weight linen thread.

The main open shapes are formed by cutting and leaving two threads alternately, both vertically and horizontally, from the back of the work. The edge of the shape is then made firm by overcasting which is worked in groups of two over the horizontal and vertical bars. The spaces are enriched with more decorative stitches and the shapes are outlined with a double row of small close chain stitches.

The working method for the second form of Hedebo is very similar, with the open drawn squares being arranged in diagonal lines to form a diamond pattern, often interspersed with floral-type surface embroidery.

Designs for Modern Hedebo

Design for modern Hedebo usually consists of an arrangement or pattern of circular, oval or lozenge-shaped cut spaces which are strengthened and then outlined with buttonhole stitch.

Choose a fine, firm linen for the work with a matching linen thread. If a linen thread is unobtainable, use a fine coton à broder or pearl cotton.

The shapes are filled with a variety of lace stitches which are looped, twisted or buttonholed into the foundation row of buttonholing. Buttonholed pyramids are a feature of this type of work and these can be incorporated into the larger shapes or used as edgings to decorate the work. Satin stitch and eyelets, rather like broderie anglaise, can be added and the work can be finished with a needlepoint lace edging. This form of Hedebo is often used for the decoration of collars and cuffs.

1 Transfer the design on to the fabric either by tacking round an arrangement of cut paper shapes or by using a very finely pointed pencil and outlining the shapes with minute dots.

2 Work a double row of running stitches

Hedebo is a form of white embroidery of Danish origin. It dates from the 16th century when the peasant women of Heden, a flat part of Denmark, used to decorate their homespun linens with it.

Types of Hedebo

There are three basic types of Hedebo.

The oldest and most traditional was adapted from wood carvings and usually consisted of formal floral shapes combining surface embroidery with a few open and drawn thread fillings. Most of the surface embroidery was in chain stitch and the finished effect was soft and graceful.

around the outlines.

3 Cut away the fabric within the shape, leaving a margin of about 0.6cm ($\frac{1}{4}$ *inch*) or 0.3cm ($\frac{1}{8}$ *inch*) for smaller spaces.
Clip into this margin and turn it on to the wrong side. Outline the space with Hedebo buttonhole stitch (see below), making sure that the fabric is turned under the needle and that the stitch is worked through both layers. Trim away the surplus fabric close to the stitches.

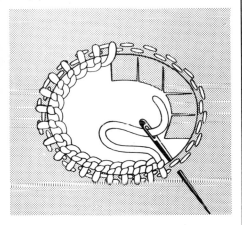

4 Fill the spaces and then add the surface embroidery.
5 Finish the work with a narrow hemstitched edge or needlepoint lace, constructed of Hedebo buttonholing to form loops, pyramids or small rings.

Hedebo buttonholing

The buttonholing used for outlining the shapes is slightly different from regular buttonholing in that it is worked in two separate movements.
1 Hold the fabric so that the edge to be worked is away from you and insert the needle into the fabric from underneath. Draw the thread through until a small loop remains.
2 Slip the needle through the loop and pull both stitch and loop tight.

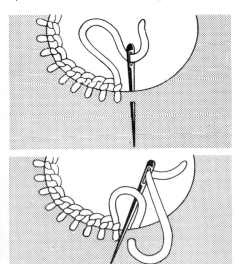

3 To join in a new thread, slip it under the last loop of thread worked and place it alongside the first thread. Work six or seven stitches over both threads and then cut off the remainder of the first thread.

Filling stitches
Circles

1 Work an inner circle of Hedebo buttonholing loosely inside the first circle, placing one stitch into every third stitch of the first circle. To obtain a loose effect, omit the final sharp pull to each stitch.
2 When the inner circle is complete, overcast or whip the looped edges.

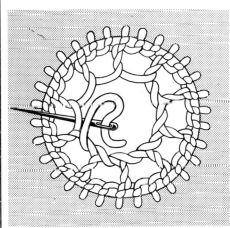

3 Fill the centre of the circle by working a woven or back-stitched wheel over four or six threads anchored into the last row of buttonholing.

Circles and lozenge shapes

Fill circles and lozenge shapes by constructing a number of bars with two or three threads across the shape. Cover these with close Hedebo buttonhole stitch.

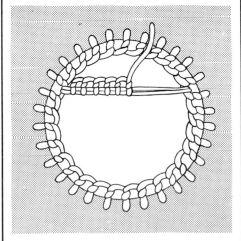

Pyramids

These are a characteristic feature of modern Hedebo and are constructed of Hedebo buttonholing stitches in increasing or decreasing rows. They can be worked singly to fill a small space or in groups of four to fill an oval or pear-shaped space.

1 Prepare the edge with a foundation row of buttonholing.
2 Start the pyramid by working from left to right, working one stitch less at the ends of each row.
3 Continue in this way until the top of the pyramid is reached, then slip the needle down the right side to start the next pyramid.

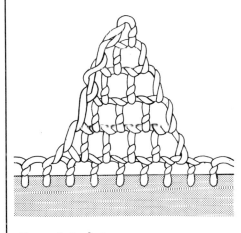

Six-pointed star

This is worked as a separate motif for insertion.
1 Wrap the thread round a pencil several times and secure the circle with a stitch.
2 Remove the circle from the pencil and buttonhole over it. This forms the foundation circle.
3 Work a further round of buttonholing, counting the stitches carefully to make a multiple of six.
4 Work a pyramid on to each multiple number of buttonhole stitches, making six points in all.
5 Secure the shape in position with a single stitch at each point.

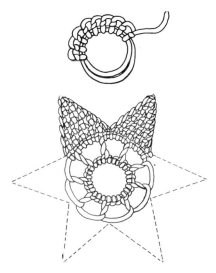

FAGGOTING

Tablemats
Size
40.5cm ($15\frac{3}{4}$ inches) × 32cm ($12\frac{1}{2}$ inches)

Fabric required
For four mats:
0.70 metre ($\frac{3}{4}$ yard) firm cotton or linen, 91cm (36 inches) wide (alternatively, you can use fabric remnants and cut the panels in sizes to suit the fabric available).

You will also need
☐ Stranded embroidery cotton or pearl cotton to match the fabric
☐ Matching sewing thread
☐ Crewel embroidery needle
☐ Four strips of firm paper, 32cm ($12\frac{1}{2}$ inches) × 4cm ($1\frac{1}{2}$ inches)

Preparing the fabric
1 Cut the fabric across the width to make two pieces 35cm ($13\frac{1}{2}$ inches) × 91cm (36 inches). Cut these pieces in half down the length to make four pieces, each 35cm ($13\frac{1}{2}$ inches) × 45.5cm (18 inches).
2 Cut each of the four pieces into three, with two sections 9cm ($3\frac{1}{2}$ inches) wide and one section 27.5cm (11 inches) wide.
3 Turn under 1.5cm ($\frac{1}{2}$ inch) on the wrong side round the edge of all the pieces and make narrow hems with mitred corners. Hem by hand two opposite sides of the large sections and one long side and two short sides of the smaller sections. Leave the remaining edges tacked in position.
4 For each mat, place the tacked hem of one small section on to the edge of the strip of firm paper so that it overlaps slightly. Tack in place. Overlap the tacked hem of the larger section on to the opposite edge of the paper and tack down, leaving a gap of 1.5cm ($\frac{1}{2}$ inch). Repeat this process with the opposite edge of the larger section and the second smaller section.

Working the faggoting
1 Mount the fabric into a frame.
2 Work the faggoting between the tacked edges, following one of the stitch patterns shown in the diagram. Make sure that the stitches worked into the edges of the fabric catch the hems securely.
3 When all the faggoting is complete, press the finished mats with a warm iron.

Faggoting is an attractive method of joining two pieces of fabric in an open-work design. It is particularly useful for tableware for which you do not necessarily need the strength of a regular seam and where a seam line would spoil the effect.

If you are making a tablecloth from 91cm (36 inch) wide dress fabric or 122cm (48 inch) wide furnishing fabric for example, and need to join panels to make it the right width for your table, you could join the panels with faggoting. The panels need not be confined to long strips but could be cut to make an attractive feature. Faggoting can be used for both square and round shapes, providing the edges to

be joined lie along the grain of the fabric – if you try to work them on the bias grain they will not lie flat.

Many of the stitches used in faggoting are common embroidery stitches but, although they are simple to work, their success depends on keeping their size and the spaces between the edges absolutely even, so it is worth mounting the work into a frame.

Faggoting can be worked in most kinds of embroidery thread of a weight to suit the fabric you are working on. You could also use a fine crochet cotton. The instructions given below are for making the mat shown in the photograph but they can easily be adapted for a tablecloth.

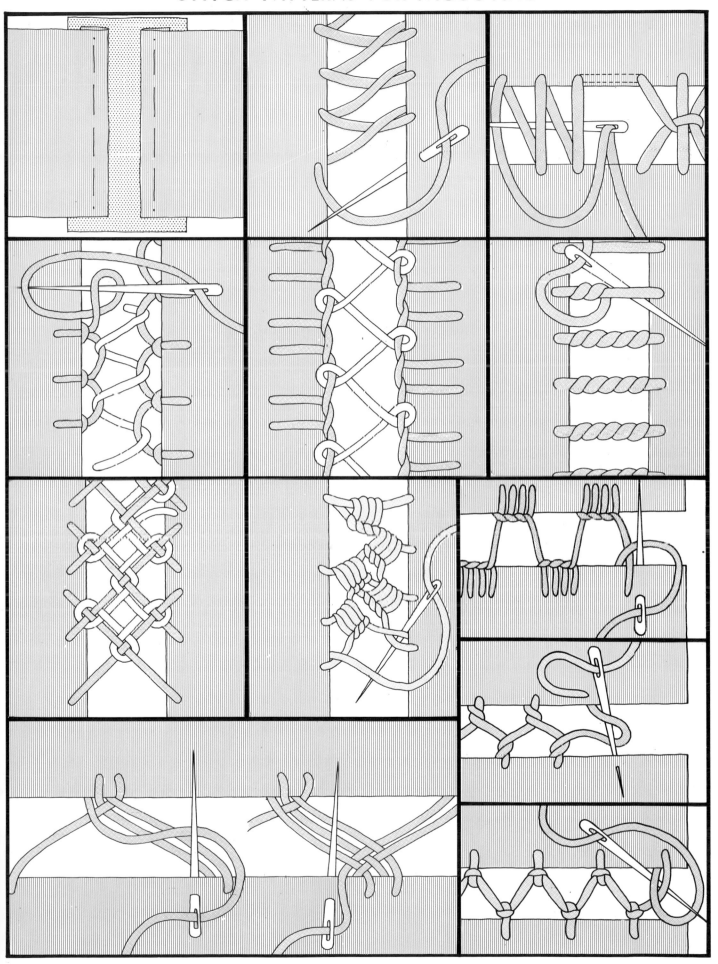

NEEDLEMADE LACE

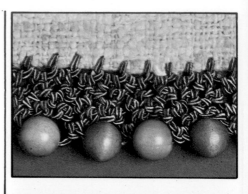

Lace-making using a needle is quite different from lace made with an implement, such as crochet or tatting, and it should not be confused with bobbin lace made on a pillow, sometimes called pillow lace. Needlemade lace is an old craft which was popular in all European countries in the mid-fifteenth and sixteenth centuries. It is directly derived from the elaborate cut and drawn work of the fifteenth century which was often used for ecclesiastical purposes and to decorate the household articles and fashionable garments of the nobility.

The stitches

The Italian name for needlemade lace is *Punto in aria*, meaning stitches in the air and the lace itself is made with nothing more than a foundation, a needle and thread.

The stitches involved are merely variations of simple embroidery stitches and the main stitches used are buttonhole (or blanket) stitch in one of its various forms, and a number of knotted stitches.

The threads

The thread should be suitable in weight for the fabric on which the edging is to be placed. If you are working on linen, use a linen thread, coton à broder, pearl cotton or crochet thread. If the fabric is heavy, such as a tweed, a heavier corded thread or heavy wool would be suitable. For working the edgings use a tapestry needle of a suitable size.

First method

This method could be used for narrow borders to decorate table linen, lampshades or a dress. It is worked directly on the folded edge of the fabric.

1 Join your thread into the side of the edge to be decorated and take a tiny stitch into the fold about 1cm ($\frac{3}{8}$ *inch*) further along (point A), leaving a small loop.

2 Go back to the starting point and make another stitch. Go to point A again, make another stitch, keeping the loops the same size. Return to the starting point again. You now have four equal loops, forming a small scallop.

3 Work over the scallop in close buttonhole stitch.

4 Make a second loop in exactly the same way and then lay the threads for a third scallop but work only halfway across in buttonhole stitch.

5 Make a loop from the centre of the third scallop to the centre of the second one and then from the centre of the second one to the centre of the first one. Repeat this until there are three loops in each of these two scallops thus forming a second row.

6 Work over the first loop and halfway over the second loop in the second row.

7 Make a loop from the middle of the second scallop in the second row into the middle of the first one. Repeat until there are three loops in the scallop and then work over them in buttonhole stitch and over the half loops left in the first and second rows.

Second method

This border can be worked into a hem or on to a foundation of buttonholing. Work all rows from left to right and fasten off the thread at the end of each row.

1 Start by working a row of spaced double knotted buttonhole stitch into the edge of the fabric.

2 For the second row, work the same stitch putting each one into a loop between the knots of the first row.

3 For the third row, work two double knotted stitches into the first loop, an ordinary single buttonhole stitch into the next loop, and so on alternately to the end of the row.

4 For the last row, work two ordinary buttonhole stitches into the loop on each side of the single stitch in the third row and with two double knotted stitches into each space between the double knots.

Working a separate strip

If you prefer to make the lace in a separate strip and then sew it on later (this would be more convenient on a large or heavy item), use a piece of stiff linen or bookbinding cloth as a foundation. The strip should be the same length as the required piece of lace and about 5cm (*2 inches*) wider.

1 Rule a line along the strip about 1.3cm ($\frac{1}{2}$ *inch*) from the top edge.

2 Couch a double thread of crochet cotton or other firm thread along the line (using a contrasting colour for the stitches to hold the thread will make it easier to remove).

3 Work the lace on to the couched thread and remove the small stitches holding the thread when the lace is complete.

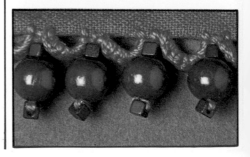

VENETIAN LACE

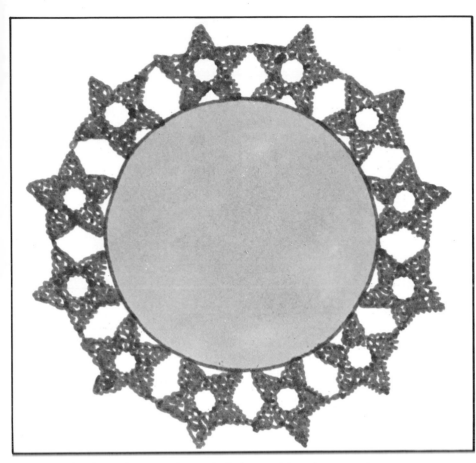

Make a border with stars or buttonholed pyramids to form a circle.

Venetian lace is the oldest type of needle-made lace. The motifs are geometric in design and, like the narrow edgings described in the previous chapter on needle-made edgings, they are made with fine, closely worked buttonhole stitches and knotted stitches.

They are worked on to couched threads, which are held with temporary stitches on a firm foundation, while the lace is being made.

The finished motifs, depending on the weight of the thread used, could be stitched on to lingerie, blouses and dresses, and on to sheets, pillowcases and table linen.

The threads and equipment

Linen thread is usually the best for working most types of lace, although fine crochet cotton, pearl cotton, and coton à broder are suitable.

For the couching, use a linen thread or mercerized crochet cotton, and for the final padding, a soft thread such as Sylko Size 5.

You will also need fine tapestry and crewel needles to suit the weight of the thread and a pair of finely pointed embroidery scissors.

For marking the design and for the foundation you will need either white paint and strong black paper with a matt texture, or Indian ink or a black felt-tipped pen and tracing paper. Both kinds of foundation should be backed with strong muslin or book-binding cloth. Alternatively you can use book binding cloth alone as the foundation.

Marking the design

1 Start by planning a well-balanced geometric design on graph paper, and consider how the lines are to be joined and the spaces filled. One way of doing this is to draw parts of the design in close double lines which separate and then rejoin. The spaces can be filled with bars or bridges.

2 Draw the design accurately on to the foundation.

Tracing the design

1 Trace over the design by outlining it with couched threads. Keep the threads as continuous as possible and, where they are double, lying evenly side by side. Where one line branches to another, divide the thread and couch it as far as necessary and then double back to the starting point. Where one line touches another, thread the couching under and back again so that the pattern is joined.

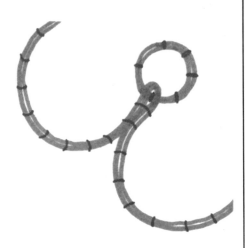

2 Secure the couching on to the foundation with small temporary stitches. These stitches can be in a contrasting colour to make them easier to remove, but if the lace is being worked in white this is best avoided if possible as the colour may leave a trace.

Filling in the design

1 Fill in the various spaces of the design by using one of the buttonhole stitches given below. Be as inventive as you like, for it is the variety of the stitches which give this type of lace its character.
2 When the filling is complete, make the final bars or bridges to link those lines which do not touch each other. These can be worked by buttonholing or by overcasting.
3 Start by laying several threads evenly across the space to be filled by taking small stitches into the outline threads on each side. Cover these threads with buttonholing or overcasting.

4 If you want a wider bar, work buttonhole stitch along both edges and decorate the bar with rings, picots or other bars.

Outlining the design

This is the stage which gives the final touch to the lace. The whole design is outlined in close buttonholing using a fine thread to bring it to life.
To give it dimension and emphasis on various parts work over a couple of strands of soft padding thread. Where one part appears to pass over another, work the under part first.
When joining in and fastening off threads, take a few neat overcast stitches into the part of the outlining nearest to you. These stitches will also get worked in with the final outlining which should cover them completely and also help strengthen the lace.

Finishing off

The last and most exciting stage is the removal of the lace from the foundation, which is done quite simply by cutting and removing the stitches which hold down the couched thread.

The stitches

These are just a few of the basic stitches which can be used to create needlemade lace. You can also invent numerous patterns by the interplay of the various stitches and the spaces created by them. You can also embellish them with picots and loops to give greater dexterity to the work. Basic buttonhole stitch, single and double knot stitch and bullion stitch were all described in the previous chapter on needlemade lace edgings.
Knotted buttonhole stitch
1 Work a row of buttonhole stitches from left to right over the couched thread.
2 Work a second row, from right to left, reversing the stitch into the loop made by

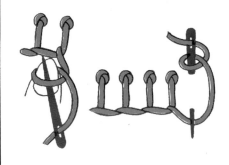

the first stitch. Work each stitch at a slight angle, pulling tight each knot thus formed before continuing on to the next stitch. Two or three buttonhole stitches can often be drawn together by working this stitch over a whole group at once.
Corded buttonhole stitch
1 Work a row of spaced buttonhole stitch from right to left.

2 Work a row of overcasting from left to right over the loops of the previous row.
3 Repeat these rows alternately for the required amount. When working the third row, check that you stitch into the loop of the buttonholing, not the overcasting.
Twisted stitches
These give a light and airy appearance to the work. It is important to keep the tension as even as possible and the stitches themselves carefully spaced. They are capable of great variety. One method is to overcast the loops, as for corded buttonhole stitch. Alternatively, they can be built up into a pyramid formation, each row having one less twisted stitch than the previous one.

Picots
1 To work a picot, make a second buttonhole stitch into the loop of the last stitch worked and then insert the needle into the loop of this second stitch just made.
2 Twist the working thread round the needle, draw up the knot and pass the needle through the loop of the original buttonhole stitch, ready to continue the row of buttonholing. The knots should twist and form into a small circle.

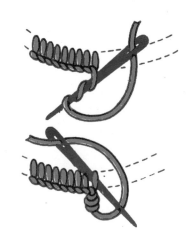

SHADOW WORK

Shadow work

Shadow work is a type of embroidery which relies for effect on a filling stitch, worked on the wrong side of a transparent fabric so that the colour of the working thread shows through to the right side of the work in a subdued tint.

It is usually worked on a very fine fabric such as organdie, organza, fine linen lawn, cotton lawn, muslin and crepe de chine in a soft shade.

Until this century it was always worked in white or a white fabric with double back stitch (a variation of herringbone). The threads of the stitches cross on the back of the work to give an opaque quality on the right side.

In more modern work the introduction of colour has changed the effect to produce an opalescence, and this type of work lends itself well to such articles as baby clothes, lingerie, party dresses and aprons as well as on the more delicate table linen and lampshades.

The design

Designs for shadow work should consist of narrow shapes which have simple outlines. Traditionally the work was always floral in design with the addition of a little surface stitchery but nowadays abstract shapes of suitable proportions can be used.

The shapes are nevertheless restricted in width by the double back stitch or herringbone stitch which fills and outlines them. To transfer the design on to the fabric, simply place the fabric over the design with the right side facing down and trace the design with a fine pencil.

Threads and needles

Choose a fine thread – either pure silk, stranded cotton or fine coton à broder – in a darker or brighter colour than the fabric so that you can achieve the desired finished effect.

Use fine crewel or betweens needles.

The working method

When the design has been traced on to the wrong side of the fabric, work all the main areas in close herringbone stitch (or double back stitch). Extra wide shapes can be filled in with two rows of herringbone, but this is best avoided.

Close herringbone stitch is worked in the same way as ordinary herringbone but with the stitches touching each other at the top and bottom, thus building up two parallel lines of back stitch on the front of the work with the opaque area between them.

Form the stitches as evenly as possible, following the outline of the shapes and working into all the corners and points in order to complete the outline accurately on the right side.

Work the stitches slightly smaller and closer together on the inside of curves and slightly larger on the outside. Take care that the stitches do not slope and always remain perpendicular to the base line.

When all the main areas are filled in, any additional stitchery such as linear detail, eyelets and spider's web wheels can be worked on the right side.

Because the fabric is transparent, take care to conceal all ends of threads.

Do not use knots but darn all ends back into the work securely and neatly.

French shadow work

This is extremely easy to work and produces quick and attractive results.

The motif most normally used is the square, which is marked on to the fabric by drawing a thread from side to side to ensure an accurate outline.

The squares are first worked one way and then the other, taking up an equal number of threads each time. The threads must be counted carefully so that the blocks of stitches are perfectly even.

Several variations of the square can be developed and the Greek fret design is always a good stand-by. The addition of eyelet holes adds variation to this type of design.

Indian shadow work

This has almost the same effect as traditional shadow work but a slightly different working method is used.

Instead of the stitches crossing on the back of the work they are taken from side to side, picking up a small amount of fabric each time and zig-zagging between the lines of the design.

Take care to pick up a small stitch each time or the threads will be too openly spaced on the back of the work, thus spoiling the shadow effect on the front.

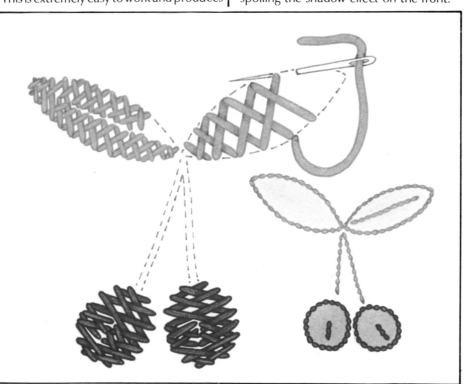

Shadow work for sheers

Fabric required

Length of fine pale green nylon or organdie to fit window, plus 3.5cm (1½ inch) turnings at top and bottom and 0.5cm (¼ inch) turnings at side.

You will need

- ☐ Required length of lightweight Rufflette nylon curtain tape.
- ☐ Anchor Stranded Cotton in the following colours and quantities (to work 8 motifs): 2 skeins each 0210 laurel green and 0402 white; 1 skein 036 blossom pink.
- ☐ Alternatively, Anchor Pearl Cotton No. 8: one 10 grm ball each 025 carnation, 0243 grass green, 0402 white.
- ☐ Circular embroidery frame to keep the fabric taut while working
- ☐ Tracing paper
- ☐ Milward 'Gold Seal' crewel needle No. 7

Transferring the motif

Two complete motifs are illustrated to size in the trace pattern. Trace the motifs and transfer them to the fabric either with dressmakers' carbon paper or by outlining with small tacking stitches.

Alternate the motifs evenly along the edge of the fabric, placing them above the final hem turning.

The design

1 No special skill is required for shadow work but it is important to work neatly so that the double lines of back stitch lie closely together. This will be easier to do if the work is held taut in a circular embroidery frame.

2 Using 3 strands of cotton throughout, follow the working chart as a guide to the colours and stitches used for each part of the motif.

3 Double back stitch, or closed herringbone stitch, can be worked either from the right or the wrong side of the fabric. Figure 1 shows how a small back stitch is worked alternately on each side of the traced double lines. The dotted lines on the diagram show the formation of the thread on the wrong side of the fabric, with the colour showing delicately through.

4 Figure 2 shows closed herringbone stitch worked on the wrong side of the fabric with no spaces left between the stitches. Both methods achieve the same results. But whichever method you choose, take care that the work is as neat on the back as on the front as the curtain will be seen from both sides.

5 To finish off, press the embroidery on the wrong side, turn up the side and bottom hems and sew on the curtain tape at the top.

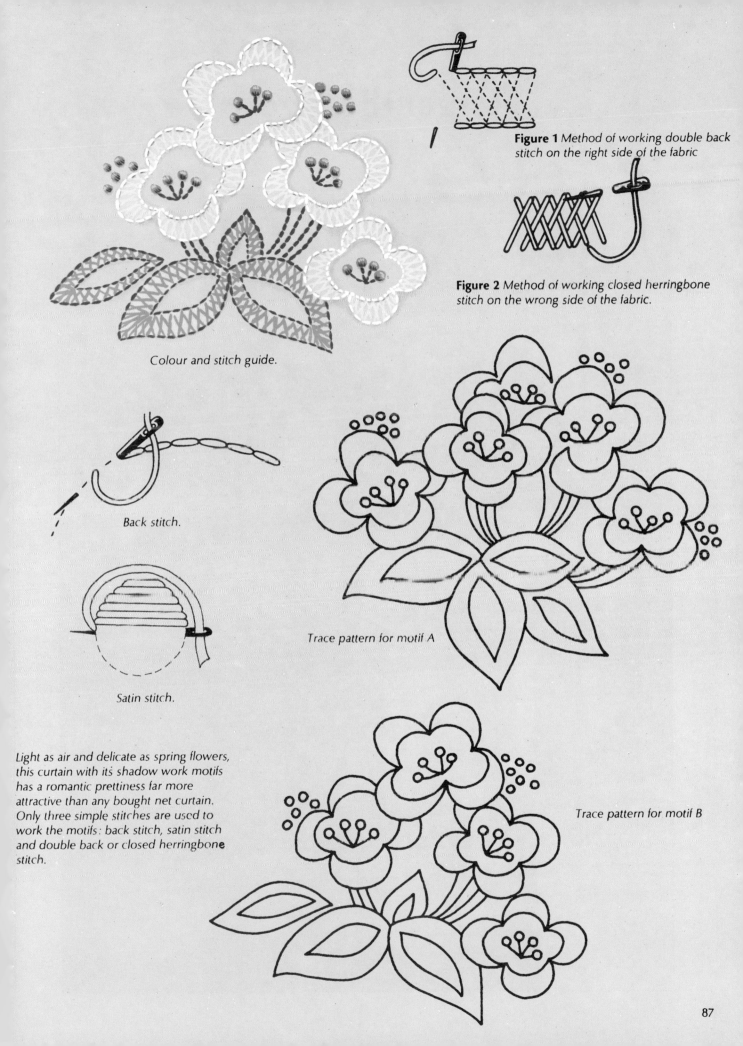

Colour and stitch guide.

Figure 1 Method of working double back stitch on the right side of the fabric

Figure 2 Method of working closed herringbone stitch on the wrong side of the fabric.

Back stitch.

Satin stitch.

Trace pattern for motif A

Trace pattern for motif B

Light as air and delicate as spring flowers, this curtain with its shadow work motifs has a romantic prettiness far more attractive than any bought net curtain. Only three simple stitches are used to work the motifs: back stitch, satin stitch and double back or closed herringbone stitch.

87

Organdie apron

Size

The length can be adjusted to fit the size you require.

Fabric required

1.15 metres (1¼ yards) cotton organdie, 112cm (44 inches) wide

You will also need

- [ ] Matching pure silk thread
- [ ] Stranded embroidery cotton in a darker and lighter shade of main colour
- [ ] Pearl cotton embroidery thread in a lighter shade of main colour
- [ ] Fine crewel needle
- [ ] Fine tapestry needle

Cutting out

Fold the fabric in half lengthways placing the selvedges together. Cut out the pieces as shown in the chart.

Making up

1 Place the facing strip to the bottom edge of the main section and tack together all round the edge. This now forms the wrong side of the apron.

2 Using a sharp pencil and a small plate or saucer as a guide, draw a scalloped edge on the wrong side of the fabric along the top edge of the facing. Start from the centre-front and work outwards to the sides so that the scallops are balanced.

| | right side | | wrong side |

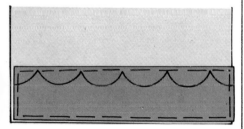

3 With the tapestry needle and pure silk thread, work pin stitching along the scalloped line on the wrong side of the fabric. Use sharp embroidery scissors to trim the excess fabric back to the stitching line.

4 Place the fabric, wrong side facing up, over the motif and trace it, placing one motif above each scallop as shown.

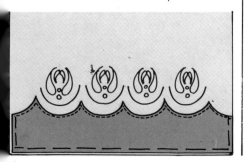

5 Still working on the wrong side, fill in the two inner shapes in herringbone stitch, using the darker shade of stranded cotton and the fine crewel needle. Keep the top and bottom of the stitch equal in width so that the work will be even on the right side.

6 Work the two outer shapes in the same way, using the lighter shade of the stranded cotton.

7 Using the fine pearl cotton complete the surface stitchery on the right side of the work.

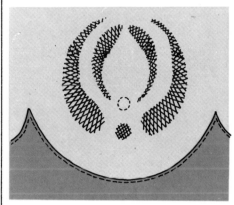

Work a back-stitch spider's web in the middle.

8 For the stitching enclosing the bottom of the motif, work a graduating line of fine satin stitch, 0.3cm (⅛ inch) apart, starting with a very small stitch and gradually getting wider then tapering off to a very small stitch at the beginning of the line.

9 On the satin stitch line work a row of raised chain band, making it a double row where the line thickens in the centre and tapering it by starting and finishing with several stem or split stitches.

Work a motif on to the pocket in the same way.

The frill

10 Finish each side of the apron with a 1.3cm (½ inch) hem.

Join the pieces for the frill along the narrow edge with a French seam.

Make a narrow hem along the short ends and bottom edge of the frill. Work a row of gathering along the top edge.

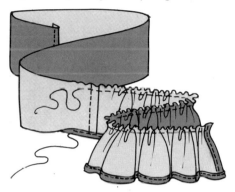

11 Remove the tacking thread from the bottom edge of the apron. With right sides together tack the top edge of the frill to the bottom of the apron, arranging the gathers evenly and leaving the edge of the facing free. Machine stitch, taking 1.3cm (½ inch) turnings.

12 Press the turnings upwards, turn under the edge of the facing and place the fold to the stitch line. Hem into place.

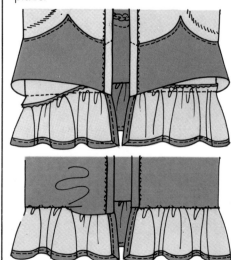

The pocket

13 Prepare the pocket frill in the same way as for the main frill.
Place the frill, wrong side down, on the right side of the pocket so that the raw edges are level along the top. Arrange the gathers evenly and tack in position.

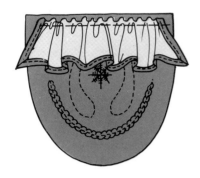

14 Work a very narrow hem along one long edge of the pocket facing. Place the facing on to the top of the pocket so that the raw edges are level along the top and sides. Tack and machine stitch along the top and sides, taking 1.3cm (½ inch) turnings. Turn the facing on to the wrong side of the pocket and press.

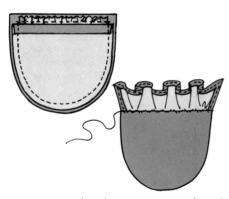

15 Turn under the remaining sides of the pocket. Place the pocket in position on to the apron. Tack and machine stitch.

The waistband

16 Fold under the short ends of the waistband for 1.3cm (½ inch) on to the wrong side and tack. Fold the waistband in half lengthways.

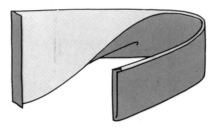

17 Try on the apron for length and adjust it at the top edge if necessary. Work a row of gathering along the top edge. With right sides together, pin the gathered edge to one long side of the waistband, arranging the gathers evenly. Tack in place.

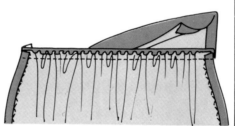

18 Make narrow hems along the two long sides and one short side of the apron ties. Place the fourth side to the ends of the waistband, gathering the fullness as shown.

19 Stitch, taking 1.3cm (½ inch) turnings from the left edge at the top of the tie, across the front and over the tie at the right edge.
Fold under the remaining edges of the waistband and hem to the stitch line.

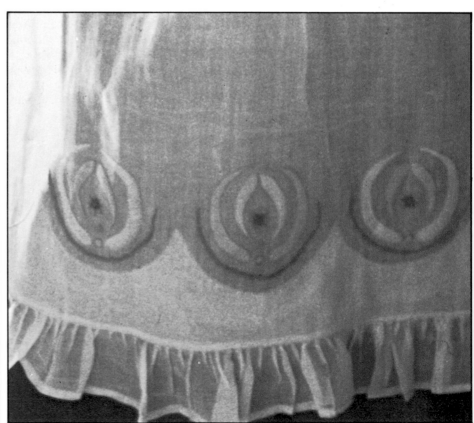

Cutting layout for apron

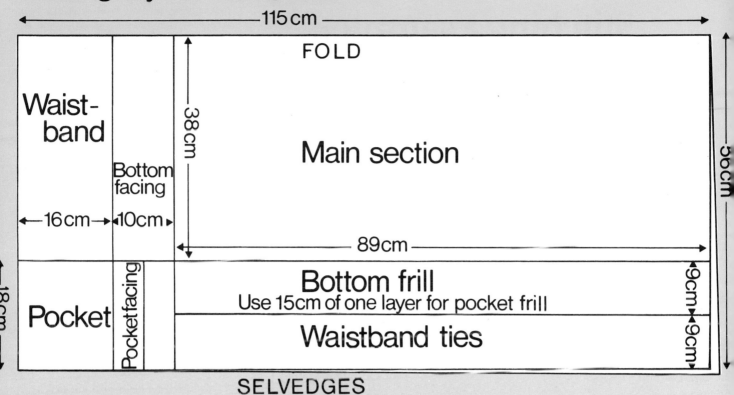

Trace pattern for embroidery

Stitching a sampler

For centuries the sampler was an essential part of every girl's education. Many survive today as beautiful examples of fine needlework. Now you can work your own sampler in the traditional manner. Nearly 20 different stitches, including drawn thread work, are included to make this sampler a technical exercise for the experienced needlewoman as well as the beginner. Add your name and the date of completion at top or bottom for a really authentic touch.

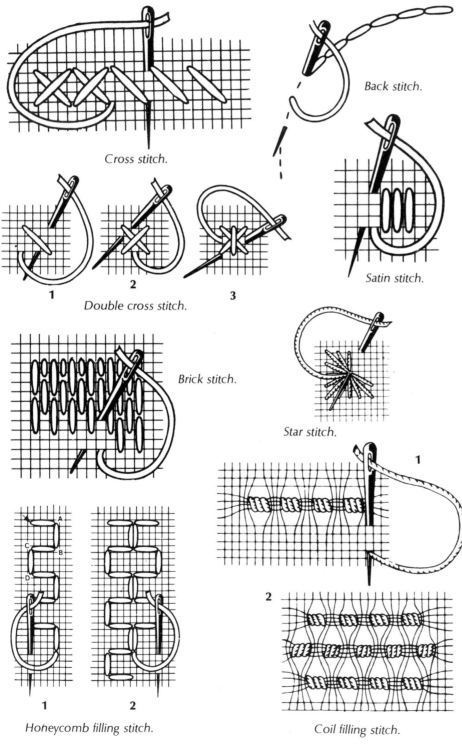

Cross stitch.

Back stitch.

Double cross stitch.

1   2   3

Satin stitch.

Brick stitch.

Star stitch.

Honeycomb filling stitch.

1   2

Coil filling stitch.

Fabric required

90cm (36 inches) beige medium weight evenweave fabric, 21 threads to 2.5cm (1 inch), 150cm (59 inches) wide

You will also need

☐ Anchor Stranded Cotton in the following colours and quantities: 2 skeins tapestry shade 0905, 2 skeins each tapestry shades 0843, 0845, 0887; 1 skein each tapestry shades 0848, 0850, 0851, 0885, 0888 geranium 06, 010 and 013.

☐ Picture frame with mounting board or cardboard to fit embroidery

☐ Milward 'Gold Seal' tapestry needles Nos. 20 and 24 for 6 and 3 strands respectively

The design

1 Cut a piece from the fabric to measure 90cm (36 inches) square. Mark the centres both ways with a line of tacking stitches.

2 Diagram I gives slightly more than half the design with the centre indicated by black arrows. Each background square on the diagram represents 2 threads of the fabric.

3 Use 6 strands of thread and needle size 20 for Swedish darning, satin stitch, couching and oblique loop stitch. Use 3 strands and needle size 24 for the rest of the embroidery.

4 Diagram 2 shows the Swedish darning and satin stitch tree. The background lines on this diagram indicate the threads of the fabric.

5 Begin working the sampler centrally with four sided stitch filling, 2 threads down and 6 threads to the right of the crossed tacking stitches. Follow Diagram 1 and the stitch and colour key for the main part of the design. Repeat in reverse from the lower black arrow to complete the second half of the sampler.

6 Couching is worked horizontally between satin stitch C9 on the diagram.

7 Once the embroidery for Diagram 1 has been completed, work Diagram 2 in the position indicated, following the key for the design and stitches used. The four drawn thread borders are worked one on each side of the completed design, linked by woven bars and oblique loop stitch as shown in the photograph.

Finishing off the sampler

Press the completed sampler on the wrong side. Place it centrally over the mounting board, fold the surplus fabric to the back of the board and secure it all round with pins stuck into the edge of the board. Lace the fabric across the back both ways with strong thread. Remove the pins and mount the sampler in a frame.

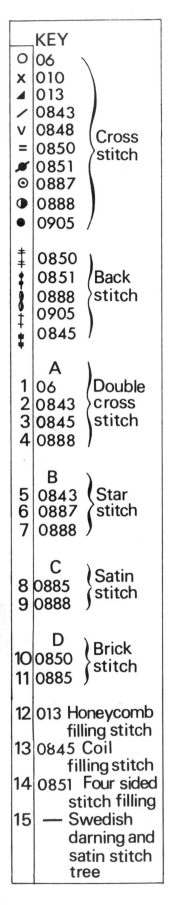

KEY

O	06	
x	010	
◢	013	
/	0843	
v	0848	Cross stitch
=	0850	
◗	0851	
⊙	0887	
◑	0888	
●	0905	

‡	0850	
◆	0851	Back stitch
◗	0888	
◍	0905	
+	0845	

A		
1	06	Double cross stitch
2	0843	
3	0845	
4	0888	

B		
5	0843	Star stitch
6	0887	
7	0888	

C		
8	0885	Satin stitch
9	0888	

D		
10	0850	Brick stitch
11	0885	

12	013	Honeycomb filling stitch
13	0845	Coil filling stitch
14	0851	Four sided stitch filling
15	—	Swedish darning and satin stitch tree

DIAGRAM 1 ▶

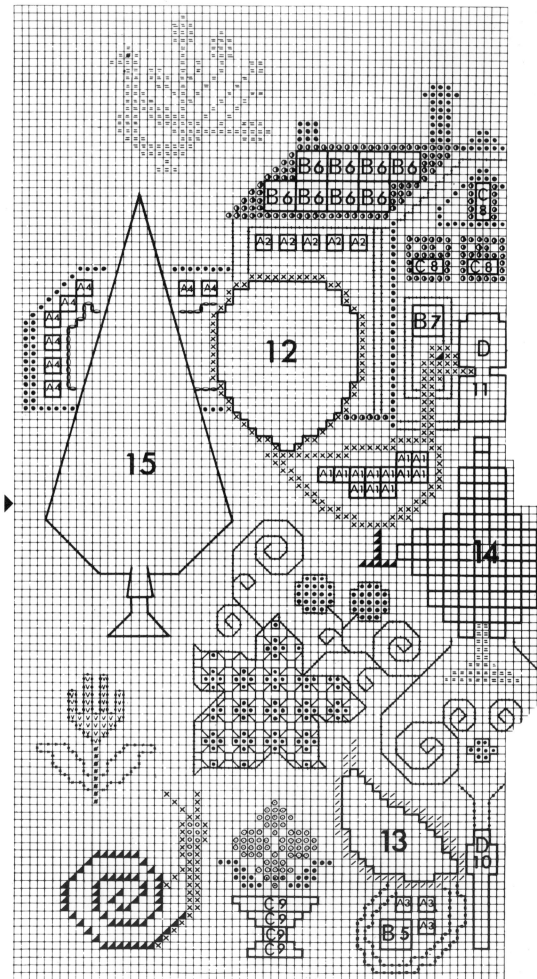

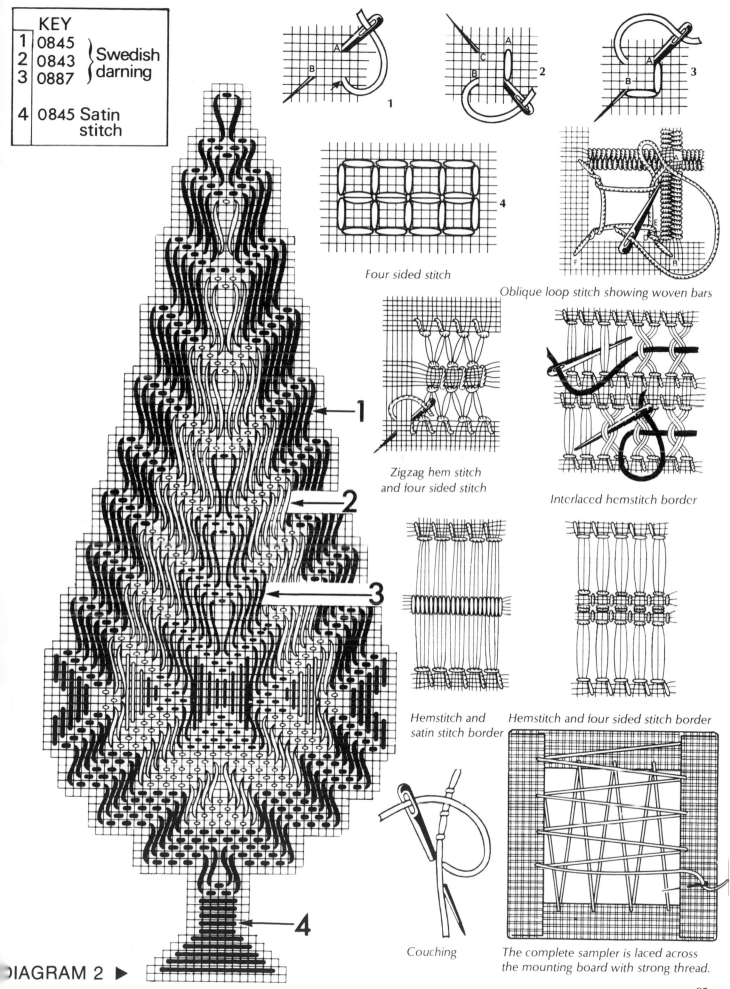

KEY

1	0845	} Swedish darning
2	0843	
3	0887	
4	0845	Satin stitch

Four sided stitch

Oblique loop stitch showing woven bars

Zigzag hem stitch and four sided stitch

Interlaced hemstitch border

Hemstitch and satin stitch border

Hemstitch and four sided stitch border

Couching

The complete sampler is laced across the mounting board with strong thread.

DIAGRAM 2 ▶

CANVAS WORK
Basic equipment

Canvas work

Canvas work is a relaxing form of embroidery. It requires little mental effort and can be most effective when worked in one stitch. Carried out on a stiff, open-weave fabric, it is hard-wearing for use in the home as chair seat covers, stool tops, cushions, lamp bases, etc. It can also be made into exciting and useful accessories, such as belts, bags and slippers. Its use for clothes, however, is more restricted because of its stiffness although it could be made up into a simple garment such as a waistcoat. Canvas work is often known as needlepoint or – mistakenly – tapestry work. Tapestry is the name given to a form of weaving, usually of a pictorial kind and this has led to the canvases sold with the design ready painted also being called tapestries.

The equipment

Canvas work can be done without a frame if you are able to maintain an even tension throughout, but it frequently does become distorted as the heat of the hands affects the stiffening in the threads of the canvas. This usually results in the work having to be pinned and stretched over layers of damp blotting paper to restore it to its former shape.

It is much better to use a slate frame or a canvas work frame to prevent this and also to protect the canvas from being creased or crumpled while working as this affects the rigidity that keeps the stitches in place.

Types of canvas frame

There are two types of canvas frame, the flat bar and the screw bar. The flat bar frame is more suitable for large pieces of work using conventional stitches and threads because the canvas is rolled up as the work progresses. It is not so suitable for more adventurous designs using wooden beads, rings, plastic or leather shapes, because these additions prevent the work rolling smoothly.

The screw bar frame has adjustable side pieces which fit into rollers at both ends. This sort of frame has to be large enough to take the fully extended canvas because it cannot be rolled.

An old picture frame or artist's painting stretcher can be used successfully as a substitute frame. To attach the canvas to it, machine-stitch wide tape over the edge

of the canvas to strengthen it and then fix firmly to the frame with drawing pins placed at 1.3cm ($\frac{1}{2}$ inch) intervals.

A circular or tambour frame is suitable only for small pieces of work where the part of canvas enclosed by the rings will be cut off as it will have become distorted from the pressure.

The canvas

Canvas is made from linen, hemp and cotton. Single canvas has the threads interwoven singly and is the variety most often used because all types of stitches can be worked without difficulty.

Double canvas has the threads woven in pairs and is normally used when fine

detail and small stitching is wanted in the design. The stitches are mostly worked over the pair of threads for the background of the design and over one thread of the pair for the detailed sections.

The number of the mesh indicates the number of threads to the centimetre or inch.

Good quality hessian or wide-meshed linen scrim can be used instead of canvas where you want a more pliable effect and these can be worked with all the usual canvas work stitches (see the following chapter) but often with much more expressive results.

Fine wire mesh and wire gauze have also been used for experimental canvas work.

The needles

Tapestry needles, which are blunt-ended with a large eye to enable the thread to be pulled through easily, are sold in a variety of sizes to suit the canvas and thread used. Before threading a needle with wool, hold the wool up to the light to see the direction of the fibres (drawing the thread through your fingers will show you if the fibres are lying in the right direction). Thread the wool into the needle so that the fibres are lying away from the threaded end. In this way the fibres will be stroked downwards when pulled through the canvas, thus reducing tension on the wool and ensuring a smoother finish to the work.

You will also need two pairs of good scissors, one for cutting the canvas and paper for designs, and another small sharp-pointed pair for cutting threads. A pair of tweezers can be very useful if you have to unpick any stitches.

The designs

In Victorian times canvas work was used for elaborate pictorial designs such as wreaths of full-blown roses, baskets and fruit and other still-life scenes, usually worked in tent stitch or cross stitch. Nowadays, however, canvas work is at its most attractive when used for geometric designs which allow a variety of textures, threads and stitches to be used.

Cut paper shapes arranged in a geometric pattern are perhaps the easiest form of designing for a beginner.

Squared paper or graph paper is best for drawing the final designs for canvas work because each square of paper can be used to denote one stitch worked over two threads of the canvas. It is often possible to buy the graph paper with squares corresponding to those of the canvas which enables intricate designs to be worked out in detail.

A useful economy is to copy the design on to greaseproof or tracing paper and to place this over the graph paper to redraw and 'square off'. In this way the graph paper can be re-used several times.

To transfer the design on to the canvas, tack the tracing to the canvas round the edges and then tack along each line of the design using a coloured tacking thread and small stitches.

An alternative method is to outline the tracing with black poster paint, Indian ink or felt tipped pen. The canvas is then centred over the design and the outline traced on to the canvas with waterproof Indian ink. It is advisable to mark the centre of each side of both the tracing and the canvas so that they can be matched accurately and to secure the tracing with drawing pins if you are using this method.

The threads

It is extremely important that the yarns and threads used for canvas work should match the mesh of the canvas so that the stitches cover the canvas completely. A large mesh canvas is obviously unsuitable for fine yarn and vice versa.

The type of thread depends largely on the nature of the work and how it will be used. Wool is the traditional thread for canvas work and is the most hardwearing Crewel wool is sold specially for canvas work and can be used with two or three strands to suit the mesh. Knitting wool can also be used if crewel wool is unobtainable.

There is an almost unlimited choice of other threads which can be used – pearl cotton in various weights, stranded cotton, twisted silks, tapisserie wool, coton à broder, soft cotton, lurex and even raffia and string.

Canvas work stitches

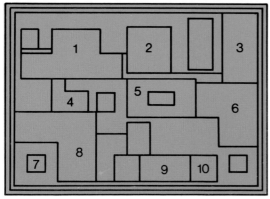

Key to Chart
1 Padded satin stitch
2 Hungarian stitch
3 Large cross stitch worked alternately with Hungarian
4 Long-legged cross stitch
5 Brick stitch
6 Long-legged cross stitch
7 Norwich stitch
8 Large cross stitch and straight cross stitch
9 Paris stitch
10 Eye stitch
Background: tent stitch

There are a great number of canvas work stitches, many of which are similar to those used in regular embroidery. Here are a few of the most useful stitches.

Smyrna or double cross

This is double cross stitch worked in two directions. Work cross stitch over four threads and then complete each stitch by

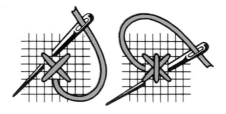

working another cross stitch vertically over the first stitch as shown.

Long-legged cross

This is a useful stitch because it can be worked in horizontal rows from left to right and from right to left, or in vertical rows from the top down and from the bottom up. Work as shown in the diagram, always beginning and ending each row with a regular cross stitch. If used to fill in a background, the rows can be worked alternately in each direction. The long-legged cross stitch can also be combined with the tent stitch in alternate rows.

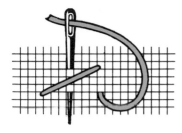

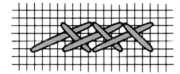

Tent stitch

This looks similar to a half cross-stitch but is so worked to give more coverage on the back of the canvas. It can be worked from right to left, in vertical rows or diagonal rows. It is a good background stitch and throws into relief more chunky stitches.

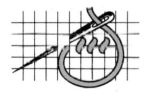

Knot stitch

This is another variation of cross stitch with one of the obliques worked over three threads and the other oblique worked over one thread to tie it. It is a useful filling stitch giving a good texture for backgrounds.

Rice stitch

This is a development of cross stitch. Work the crosses in a thick yarn over four threads. Then using a finer thread in a contrasting colour or texture work a single oblique over each corner. Work these stitches in two horizontal rows, tying down the two upper corners of each cross in the first row and the two lower corners in the second row.

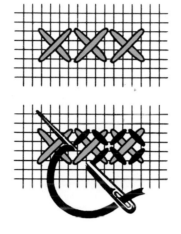

Hungarian stitch

This is a simple stitch which is more effective when worked in two colours or two textures. It consists of straight stitches worked in groups of three. For the first row, work the first stitch over two threads, the second over four threads and the third over two threads. Leave two threads and repeat to the end of the row. Work the second row as for the first, fitting the longer stitches into the spaces left by the previous row as shown.

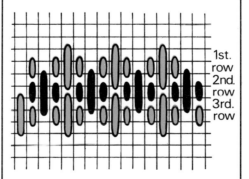

Paris stitch

This is a good background filling stitch made by working alternately over one and then over three threads of the canvas in alternate rows from left to right and right

to left. The short stitches in the second row fit in under the long stitches of the rows on each side.

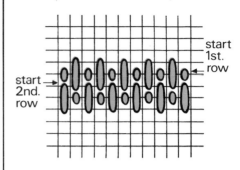

Eye stitch

This consists of 16 stitches worked over eight threads, all radiating from the same centre hole.

Norwich stitch

This is not as complicated as it appears. It can be worked over any size square, providing that the square consists of an uneven number of threads. Start at point 1 and take a straight stitch to point 2. Go to the opposite corner and take a stitch from point 3 to point 4. Continue in this way round the square, taking stitches between the points shown on the diagram, thus giving the effect of a square on the diagonal.

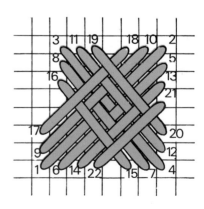

Canvas work sampler

This cushion can be worked as a sampler to practise many different stitches making up an interesting collection of textures. The simple use of one colour also emphasises the variation of stitches, although other colours may be used to complement the subtle variety of stitches.

Size
43cm (17 inches) square

Fabric required
Cream fabric for backing, 48.5cm (19 inches) square

You will also need
- [ ] Anchor Tapisserie Wool: 43 skeins 0386 cream
- [ ] 0.60m (⅝ yard) single thread tapestry canvas, 68.5cm (27 inches) wide, 18 threads to 2.5cm (1 inch)
- [ ] Cushion pad to fit
- [ ] Tapestry frame with 68.5cm (27 inches) tapes
- [ ] Milward 'Gold Seal' tapestry needle No. 18

The design
1 Mark the centre of the canvas along a line of holes in both directions with tacking stitches. Mount the canvas in the frame, with the raw edges to the tapes. When working fern stitch turn the frame on its side to allow the stitches to be worked in the correct direction, as indicated by the black arrows on the working chart. The working chart gives a section of the complete design. Blank arrows indicate the centre of the design, which should coincide with the tacking stitches.

2 Follow the working chart using the stitch key for the design. Each background square represents two threads of the canvas. Detailed stitch diagrams are given showing the number of threads over which the stitches are worked. When working cross stitch it is important that the crosses cross in the same direction.

3 Begin the design at the small black arrow 6 threads down and 14 threads to the left of the crossed tacking stitches in the centre of the canvas, and work the section as given on the working chart. Omit the centre section and repeat the stitches in reverse from the blank arrow to complete one quarter of the design. Work the other three quarters to correspond. The completed canvaswork should be dampened, then pinned and stretched to the correct shape, on a clean dry board with rustless drawing pins and left to dry naturally.

To work velvet stitch

This stitch resembles the pile of an oriental carpet. It is worked from left to right in rows working from the bottom upwards. Follow the stitch diagram, bringing the thread out at the arrow and insert the needle at A (2 threads up and 2 threads to the right), then bring it out again at the arrow. Re-insert the needle at A, leaving a loop of thread at the bottom, bring the needle out at B (2 threads down). Insert at C (2 threads up and 2 threads to the left), bringing the needle out again at B in readiness for the next stitch. To maintain a regular length to the loops they can be worked over a thick knitting needle. After all the rows have been worked, cut the loops and trim them evenly, taking care not to trim the tufts too short.

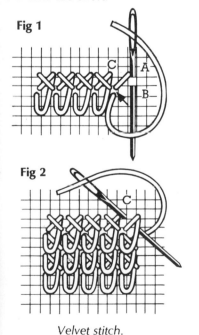

Velvet stitch.

To work brick stitch

This stitch is worked in rows alternately from left to right or from right to left. The first row consists of long and short stitches into which are fitted rows of even satin stitch, giving a 'brick' formation. The whole filling must be worked very regularly, making each satin stitch of even length and all exactly parallel.

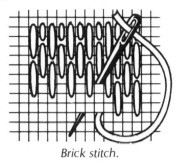

Brick stitch.

To work cross stitch and upright cross stitch

1 Work the required number of cross stitches over 4 threads, then work upright cross stitch between each cross stitch, working diagonally from the lower right to the top left corner in the following way.

2 Figure 1 – bring the thread out at the arrow; insert the needle at A (2 threads up), then bring it out at B (2 threads to the left). Continue in this way to the end of the row.

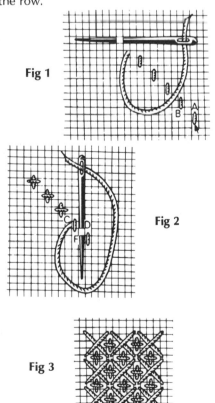

Cross stitch and upright cross stitch.

3 Figure 2 – after completing the last stitch, bring the needle through as shown at C. Insert the needle at D (2 threads to the right), and bring it though at E. Continue in this way to the end of the row. Figure 3 shows the finished effect.

To work fern stitch

Pull the thread through at the arrow and insert the needle 2 threads down and 4 threads to the right bringing it out 2 threads to the left. Then insert the needle 2 threads to the right. Bring it out 2 threads down and 4 threads to the left in readiness for the next stitch. The diagram also shows the direction of the two rows of fern stitch as they have been worked on the cushion.

Fern stitch.

To work eye stitch

This stitch is worked in the same way as star stitch, to form a square over 8 horizontal and 8 vertical threads of canvas. It consists of 16 straight stitches all taken into the same central hole but with their outer ends arranged over a square of eight threads. Finish off the square with an outline of back stitch worked over 2 canvas threads, shown in Figure 2.

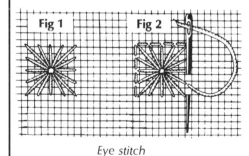

Eye stitch

To work gobelin stitch

Work a trammed stitch from left to right, then pull the needle through 1 thread down and 1 thread to the left, inserting

Straight gobelin stitch.

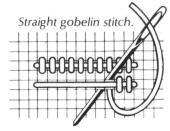

101

again 2 threads above. Pull the needle through 2 threads down and 1 thread to the left in readiness for the next stitch.

To work the cord

Measure off six 13.75m (15 yard) lengths of wool. With another person to help you, double the pieces of wool in half to make a length of 6.90m (7½ yards), then knot the loose ends together and insert a pencil at each end. Pull the threads and, keeping them taut, turn the pencils round in opposite directions following the natural twist of the wool. Continue until the cord is sufficiently tight and begins to curl. Still keeping the cord tight, place another pencil in the centre and double the cord over it until both ends meet, making a length of 3m (3¼ yards). Next twist the cord in the opposite direction, until it begins to curl naturally. Set the cord by exerting a steady pull at both ends which will cause it to stretch slightly and so retain its twist permanently.

To make the tassels

For one tassel, wind 2 skeins of wool neatly round a piece of card 7.5cm (3 inches) wide Tie them together with a piece of matching wool at one end, cut the wool at the opposite end, and then remove the card. Now take another piece of wool, about ¼ skein, and wind this round the tied ends near the top to form a head, then fasten off securely. If the wool does not lie properly when the tassel is completed, hold it for a few minutes in the steam from a kettle, or press with a cool iron.

To make up

Trim the canvas, leaving a 2.5cm (1 inch) border of unworked canvas all round. Place the canvaswork and backing fabric right sides together and sew close to the embroidery round three sides. Turn back to the right sides, insert the cushion pad, and slip stitch along the opening. Stitch the cord in position around the edge of the cushion and attach the tassels securely to the corners.

KEY
1 Velvet stitch
2 Cross stitch
3 Satin stitch
3a Satin stitch (horizontal)
4 Brick stitch
5 Cross stitch and upright cross stitch (variation)
6 Fern stitch
7 Eye stitch
☐ Petit point
☐ Straight gobelin stitch

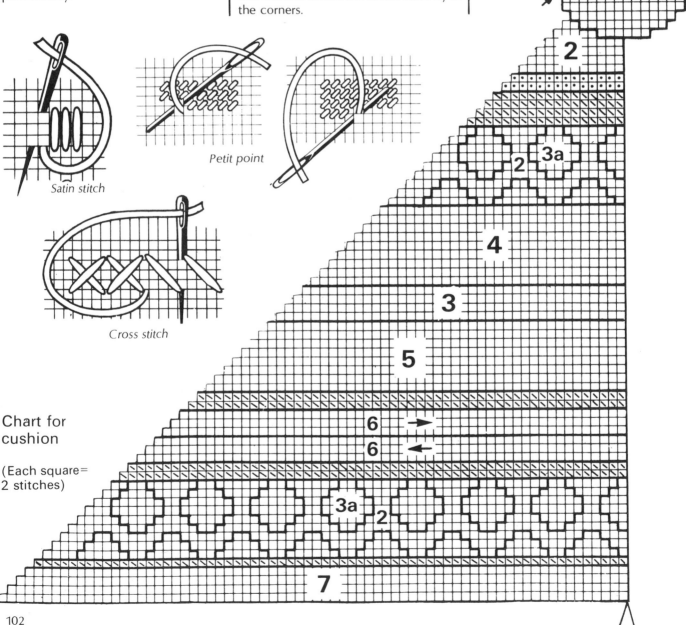

Satin stitch

Petit point

Cross stitch

Chart for cushion

(Each square = 2 stitches)

Quillwork desk set

For your desk

This smart desk set was inspired by the quillwork embroidery of North American Indian tribes. The colours, ochre, indigo and rust, are similar to those produced by natural dyes. The embroidery is worked throughout in variations of satin stitch. The simple basic design can easily be adapted to make the pieces of the set larger or smaller if you wish.

Fabric required

0.65m (⅔ yard) single thread canvas, 16 threads to 2.5cm (1 inch), 59cm (23 inches) wide 0.25cm (¼ yard) felt, 1.85m (72 inches) wide to match one of the main colours

You will also need

☐ Anchor Tapisserie Wool in the following colours and quantities: 8 skeins 0850 indigo, 7 skeins 0412 rust, 5 skeins 0315 ochre, 4 skeins 0848 light blue.
☐ Hardback address book, 12.5cm by 20.5cm (5 inches by 8 inches)
☐ 29grm (10½ ounce) soup tin, 10cm (4 inches) high, for pen holder
☐ Piece of heavy cardboard, thin plywood or plastic sheet 40.5cm by 59cm (16 inches by 23 inches)
☐ Milward 'Gold Seal' tapestry needle No. 22
☐ Sewing needle
☐ Thread to match felt

The design

1 Tape the raw edges of the canvas and, following the working charts, work the parts of the desk set. Do not cut the canvas, but leave a 5cm (2 inch) border of unworked canvas around each piece of embroidery. The embroidery is worked in satin stitch of various lengths.
2 The completed canvaswork should be dampened, then pinned and stretched to the correct shape on a clean board, and left to dry naturally.

Pen holder

Trim the canvas to 2cm (¾ inch) all round. Fold the canvas round to form a ring, trim the top layer of unworked canvas down to 4 threads. Work satin stitch, using indigo thread, over the 4 threads as shown, joining the two layers of unworked canvas. Cut a strip of felt 10cm by 2cm (4 inches by 9 inches) and sew the short ends together. Turn under the border of unworked canvas round top and bottom, slip the felt inside the canvas and slip stitch together round top and bottom. Fit the completed cover over the tin.

Address book cover

Trim the canvas all round to 2cm (¾ inch). Mitre the corners and fold down the

borders of unworked canvas. Cut a strip of felt 28cm by 21cm (11 inches by 8¼ inches). Stitch one short end of the felt to the canvas as shown in the diagram. Cut another piece of felt 10.5cm by 21cm (4¼ inches by 7¼ inches), sew this to the remaining 3 sides of the canvas. Slide the embroidery onto the front cover of the book, fold the rest of the felt around the book and inside the back cover. Slip stitch at top and bottom.

Blotter

Trim the canvas to 2cm (¾ inch) all round. Cut a piece of felt as shown in the diagram. Turn under the unworked borders of canvas and sew the two embroidered end pieces onto the felt as shown. Lay the top of the felt and fold the end pieces round to the front. Fold the excess felt at top and bottom to the back of the board and stitch down. Insert blotting paper.

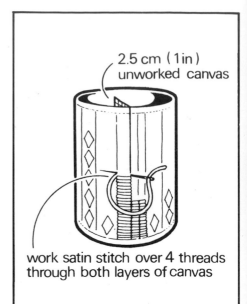

2.5 cm (1 in) unworked canvas

work satin stitch over 4 threads through both layers of canvas

Sewing the pen holder cover.

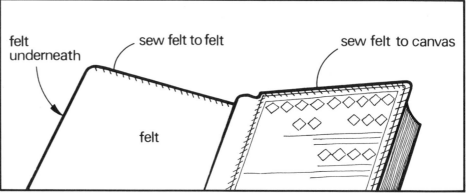

felt underneath   sew felt to felt   sew felt to canvas

felt

Fitting the cover on the address book.   *Cutting felt for the blotter.*

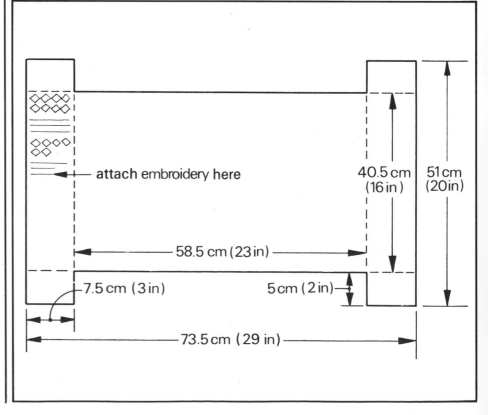

attach embroidery here

40.5 cm (16 in)   51 cm (20 in)

58.5 cm (23 in)

7.5 cm (3 in)   5 cm (2 in)

73.5 cm (29 in)

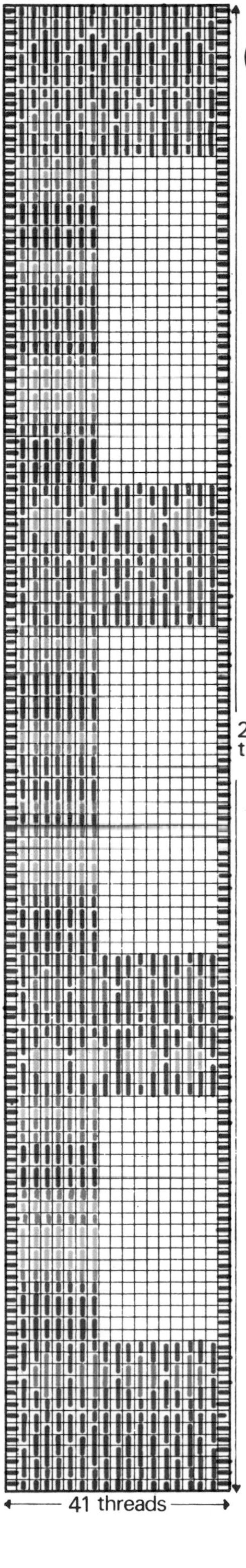

Chart for blotter cover

Each square = 2 threads of the canvas

Chart for address book cover

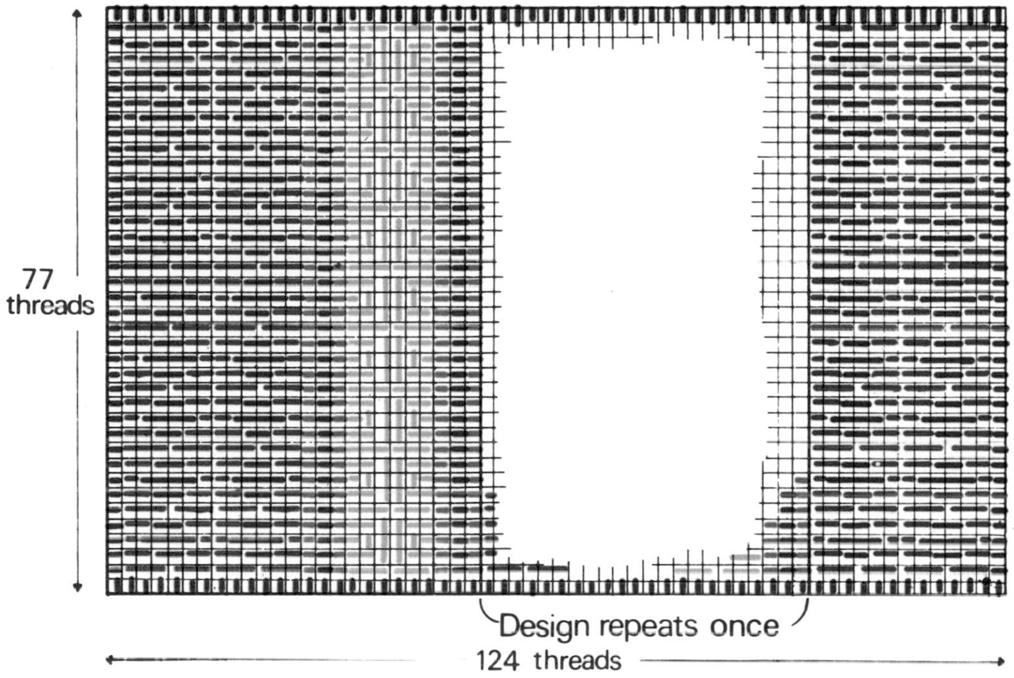

77 threads

254 threads

Design repeats once

124 threads

Chart for penholder cover

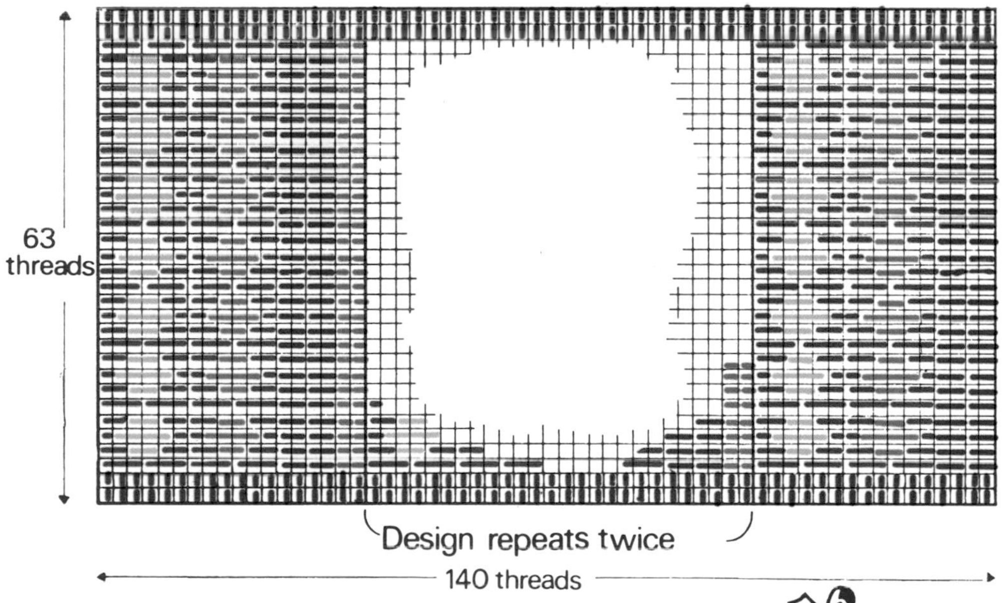

63 threads

Design repeats twice

140 threads

41 threads

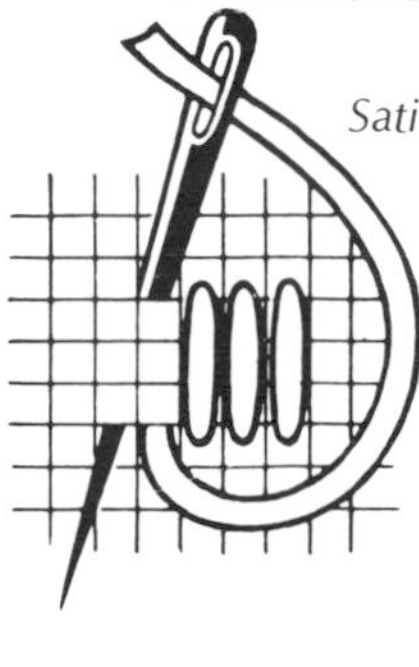

Satin stitch.

Anchor Tapisserie Wool

0412 rust
0850 indigo
0315 ochre
0848 light blue

FLORENTINE EMBROIDERY

Florentine canvas work dates back as far as the thirteenth century and is thought to be of Hungarian origin.

It is also known as Bargello, which is probably a corruption of Jagiello, the family name of the Polish King Vladislaw who married a young Hungarian princess. She incorporated the arms of Hungary and Poland in a bishop's cope which she worked in the stitch now known as Florentine.

It became known as Florentine work in the fifteenth century when one of the Medici family married a Hungarian bride who taught the art to the ladies of the Florentine court. Other names for Florentine work include Hungarian point, 'Fiamma' or flame stitch.

There is a great difference between the Florentine work of the past and that of today. The main characteristic of the work is the shading and blending of colour, but while the early work was subtle with carefully arranged colour tints, modern work is bolder and more striking.

Traditionally Florentine work was used for upholstery on stool tops, chair seats and bed drapes but it can also be made into smaller articles such as accessories like bags and purses.

Choosing the colours

As a general rule, it is advisable to use two or three basic colours with as many intermediate shades of these colours as you like. Each successive line is worked in a lighter or darker tint to the previous line, so shading gradually from one tone to another. When you are working in shades which are very close, grade and number the skeins before starting.

Materials

Use single thread canvas with yarn in the correct thickness to match the mesh and completely cover the canvas. Tapestry and crewel wools are the most frequently used being specially designed to suit a wide range of different sized canvases. Both are sold in a good colour range. Knitting wool can also be used and it is possible to incorporate silk threads on a fine mesh canvas.

Estimating the amount of yarn

1 Cut a 45cm (*18 inch*) length of yarn. Stitch as much of the pattern repeat as this length will allow and then count up the number worked. Multiply by the yarn length to calculate how much you need for a complete row and then multiply by the number of rows worked in each colour.

2 Calculate from the amount specified by the manufacturer how many skeins of each colour you will need.

Needles

Use tapestry needles of a suitable thickness for the canvas and yarn.

Frames

Technically this form of canvas work can be evenly stitched whether held in the hand or mounted in a frame so it is a matter of personal preference.

Preparing the canvas

Tack the centre lines both vertically and horizontally on the canvas and any other guide lines necessary. Count and mark the high points of any pattern where the repeat is the same throughout.

The stitch

Only one type of stitch is used for Florentine work. It is a vertical stitch usually covering an even number of threads, such as four, six or eight, and moving either upwards or downwards over one or more threads depending on the pattern.

Patterns are constructed by working blocks of stitches side by side, then moving higher or lower to make another block, and so on.

Zig zag stitch

This is the most commonly used Florentine stitch and is worked by passing each stitch over four threads and back under two. The easiest way to vary it is to take it over six threads and back under one. To avoid monotony in the pattern, vary the height of the pinnacles formed or make the slopes more gradual, perhaps by making two stitches over the same number of threads.

Flame stitch

This is worked over four threads and back under one and produces a flame-like effect. It is important to start in the centre of the canvas with the apex of the stitch at the highest point. Both flame stitch and Florentine stitch can be the basis of more complex designs using squares, diamonds or trellises.

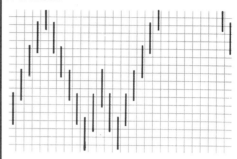

Curves

You can form the illusion of a curve by working blocks of stitches over the same number of threads by varying the rate of progression. Thus stitches or blocks of stitches worked on the 6/1, 5/1 and 4/1 principle will produce steeper curves than those worked on the 6/3 and 4/2 principle.

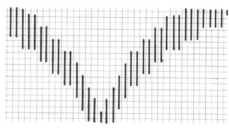

Medallion pattern

This is a popular repeating pattern where each stitch is taken over four threads and back under two, starting with four single stitches, followed by one block of two stitches, then three blocks of three stitches to form the top of the pattern.

Progress downwards, repeating the same number of stitches. This forms the outline of the pattern which can be repeated for the whole work. The spaces formed between the medallions can be filled with contrasting yarns.

The foundation row

All Florentine patterns depend on an accurate first row and in some patterns the embroidery is worked either above or below this row. In others each section is filled in from one outer foundation row or grid. When working this foundation row it is extremely important to count the threads accurately – if you make a mistake, cut it out rather than trying to unpick it which takes too long and frays the wool so badly that it is unusable again.

For patterns where symmetry is important, begin at the marked centre line of the canvas and stitch the first row from the centre outwards. The following rows can be worked from side to side in the normal way, following the pattern established by the first row.

Starting and finishing

Use a length of yarn about 38cm (15 inches) long and knot one end. Thread the needle with the other end and pass the needle through the canvas from the front about 5cm (2 inches) from the position of the first stitch. Bring the needle up in the position for the first stitch, work several stitches and then cut off the knot, leaving the tail.

Thread the tail through to the back of the canvas and work it in through the back of the stitches. Finish off by working a short length through the stitches on the back in the same way. Always avoid starting and finishing in the same place so that the work has an even finish and darn in the ends as they occur to avoid matting and tangling on the back of the work.

Florentine clutch bag
Size
19cm (7½ inches) × 30cm (11¾ inches) × 5cm (2 inches)

Fabric required
0.35cm (⅜ yard) single thread tapestry canvas, 68.5cm (27 inches) wide 14 threads to 2.5cm (1 inch)
Small skin of suede for back of bag and gussets
1 × felt square, 61cm × 61cm (24 inches × 24 inches)

You will also need
☐ Coats Anchor Tapisserie wool: 4 skeins Raspberry 071, 2 skeins each Raspberry 067, 068, 069; 1 skein grey 0398
☐ Clark's Anchor Stranded Cotton: 3 skeins rose pink 048, 2 skeins each white 0402, grey 0397. Use six strands throughout.
☐ Tapestry frame with 68.5cm (27 inch) tapes
☐ Adhesive

The design
This design is worked in Florentine canvas embroidery.
The photograph gives a section of the design with the double row of three straight stitches forming the centre.

Working the embroidery
1 Mount the canvas into the frame. Mark the centre of the canvas widthwise with a line of tacking.

2 Start the embroidery in the centre of the canvas with the double row of three straight stitches. Work the motifs on each side and repeat to the sides and above and below to the required size. Grade the colours according to the photograph showing a detail of the bag.
Most stitches are worked over six threads of canvas with some stitches over three threads to complete the design.

Making up
1 Cut out pieces of suede measuring 21.5cm (8½ inches × 32.5cm (12¾ inches) for the front; 18cm (7 inches) × 32.5cm (12¾ inches) for the back, and two pieces, 7.5cm (3 inches) × 37cm (14½ inches) for the gusset.
2 With right sides together stitch the gusset pieces along their short edges taking 1.3cm (½ inch) turnings. Press the turnings open with your fingers.
3 With right sides together stitch the Florentine flap to one long edge of the suede back. Press the seam open. Working from the right side top-stitch the suede close to the seam line.

4 Cut out pieces of felt the same size as the suede for the front and gusset and 32.5cm (12¾ inches) × 40.5cm (16 inches) for the flap and back. Stitch the gusset sections as for the suede.
5 With right sides together, stitch the felt back and flap piece to the Florentine flap as far as the fold line which is 4cm (1½ inches) from the seam.
Clip across corners, turn through to the right side and press. Clip seam allowance at the fold line.
6 Place the remaining felt pieces on to the wrong side of the corresponding pieces of suede and treat them as one piece.
7 To neaten the top edge of the front, fold under the turnings for 1.3cm (½ inch), place together and glue with adhesive. Top-stitch close to the edge.
8 With right sides together, stitch the front to the gusset, clipping the gusset turning at the corners. Repeat with the back. Trim seams and turn right side out. Top-stitch the seams through all thicknesses 0.6cm (¼ inch) from the edge.

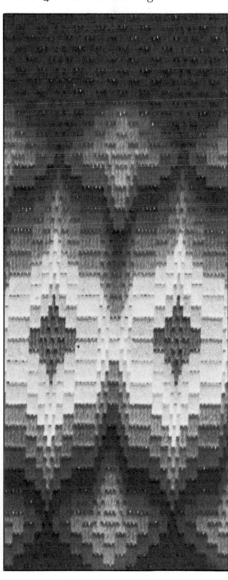

Florentine chair seat

The quantities and instructions are given for a dining chair with a larger than average drop-in seat but they can easily be adapted to fit your own chairs or even worked for the top of a foot stool or for a cushion cover.

Materials required

☐ Coats Anchor Tapisserie wool: 5 skeins each Tangerine 0311, 0313, 0315, Chestnut 0350, Black 0403, 2 skeins Flame 0334
☐ 0.70 metre (¾ yard) single thread tapestry canvas, 7 threads to 1cm (18 threads to 1 inch) 68.5cm (27 inches) wide
☐ Tapestry frame (optional)
☐ Tapestry needle No. 18
☐ Paper for making template of chair seat
☐ Upholstery tacks, 1cm (⅜ inch) long
☐ Tack hammer
☐ Wood plane (if necessary)

KEY TO DIAGRAM

 Foundation row 0403

2 - 0311

3 - 0313

4 - 0315

5 - 0350

- 0334

TAPISSERIE WOOL

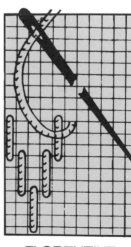

FLORENTINE STITCH

Making the template

1 Remove the seat from the chair, place it on to the paper and draw round.

2 Draw a second line 2.5cm (*1 inch*) outside the first line to allow for the depth of the padding. Draw 2.5cm (*1 inch*) squares in each corner for mitred corners. The stitching should not be worked in these squares. Cut along the outside line.

3 Pin the template on to the canvas and draw round the edge using waterproof ink. Allow at least 2.5cm (*1 inch*) unworked canvas all round so that it can be attached to the under-side of the seat.

Marking the design

1 Mark the centre of the canvas in both directions with tacking.

2 Following the chart, mark the pattern on to the canvas starting at the centre (indicated by the arrows) and working outwards. Repeat the design until you reach the outside edges.

3 Mount the canvas on to a tapestry frame if you are using one.

Working the design

1 The design is worked in Florentine stitch and satin stitch over four threads of the canvas. Work the foundation row first in the colour shown on the chart, starting at the centre and going out to the sides in both directions.

2 Work the next row below the foundation row in the colour shown on the chart. The tops of the stitches in this row should be worked into the same holes as the bottom of the stitches in the foundation row.

3 Work the following rows in the same way.

4 When the colour sequence is complete, start again with the foundation row and continue as before, working to the outline shape.

5 To complete the design work the horizontal straight stitches.

Attaching the canvas

1 Place the canvas on to the seat and fold the excess on to the underside. Try the seat in position on the chair.

2 If the canvas is too thick for the seat to fit back into the chair, remove the tacks holding the original fabric. Plane the sides of the frame by the required amount and carefully re-tack the fabric back on to the seat.

3 Mitre the corners of the canvas and attach the canvas centrally to the seat as for the cover fabric.

4 Replace the seat on the chair.

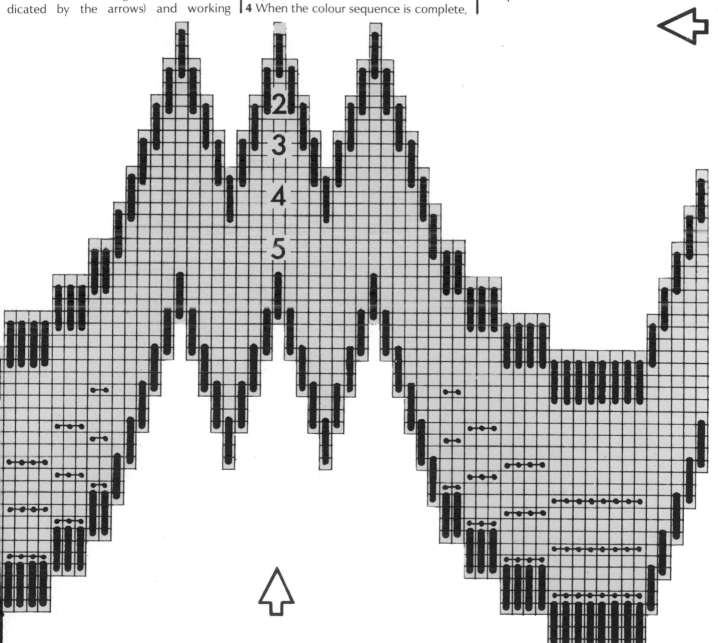

BEADWORK
Simple techniques

Beads have been used as decoration for thousands of years and have been made of many different materials such as pebbles, bone, teeth, seeds, glass and even paper. During the 19th century, embroidery with beads reached its peak when clothes and household articles were often heavily beaded; Berlin woolwork, a form of canvas embroidery incorporating beads, is a good example of this.

Today, beads – wooden, plastic and glass – are used in many ways. They can be combined with stitchery in cut work, canvas work, smocking, quilting, drawn and pulled fabric embroidery and they can be used without stitchery to decorate any number of things.

Types of beads
There are wide varieties of beads, sequins and acetate shapes, and can be obtained in many sizes. Jumble sales and junk shops often prove a good source as fragments of old beaded clothes, bags and lampshades will often yield very interesting beads which can be washed and re-used. A bag of 'sweepings' from a workroom will often provide sufficient beads and sequins for many pieces of embroidery. When choosing beads for clothes or articles which need to be washed or dry-cleaned, check that they are durable because some acetate shapes will not stand laundering or a hot iron. Most sequins can be washed with care although you should avoid touching them with a hot iron.

Designing with beads
Choose the beads to enhance the background fabric, not necessarily to contrast with it. Often the best effect can be obtained by creating a subtle contrast rather than an obvious one. Always try to avoid crude or over bright effects.

A geometric pattern is probably the easiest way of building up a pattern which can be repeated on a bag, belt or garment, and the simplest starting point is with a square. Start by placing a square acetate bead on a piece of felt and surround it with a row of medium size square or round beads and surround these with a row of flat sequins which might be oval or boat shaped. These could be followed by a small quantity of fine piping cord, securely couched on to the background fabric and covered with succeeding rows of small beads. If you prefer a circular motif, use the same principle but start with a large jewel or circular domed sequin. Another way that beaded and sequinned motifs can be used successfully is to place them on a geometrically patterned fabric, building up a pattern on the design of the fabric.

Whether you decide to build up a geometric pattern or to work out a less formal idea, the design should fill the space intended or it will look thin and meagre. Try to ensure that different parts of the design balance. A large solid shape should be balanced with several smaller ones. If you are interpreting a design based on cut paper shapes, consider the spaces formed in between the shapes as they are just as important as the shapes themselves.

Frames
It is important to use a square or rectangular frame for bead embroidery. A tambour frame is not suitable except for an isolated motif because you will often need both hands free and it does not provide sufficient tension on the fabric. When embroidering a section of a garment, mount the whole piece into the frame, complete the bead embroidery, remove from the frame and then make up the garment.

Fabric
Any type of fabric can be enhanced with

beads which are suitable for the weight and texture – naturally small glass beads would be unsuitable for a heavy tweed when large wooden or china beads would give the best effect.

It is advisable to back the fabric to be embroidered. If it is heavily beaded, a firm non-woven interfacing will support the beads on a bag or a belt. For a garment use a firm lightweight cotton or lawn as a backing for the beaded part only. Cut away the surplus before making up that part of the garment.

Thread

The thread you use will depend on the size and type of fabric and beads. Never use a polyester thread because it will stretch too much. The beads should lie on the fabric without being too loose or puckering it. Pure sewing silk is the most satisfactory – choose a colour to match the bead or sequin. Always wax the thread with beeswax to strengthen it and prevent the beads – particularly bugle beads – from cutting it.

Needles

Use special beading needles which are long and pliable and are available in sizes 12–18. Choose the size to slip through the beads easily.

Attaching beads

Beads, depending on their size, can be attached to fabric in one of four ways.
1 They can be sewn on to the background fabric with a straight stab stitch. The thread is brought through the fabric, the bead is threaded onto the needle and the needle is passed through the fabric again. The bead will then lie on its side.

2 The bead, if large enough, can be secured by two or four stitches through the centre hole so that it will then lie with the hole upwards.
Square beads are more effective when used in this way but it will depend on the effect you are trying to produce.

3 Beads can be sewn on with a back stitch or several beads can be threaded on to a needle and couched down to follow a line of the design.

4 A large bead can be sewn on by bringing the threads through the fabric, sliding on the large bead and then one small toning or contrasting bead. The needle and thread then re-enter the large bead and the fabric. This secures the large bead so that it is free-standing.

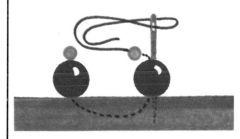

It is advisable to fasten the thread off after sewing on each heavy bead, rather than carry the thread on the back of the work from bead to bead.

Attaching sequins

Sequins are available in flat and cupped shapes in a number of sizes. They can be attached as for beads or jewels when used as isolated units or they can be sewn on in line so that they overlap.
1 Bring the needle up through the fabric and through the hole in the centre of the first sequin. Pass the needle back through the fabric at the edge of the sequin and bring it up again immediately next to the point that it entered.
2 Thread on the next sequin making sure that cupped sequins all lie in the same direction with the domed side uppermost. Continue in this way for the whole line. Each sequin should evenly overlap the preceding one.

Sewing beads over cord

Piping cord can be used as a base and can be dyed to show through glass beads.

To attach the cord, place it on the line of the design and secure it with three over-casting stitches at each end and with three straight stitches from the fabric to the centre of the cord alternately each side. To cover the cord with beads, bring up the thread at the side of the cord, slide on enough beads to cover the cord from side to side and insert the needle into the fabric on the opposite side of the cord. Repeat this over the entire length of the cord, keeping the beading tightly packed and with the same number of beads for each stitch.

Attaching bugle beads

Bugle beads can be sewn flat, arranged in regular numbers to produce a repeat pattern. For example three or four beads could be placed vertically followed by the same number placed horizontally. Or they could be arranged in blocks in a brick pattern.

Some beads are set in metal mounts which have channels through which the thread passes or they might have a hole in the centre or at either end. Both kinds can be attached as for heavy beads.

Fastening on and off

Never use a knot for fastening on and off. Work all ends in securely on the back of the work, keeping it as neat as possible.

A touch of luxury

Add a touch of exclusive luxury to your clothes with this spray motif of beads and paillettes. For a very individual look, beading has been worked here onto the patterned velvet bodice of a smock dress. Tiny pearls and beads in shades of brown and gold subtly pick up the colours of the fabric. Paillettes and feather stitch trim give the dress an exotic air.

To work the embroidery

1 If the beading is to be worked on a garment you are making yourself, do it before sewing the seams. Outline the shape of the pattern piece, then position and trace the outline of the motif, either with tacking stitches or light chalk lines.

Attaching the beads

2 On a casual dress which will receive more wear than a special occasion dress, the beads should be attached as securely as possible. Thread used for beading should be the finest and strongest silk or cotton available and should match the background fabric. Use the thread double and draw it across a piece of beeswax for extra strength. Special beading needles, long and very fine, are available in sizes 10–13. To sew the beads on, fasten the thread securely on the underside of the fabric. Bring the beading needle to the front of the work and slide one bead along the needle and onto the thread. Pick up a tiny piece of fabric, the length of the bead along the design line. Draw the needle through the fabric and place the bead in position. Pick up the second bead.

Attaching the paillettes

1 Use stranded cotton, either matching or in direct contrast to the colour of the paillettes and fabric. The web of stitchery circling the paillette is attractive enough to be a feature of the design. Work with 3 strands of cotton in the needle. Hold the paillette in place with your left thumb and take a stitch across it four times (Figure A). Make a small stitch over the crossed threads at each of the four corners (Figure B).

2 Place the needle at right angles to the square of thread and pick up a small piece of fabric just outside the edge of the paillette, keeping the thread to the right and under the needlepoint. Draw the thread through, keeping the stitch flat (Figure C). Still with the thread to the right, push the needle under the thread forming the square and over the thread emerging from the fabric (Figure D). Repeat the last two steps, working clockwise round the paillette until the circle is complete and the foundation threads covered.

Ideas for using the motif

Work the spray motif as a bold contrast or as a subtle highlight on a dress bodice, a wide waistband, or on the flap of a velvet bag. Try making up your own motif; this one is the simplest possible arrangement of curving lines. Play around with simple flowing shapes, place beads on a scrap of fabric, move them around and see how they look.

Beware of enthusiatically over-beading. A simple motif has impact, while too many beads, especially on a printed fabric, can look unattractive.

Chart for position of beads and paillettes

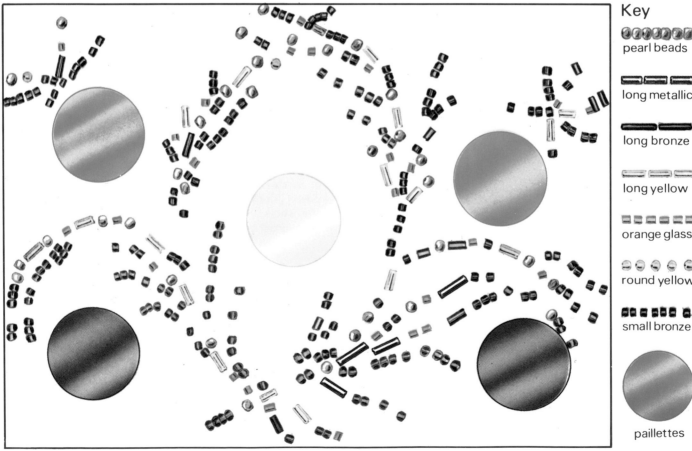

Key

pearl beads

long metallic

long bronze

long yellow

orange glass

round yellow

small bronze

paillettes

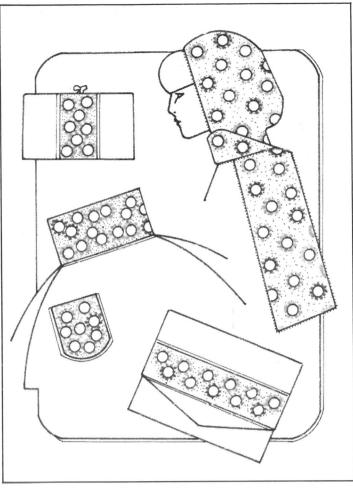

Other ideas for using the bead motif

A
B

Attaching the paillettes

C
D

Feather stitch

BEAD WEAVING

Bead weaving is an ancient craft used to make a garment, jewellery or a wall decoration. Traditionally it has been a craft associated with South America. Bead weaving is used to decorate parts of some national costumes, and has developed into a highly decorative and sophisticated art form. Egyptians also used bead weaving and traces of it have been found in tombs dating back over 3,000 years.

The equipment

Little equipment is needed for bead weaving apart from a beading loom and beading needles. The looms are inexpensive to buy or you could construct one from a wooden or cardboard box by cutting notches along the edge or by hammering tacks along the edge for small pieces of work. The notches or tacks hold the warp threads and the spaces between them should be equal to the length of the beads.

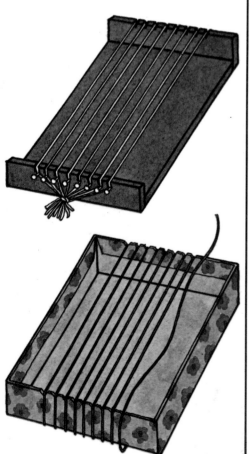

The beads

Any type of bead can be used, although glass, ceramic, wooden or plastic ones are the easiest to work with. Choose beads of equal size for an even piece of weaving.

Needles and thread

Both the beading needle and thread must be fine enough to pass twice through the bead. Depending on the size of the beads, pure silk, linen, cotton, or carpet threads can be used. Do not use a synthetic thread because this tends to stretch. All threads should be waxed with beeswax to strengthen them and make the beads slide on easily.

The pattern

The finished bead weaving can be used for a belt, an evening bag, cuffs and collar for a dress, or a piece of jewellery such as a bracelet or necklace.

It is easiest to work from a chart which you can draft out for yourself on graph paper, with each square representing one bead of the design. Colouring the chart with ink or crayon in shades to represent the colours of the beads being used, enables the chart to be read easily while you are working.

A geometric pattern will often produce the most effective pieces of bead weaving, and is easiest to follow if you intend to build up your own pattern. Alternatively, charts for canvas embroidery or cross-stitch can be used and adapted so that one bead represents each stitch marked on the chart.

Setting up the loom

The vertical threads of the design are known as the warp, and these fit into the grooves cut into the combs or bridges on the loom. The beads lie between the warp threads so you should decide how far apart to position the threads and set up the loom accordingly. There should always be one more warp thread than there are beads in the width of the pattern. The weaving is strengthened when you are using fine threads if the two outer warp threads are made double. To set up the loom:

1 Cut the warp threads to the length of the beading you require plus 15cm (6 *inches*).
2 Knot the warp threads into small equal

bunches, pass them over the roller at the end of the loom and tie them securely to the nail or hook supplied on the roller.
3 Stretch the warp threads tightly across both combs or bridges on the loom making sure that each warp thread lies in the correct groove. If you are using small beads, the warp threads should lie closely together. With larger beads they should be spaced further apart so that the beads will fit easily between them.
4 Wind the surplus warp thread around the pegs or nails at the opposite end of the loom, making sure that they are evenly taut to give a good tension to the weaving.

Starting to weave

1 Thread the needle with the working thread and attach it securely with a knot to the double thread on the left of the warp threads. If you are using very fine beads, you can give a firm edge to the weaving by working a few rows of darning stitch under and over the warp threads before starting to use the beads.
2 Thread the required number of beads on to the needle for the first row of the pattern, working from left to right.
3 Place the string of beads under the warp threads and position each bead between two warp threads. Press the string of beads up between the warp threads with the fingers of your left hand.

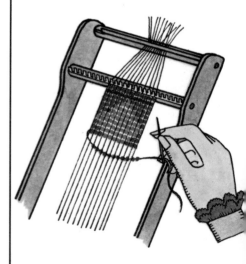

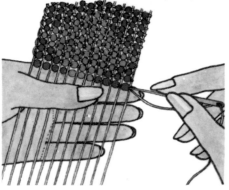

4 Bring the needle out round the last warp threads and pass it back from right to left over the warp threads and through the hole of each bead, thus securing the beads in position. Keep the tension as even as possible to avoid distorting the edge of the weaving.

5 Work the remaining rows of the pattern in the same way.

6 When the work is the required length, work a row, or two of darning stitch if you are using fine small beads, and then take the working thread back through the

last but one row of beads and cut the end. Lift the warp threads from the loom and darn each thread back through the beads or in and out of the thread between the beads. Cut the thread, making sure you leave no loose ends.

7 If you are making a long length of weaving, work over the warp threads on the loom, then loosen them, wind the weaving round the roller and stretch the unwoven warp threads into the correct position for weaving. Tighten the roller by re-positioning the pin which secures it.

SMOCKING:
Basic techniques

No other form of embroidery is quite so simple or so effective as smocking. Through the combined devices of gathering into pleats and subsequent decorative stitching, the appearance of the surface of a fabric and of a whole garment is altered in the most attractive way.

The history of smocking

The initial purpose of smocking was utilitarian; it was found to be an effective method of controlling fullness in an English labourer's garment. By the eighteenth century, the popular 'smock frock' had become decorative as well as durable and, in the next century, this garment reached its peak in elaboration. Ultimately the smocked area was combined with a variety of embroidered patterns, the pattern chosen depending on the trade of the wearer. This embroidery usually adorned the 'box', an area on either side of the smocking, and sometimes the collar and cuffs. Many surviving smocks are identifiable as having belonged to gardeners, shepherds and milkmaids, by the pattern of flowers, staffs, hearts and other similar forms on each.

The designs worked on these hardwearing linen smock frocks were seldom drawn on to the fabric before working, as the needlewomen who worked them developed a keen eye for following the thread of the fabric. The most frequently used fabric was heavy weight linen, often in a natural, unbleached colour, with the embroidery worked in a twisted linen thread. Both materials were sturdy enough for a garment which had to accommodate activity and ease of movement.

There were no curves at all in the design of the basic smock; it was, instead, entirely a composition of squares and rectangles. One popular style was reversible, with a square opening for the head, and another had a wide embroidered collar. Although all the working in the smocked area was traditionally a variation of stem or outline stitches, a number of stitches were used for other decorative embroidery on a garment. Among these stitches were feather stitch, chain stitch, stem stitch, satin stitch and faggot stitch. As in smocking today, the success of these smocks depend upon accuracy and even tension in smocking, as well as a carefully executed choice of stitches.

Smocking today

Over the years, the range of uses for smocking has widened to include an attractive variety of garments for children and adults. Children's clothes, women's nightdresses, blouses and dresses are all particularly suited to the texture and shape which smocking gives.

Fabric

Among the materials suitable for smocking are linen, cotton, nylon, voile and velvet. Any fabric that can be easily gathered is ideal for this purpose. The garment itself will determine the most suitable weight for the fabric to be used. Be sure to allow adequate width for the smocking – about three times the finished width is a general

Surface honeycomb stitch reduces fullness at waist and upper sleeve.

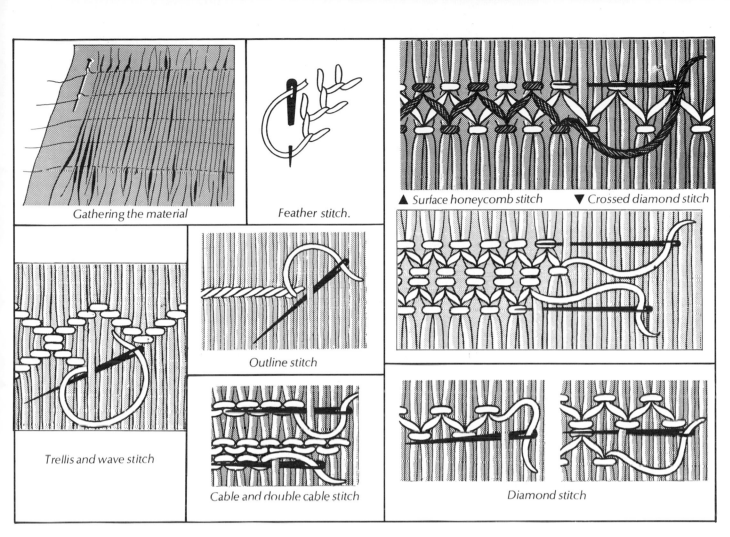

Gathering the material

Feather stitch.

▲ *Surface honeycomb stitch*　▼ *Crossed diamond stitch*

Outline stitch

Trellis and wave stitch

Cable and double cable stitch

Diamond stitch

rule, although this depends upon the tension and elasticity of the stitches, the weight of the fabric used and the depth of the gathers.

Colour possibilities

As the decorative value of smocking does not depend on the colour – too much colour actually detracts from the effect of the stitching – plan ahead to make quite certain that the colour scheme is kept simple. There are three possibilities to consider when smocking: one may use threads in the same colour as the background fabric, threads in a contrasting colour, or threads of various colours. The effectiveness of matching threads is exemplified by the blouse illustrated. On this blouse a little colour has been introduced with some floral embroidery on the bodice, whereas the smocking itself is merely a part of the textured backdrop.

Thread

It is most important that the thread used for the smocking is suitable for the fabric on which it is being worked. Traditionally, a linen thread was used on linen fabric and cotton thread on cotton or similar fabric. In fact, most kinds of embroidery thread are suitable but, for most work, coton à

broder or pearl cotton may be used in a medium sized crewel or embroidery needle. Always work the smocking before a garment is made up. Mark the area to be smocked with a tacking stitch following the thread of the material.

Smocking transfers

Ideally, transfers should not be used for smocking, as they are rarely evenly printed and it is difficult to follow the thread of the fabric. If, however, a smocking transfer is used, the spacings between the dots should be determined by the weight of the fabric (a coarse material requiring more widely spaced dots than a fine material). Iron the dots on to the wrong side of the material, aligning them with the weave of the material as accurately as possible. An alternative method of using a transfer is to mark the dots on the fabric with a sharp pencil and a ruler. This is, in most cases a more accurate way of aligning the dots on the fabric.

Gathering up the fabric

To gather up each row, use a strong thread with a secure knot at one end. Begin on the right side of the first row of dots and pick up a few threads at each one. At the end of the row, leave the thread unknotted.

Then, after running across the second row of dots, tie the two loose ends together. Continue in this way, tying each pair of threads together along the left hand side of the work. Remember, too, that when it is worked, smocking is flat on the surface but has a certain amount of bulk underneath.

The gathered lines should be pulled up so that the folds in the fabric become a series of close, parallel tubes. After drawing up all the rows of gathers, turn the fabric over and begin to smock.

Smocking stitches

Feather stitch, honeycomb and similar stitches are a modern innovation in smocking; the original smock frocks were worked only in variations of stem or outline stitch. Most smocking stitches are worked from left to right with two notable exceptions, which are worked from right to left. It is particularly important to remember that the only knot in the stitchery must be at the beginning of the row; remember, therefore, to have enough thread in the needle at the beginning of a row to complete that row. After completing the work, remove the tacking threads and discover the elasticity of the stitchery on the garment.

Smocking on heavy fabrics

A mixture of stem, wave and straight stitches ideal for working on heavy fabrics.

Smocking can be just as attractive when worked on heavier fabrics as on traditional fine lawns and cottons.

Many of the same stitches can be used, although the fabric should be prepared in a slightly different way. The stitch used here is particularly suitable for heavy fabric.

Preparing the fabric

Because of the extra bulk when using heavy fabrics for smocking, allow only twice the required final width before gathering instead of the more usual three widths. If the fabric is spotted, striped or checked, the gathers can be worked using the pattern as a grid. If you are working on corduroy or needlecord the gathers can be worked by picking up alternate ribs, unless it has widely spaced ribs in which case a stitch should be worked on each one. If you are buying commercially printed dot transfers or are marking the grid yourself, they should be fairly widely spaced – approximately 1.3cm ($\frac{1}{2}$ *inch*) apart or even more for very heavy fabrics. If you are unsure, it is advisable to make some trial gathers on a small piece of spare fabric to see how tightly gathered it should be. The fabric should look well pleated and there should be no need to stroke the gathers down as they should lie in flat and even folds.

If you are smocking a definite pattern, count the number of rows and gathers required to complete the pattern accurately, and work the gathering to allow for this. This is particularly important with wide patterns such as open diamond, feather stitch and chevron.

The threads

Use pearl cotton, coton à broder, stranded cotton (use all six strands) or pure silk twist when smocking on heavy fabrics. It is possible to use a fine string or carpet thread on hessian and linen scrim.

The design

Plan the smocking design carefully before you start work as it could be spoilt unless a good balance is worked out with the

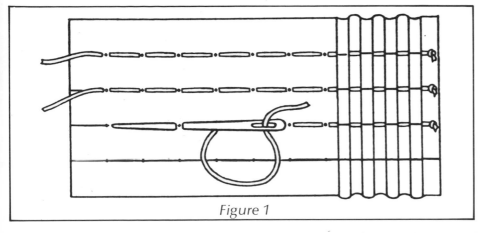

Figure 1

not pull too tightly as the finished garment must have elasticity.

Figure 2 indicates a section of the design repeated across the fabric. The dotted lines at the left hand side indicate the lines of gathers and the placing of stitches in relation to the rows. The vertical broken lines indicate the pleats.

Stem stitch Working from left to right, fasten the thread on the wrong side and bring the needle up through the first pleat. Pick up the top of the next pleat inserting the needle at a slight angle with the thread below the needle. Always work

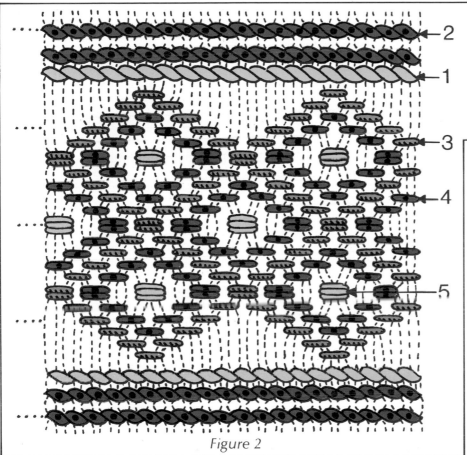

Figure 2

Key

1 – 0303	Stem stitch
2 – 0352	
3 – 0309	Wave stitch
4 – 0352	
5 – 0303	3 straight stitches

the thread over two pleats but pick up only one (figure 3).

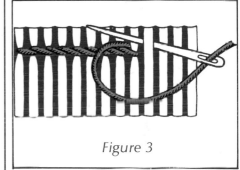

Figure 3

Wave stitch Working from left to right fasten the thread on the wrong side and bring the needle through to the left of the first pleat. Take a stitch through the second pleat on the same level with the thread below the needle. Take a stitch on the third pleat slightly higher than the previous pleat with the thread still below the needle. Continue in this way for five stitches finishing the top stitch with the thread above the needle. This completes the upward slope. Work in the same way on the downward slope except with the thread above the needle (figure 4).

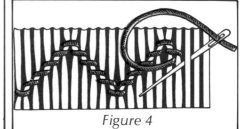

Figure 4

various patterns. The fundamental smocking stitch is stem or outline stitch and this should be used at the beginning of the work along the edges of the border to give it a firm foundation. The modern introductions of feather stitch and herringbone stitch are better used sparingly as they tend to mask the pleated background which is such an important characteristic of smocking.

The pattern shown in the photograph is a simple design using stem stitch and wave stitch and it can easily be adjusted for garments made from heavy fabrics.

Stem stitch and wave stitch pattern

Mark the areas to be embroidered on the wrong side of pieces to be smocked within the rectangles already marked. Use a soft pencil or tailor's chalk for this and draw fine parallel lines 1.3cm ($\frac{1}{2}$ *inch*) apart. Using the horizontal lines as a guide, work five rows of gathering stitches, making sure that the stitches correspond exactly on each line (figure 1). Pick up a small thread only at regular intervals and leave a loose thread at the end of each row.

Pull up the lines of gathering, easing gently to form pleats. Do not pull up too tightly as the pleats must be flexible enough to work the stitches over. Tie the loose ends together in pairs close to the last pleat.

When working the smocking stitches, do

Honeycomb smocked bedspread

Fabric required

Cotton gingham with 2.5cm *(1 inch)* checks. To calculate the amount of fabric needed, measure the width and the length of the bed. Add 1.3cm *($\frac{1}{2}$ inch)* for turnings and 10cm *(4 inches)* for the pillows.

For the gathered flounce, measure from the edge of the bed to the floor and, to allow fullness and a half for the gathering, multiply the length of the bed by 3 and the width by $1\frac{1}{2}$.

You will also need

☐ 6–7 skeins stranded embroidery cotton to match the gingham
☐ Crewel embroidery needle
☐ Regular sewing thread

Making up

1 Mount each piece of gingham with a plain piece of fabric. Tack all round the edge.
2 Join the pieces for the flounce, matching the checks of the gingham carefully. Press the turnings open.

Working the smocking

The smocking is different from regular smocking in that the fabric is not gathered first. The stitches are worked on the corners of the gingham squares and form a honeycomb pattern.

1 Working from right to left on the right side of the fabric, leave a complete gingham square along the top and right hand edge of the flounce. Using three strands of embroidery thread, knot the end of the cotton and make a small stitch at the bottom right hand corner of the first square.
2 Pass the thread along the front of the fabric and make another small stitch at the bottom right hand corner of the next square. Pull the thread tight, thus drawing the first and second stitches together. Make another half back stitch and pass the needle on to the wrong side of the

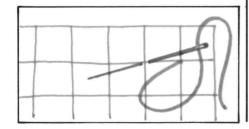

fabric. This completes the first honeycomb stitch.

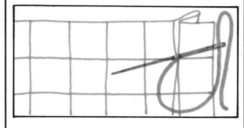

3 Still with the needle on the wrong side, bring it out at the corner of the next square.
4 Keep the fabric flat between the previous stitch and this point and make a small back stitch to secure the thread. Then pass the needle along the front of the fabric and make a small stitch at the corner of the next square.
Pull the thread tight to draw the third and fourth squares together.
5 Continue like this until six honeycomb stitches have been made.
6 Move to the row below and work five honeycomb stitches in the alternate

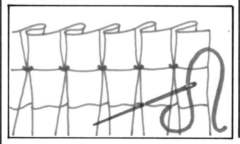

spaces to the row above so you are joining the second square to the third, the fourth to the fifth and so on.
7 Work four honeycomb stitches centrally in the third row so you are omitting the first and sixth stitches of the first row.
8 Work three honeycomb stitches in the fourth row, two stitches in the fifth row and one stitch in the sixth row to complete the V shape.

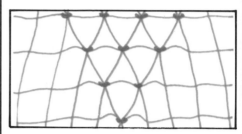

9 Work the next blocks of stitches in the same way all along the length of the flounce. You will now see how the space between the blocks forms an inverted 'V' shape.

Attaching the flounce

1 When all the smocking has been worked, it will form into pleats automatically along the top edge of the flounce. Pin these down and secure with tacking.
2 Make narrow hems along the side edges of the flounce.
3 Pin the top edge of the flounce round the edge of the main section of the bedspread and machine stitch taking 1.3cm ($\frac{1}{2}$ inch) turnings. Neaten the turnings and press them on to the main section.
4 Make a hem along the top edge of the main section.
5 Try the bedspread on to the bed and mark the hem line so that it just clears the floor.
6 Stitch the hem and press the finished bedspread.

Pleated smocked cushions

Sizes

Square cushion: 38cm (*15 inches*) square
Round cushion: 40.5cm (*16 inches*) diameter, 10cm (*4 inches*) thick

Fabric required

For square cushion:
61cm (*24 inches*) lightweight furnishing velvet, 122cm (*48 inches*) wide
For round cushion:
90cm (*36 inches*) lightweight furnishing velvet, 122cm (*48 inches*) wide

You will also need

☐ Buttonhole thread to match velvet
☐ Graph paper for making pattern
☐ Tacking thread in different colours
☐ 2 button moulds, 2.5cm (*1 inch*) diameter
☐ Cushion pads in the same sizes as the finished covers
☐ Transfer pencil (optional)

The smocking

This sort of smocking is different from conventional smocking in that the stitches are all worked on the wrong side of the fabric and do not show on the right side. The fullness is not reduced by gathering but simply by drawing points of fabric together to give a decorative pleated finish on the right side.

Although velvet has been used for the cushions in the photograph, this method of smocking is also very attractive on satin or gingham.

The pattern

Each line of smocking is worked over three vertical rows of dots, spaced 2.5cm (*1 inch*) apart. It is possible to buy transfers of the dots which can be ironed on to the fabric but it is quite simple and much less expensive – particularly if you are making several cushions – to draw your own pattern and transfer the dots to the fabric with tailor's tacks. Alternatively, you could mark the dots on the pattern with a transfer pencil and then iron on to the fabric with a cool iron.

Making the pattern

Using graph paper, draw the pattern for the cushion shape you are making to scale. One square = 2.54cm square (*1 inch square*). If you are making the square cushion, mark the dots for each line of smocking in different colours as shown so you can easily see where the rows overlap. Repeat rows two and three until you have ten rows in all.

The square cushion
Cutting out

Cut the fabric in half to make two pieces, 61cm square (*24 inches square*). Place the pieces together and pin pattern centrally to them. Mark the dots with tailor's tacks, using different coloured thread for the rows as indicated on the pattern. Unpin the pattern, cut through the tacks and open out the fabric. Work the smocking on each piece separately.

Working the smocking

For ease of working the dots are numbered to show the order of the stitches. It may seem very confusing as you start but after the first few smocked pleats are formed you will soon get into the rhythm.

1 With the wrong side of the fabric facing up, start at dot 1 in the top left hand corner. Using a long length of buttonhole thread, knot the end and make a small stitch at dot 1. Pass the thread along the fabric and make another small stitch at dot 2 in the line of dots to the left.

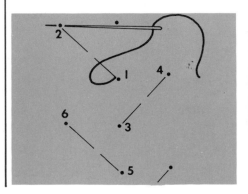

2 Go back to dot 1, make another small stitch over the one already there and then pull dots 1 and 2 together. Knot them tightly by making a loop of the thread above the stitches and passing the needle under the stitches and through the loop. Be careful not to catch the fabric as you do this or the stitch will show on the right side.

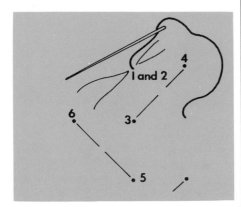

3 Pass the thread along the fabric to dot 3 and make a small stitch. Keep the fabric completely flat between dots 1 and 3, make a loop of the thread above dot 3 and slip the needle under the thread between the dots and above the loop to make another knot. Do not draw up the thread between the dots.

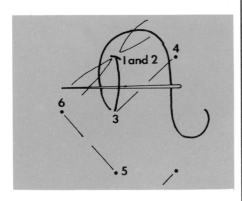

4 Pass the thread along the fabric to dot 4, make a small stitch, go back to dot 3 and make another small stitch. Pull dots 3 and 4 together and knot them as for dots 1 and 2.

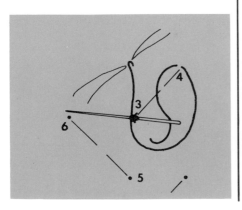

5 Move down to dot 5 and knot the thread keeping the fabric flat, as at dot 3. Pick up a small stitch at dot 6 and join it to dot 5 in the same way as before.

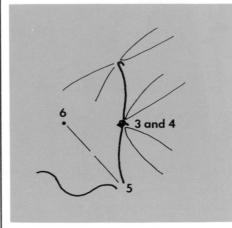

6 Continue down the whole line in this way, picking up a dot on the left, moving down to the next dot in the middle row and then picking up a dot on the right.

7 Work all the lines of smocking in the same way, and then smock the other side of the cushion cover.

Finishing off

1 When the smocking is complete, you will find that pleats have formed all round the edge. Pin these down evenly and tack in position, checking that each side of cover measures 38cm (15 inches). Pin the pleats on the other side of the cover in a similar way, but with the pleats facing the opposite direction so that when the sides of the cover are put together the pleats will match.

2 Place the sides of the cover together and tack and machine stitch round three sides, taking 1.3cm (½ inch) turnings.

3 Insert the cushion pad, fold under the turnings of the opening and slip-stitch the folds together.

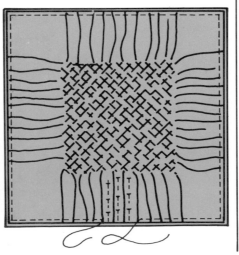

The round cushion
Cutting out

Cut the fabric in half to make two pieces, 90cm × 61cm (36 inches × 24 inches). Join the pieces along the longer edges, taking 1.3cm (½ inch) turnings and making sure that the pile runs the same way on both pieces. Trim the length of the fabric to 178cm × 53cm (70 inches × 21 inches) and use the spare piece to cover the button moulds.

Fold the fabric right side out along the seam line. Place on the pattern with the line indicated to the fold. Mark all the dots with tailor's tacks. Unpin the pattern, cut through the tacks and open out the fabric.

Working the smocking

1 Join the short ends of the fabric, taking 1.3cm (½ inch) turnings. The smocking is then worked in a continuous round.

2 Work the smocking in a similar way as for the square cushion. The finished effect will be less tightly plaited than the square cushion because the lines are spaced apart.

Finishing off

1 Using strong thread, attach the end securely 0.6cm (¼ inch) from the edge of the fabric.

2 Form the nearest pleat with your fingers and make a small stitch through the fold. Draw up the thread tightly.

3 Form the next pleat, take a stitch through the fold and pull it up to meet the first pleat. Continue all round the cushion.

4 Insert Pad. Repeat on other side.

5 Sew the covered buttons to the centre of each side of the cushion.

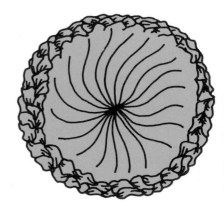

Graph for square cushion
1 Square = 2·5cm (1 inch)

ROW 1		ROW 2		ROW 3	
2		2		2	
	1	4	1	4	1
6	3	6	3	6	3
	5	8	5	8	5
10	7	10	7	10	7
	9	12	9	12	9
14	11	14	11	14	11
	13	16	13	16	13
18	15	18	15	18	15
	17	20	17	20	17
22	19	22	19	22	19
	21	24	21	24	21
26	23	26	23	26	23
	25	28	25	28	25
30	27	30	27	30	27
	29	32	29	32	29
34	31	34	31	34	31
	33	36	33	36	33
38	35	38	35	38	35
	37	40	37	40	37
	39		39		39

Graph for round cushion
1 Square = 2·5cm (1 inch)

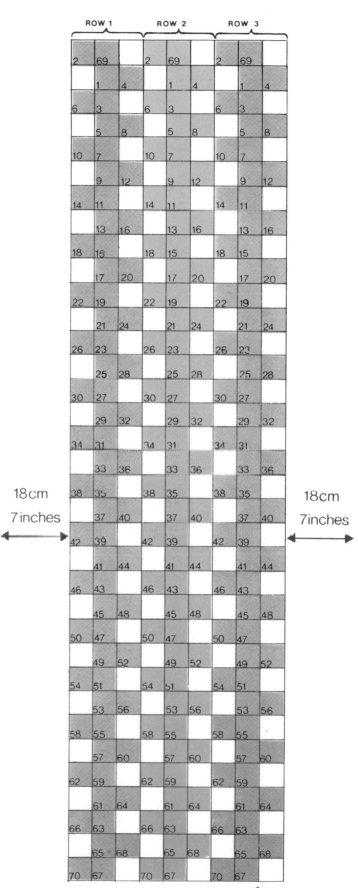

18cm 7inches

18cm 7inches

PLACE THIS LINE ON FOLD ▲

125

CANDLEWICKING

Candlewick originated in the United States in early Colonial days when, with a severe shortage of sewing materials of all kinds, women settlers used the thick cotton wick intended for candlemaking as an embroidery thread, working it into knotted and tufted designs on bedspreads. For many years the use of candlewick was restricted to bedspreads, but it looks effective in many other forms and can be used for cushions, rugs and bath mats as well as for warm garments such as dressing gowns.

Materials for candlewick

There are two kinds of candlewicking, tufted and smooth, but for both types it is essential that the material on which the embroidery is worked should shrink on the first washing to secure the candlewick in the fabric.

Usually, unbleached calico is used for candlewick, but linen can also be used. It is important to choose a weave which will take two thicknesses of the candlewick cotton.

The trace design given in this chapter is adaptable for almost any use and builds up extremely well, placing the motifs as linking squares. It can be used for both tufted and smooth types of candlewicking and parts of the design might be adapted for a matching border motif.

Yarn

Strutts Candlewick Cotton is used for candlewick and is sold in skeins, available in a variety of colours. Skeins can be cut into 122cm (*48 inch*) lengths or wind the yarn into a ball and use as required.

Needles

A special candlewick needle is used; this is fairly large with a flattened, curved point and a big eye.

Scissors

It is essential to have scissors which are extremely sharp for cutting the loops. A blunt pair will drag and pull the tufts out of the fabric.

Designs

Designs for candlewick are most effective when based on geometric shapes, but flowing designs can also be used if they are large sized. Small, intricate patterns are difficult to work and the shapes become distorted with the tufting. The candlewick can follow the outlines of the design, can fill in some areas, or cover the background completely as an all over design, giving a solid area of pile texture.

Tufted candlewick

In some early examples of candlewick French knots and backstitch were used, but in modern embroidery the stitch mainly used is running stitch worked 0.6cm to 1.3cm ($\frac{1}{4}$ to $\frac{1}{2}$ *inch*) apart along the line of the design, leaving a small loop between each stitch. To keep the loops of even length place a pencil under the cotton as each loop is made. The candlewick yarn is used double. Cut a length twice as long as is required and thread it through the needle until the ends are level. It is not necessary to finish off the ends when starting or finishing – begin on the right side of the fabric, leaving an end equal to the size of the completed tuft and end in the same way.

When all the design is completely worked cut the loops evenly with a very sharp pair of scissors.

Smooth candlewick

This type of candlewick is worked simply in running stitch. One double length of cotton is used in the needle as for tufted candlewick and the stitches are worked about 0.6cm ($\frac{1}{4}$ *inch*) long and 0.6cm ($\frac{1}{4}$ *inch*) apart. This results in a bead-like stitch giving a beautifully raised, sculptured effect. This type of candlewick is at its best worked in geometric designs built up into solid shapes and covering the entire area of the fabric.

Finishing candlewick

The completed work should be washed

A trace design for working in either tufted or smooth candlewicking.

A detail of the design above worked in tufted stitch and showing the reverse.

Smooth candlewick in a modern bedspread.

so that the fabric shrinks to fix the tufts more securely and to fluff them up. If a washing machine is used, wash for at least 20 minutes in warm soapy water. If washing by hand let the work soak for three to four hours. Do not wring or squeeze, just shake out.

Dry the work out of doors in a strong breeze and shake it frequently whilst drying to eliminate creasing and to make the tufts fluffier. Brush the tufts lightly with a soft brush before they are quite dry to fluff them up.

It is best to avoid ironing candlewick as this will flatten the tufts.

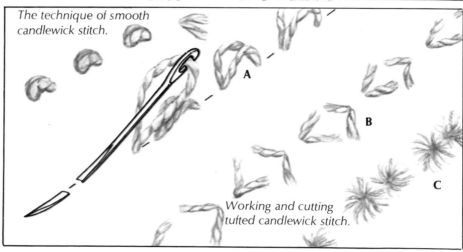

The technique of smooth candlewick stitch.

A

B

C

Working and cutting tufted candlewick stitch.

MACHINE EMBROIDERY
BASIC EQUIPMENT

Although the sewing machine is a standard piece of equipment in so many homes, it is seldom used for embroidery and many people are not even aware of its decorative potential. In these chapters we introduce you to the simpler aspects of machine embroidery and a whole new range of decorative effects and stitches, many of which can be created with even the simplest straight stitch machine.

Machine embroidery is not only a quick method of decorating clothes and furnishings. It can be as delicate as traditional hand embroidery or as bold and chunky as a rug or a heavy woven wall hanging. The possibilities are endless. The other important aspect of the craft is the use of the machine to hold applied fabrics, braids, wool, weaving yarn or even string to the background. In this case the machining may be nearly invisible or used to supplement the texture of the applied material.

Basic Equipment

The only equipment needed for machine embroidery is a sewing machine, fabric, thread, a frame and tracing paper.

Your Machine

It is a common misapprehension that a special sewing machine is needed for machine embroidery. This is not so. There is a great deal you can do on a straight stitch machine and if your machine does even a simple zig-zag you can do a great deal more, whilst the effects with an automatic machine are unlimited.

Most modern machines have a drop feed, that is a control to lower the feed for darning and embroidery while others require a plate which will fit over the feed. To adapt a machine, when it is not possible to obtain a plate, the throat plate may be removed and small washers inserted under it before returning the screws. This raises the throat plate to the level of the teeth at their highest point.

Whichever machine you use it is essential that it is in perfect working order as it receives far more wear during embroidery than dressmaking due to the speed at which it is worked. The machine must be cleaned and oiled regularly. Oil before use rather than after as fine oil tends to evaporate. Run the threaded machine over a spare piece of fabric before starting your work to remove the excess oil. Check foot controls and motors occasionally for overheating and if this occurs have your machine serviced.

Fabrics

Many fabrics are suitable for machine embroidery. It is important however that the fabric being worked should be firmly woven so avoid stretch and knitted fabrics such as jersey or crepe which pull out of shape when framed. Embroidery will not give with these fabrics. However, for a technique such as appliqué work, where the individual shapes need not necessarily be held in a frame, this elasticity is in fact an advantage.

As framing is so important, and practice is needed to get the fabric into the rings tightly without tearing, the beginner should choose to work on medium weight fabrics such as sailcloth or dress-weight linens. With more experience exciting and varied effects can be achieved using net, and fine fabrics such as cotton organdie and even plastics and leather.

Thread

Machine embroidery thread is supplied in two thicknesses, 50 and 30. The 50 is the finer of the two while 30 is comparable in weight to ordinary machine dressmaking thread. 50 should always be used in the

spool unless a thicker thread is needed for special effect. 40 and 50 sewing cotton are needed for variety in the weight of stitching and for whip-stitch, while a collection of wool and hand embroidery thread is always useful.

Invisible thread is invaluable to the more experienced embroiderer. It is available in light and dark tones and is useful for sewing on fabric pieces when an exact colour match cannot be made. It gives a rich glint to the work when used for free embroidery and is best used with machine embroidery thread in the spool partly to provide colour interest and partly because it will not stand a warm iron. Therefore work should be pressed from the back.

Glitter threads are also available and handicraft shops will provide a variety of textured threads for appliqué work.

Frames

The frame comprising of two interlocking frames with an adjustable screw is an essential piece of equipment. A 20.5cm – 25.5cm (8 inch – 9 inch) frame is ideal for beginners. The more experienced embroiderer may prefer a 30.5cm (12 inch) frame. A very small frame is useful for eyelets and working in corners. The most satisfactory frames are made of wood, are narrow enough in depth to pass under the raised machine needle and have a screw adjustment for extra tightening. Plastic frames are not as good as they do not grip the fabric so well, particularly if it is slippery, although covering the inner ring with tape or bias binding may help. Metal frames have the disadvantage of being too deep to slide easily under the needle on most machines and need complete screw adjustment every time the frame is moved on the fabric.

Tracing paper

For marking out designs use dressmaking tracing paper. It can be pricked and pounced as for hand embroidery (see the chapter on Transferring designs). If the structure of the design is in a straight stitch the main lines may be transferred to the cloth by machining over the paper with the presser foot down, then tearing the paper away. If the design is heavily drawn on the paper with felt tip pen, it is possible

o trace it directly on to the fabric by
aping the paper to a window with the
abric over it. Use a tailors chalk pencil for

a dark fabric and a sharp, hard pencil for
a light fabric, making a dotted rather than a
solid line.

This striking fish design is an example of
machine embroidery used to great effect
on the table mats shown above.

STITCHES
Automatic stitches

Automatic stitches can be used for a wide variety of pleasing designs on clothes and furnishings. They can be used to good effect with applied pieces of fabric, braid or ribbon, for border patterns and decorative motifs for casual wear, for children's clothes and to give the most ordinary household linens a luxury look. Automatic stitches must be used selectively; if too many stitches are combined in one design, the results can be confused and unattractive.

Many machines only make stitches based on the side to side throw of the needle, but some combine this with a backwards and forwards motion of the feed thus making a much wider range of stitches available.

Automatic stitching is normally worked using the presser foot in the usual way without framing the fabric. Worked freely in the frame they completely lose their effect unless you have acquired the skill of moving the frame smoothly with your left hand while operating the stitch lever with your right hand. This will come with practice. Free machine embroidery will be described in more detail later in this section.

The stitching can be done with 30 or 50 machine embroidery cotton which gives a smoother and more lustrous effect than sewing cotton or with a thicker thread to give a bolder effect. To prevent the thread fraying, it is essential that the needle is large enough for the thread to pass easily down the groove and through the eye. If a very thick thread is used it must be put in the spool, a technique which will be more fully described in a later chapter. The stitch should always be tested on spare fabric before you begin your design. The space between the stitches should be adjusted to achieve the desired stitch density according to the thickness of thread.

Some degree of tension is essential on upper and lower threads but swing needle work tends to pull up the fabric more than straight stitching. To counteract this, the upper tension should be slackened as much as possible without affecting the even appearance of the stitching. The

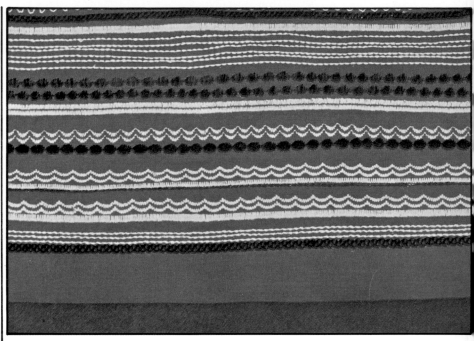

lower tension may also be loosened but in the absence of a numbered dial remember to memorise the pull of the thread and the position of the screw groove in relation to its socket. In this way the tension may be easily reset for normal sewing. It is often necessary to back the fabric to prevent it pulling up when the needle swings, or stretching when machining on the bias. The finer the fabric the more important it is to back it. The ideal backing is vanishing muslin which tears away easily after stitching but medium weight paper is a good substitute. Vilene should only be used if a permanent stiffness is required. The fabrics should be firmly tacked to whatever backing is used.

Automatic patterns need not be limited to straight lines of stitching along the straight grain of the fabric. It is not difficult to follow gently curving lines using the right hand to open and close the stitch width lever to give further variety. It is also possible to put the fabric into an embroidery frame, replacing the presser foot when the frame is under the needle. This method is suitable for a series of small shapes or a design with short lines radiating out from the centre. Check that your frame is small enough in diameter to pass

completely round the needle while resting on the throat plate of your machine. Framing will be described in more detail later in this section.

These patterns may be made even more exciting if shaded threads are used. An interesting effect is sometimes achieved by using different coloured threads above and below and tightening the upper tension or loosening the lower tension to give the stitch spool coloured edges.

You could use any simple smock pattern with plain square yoke and cap sleeves. The design, embroidered in two colours, use twin needles for the double patterns such as the scallops and a stretch stitch for the heavy lines. The satin stitch is used to stabilize the whole design. Automatic stitches will differ from machine to machine but similar effects can be achieved on most machines.

The design is worked before the smock is made up. Be sure to cut out the pattern pieces allowing approximately 5cm (inches) all round to make handling easier during embroidery. Allow extra when buying your fabric. Mark each pattern piece and the design areas with tailor chalk or tacking and work each piece starting at its lowest edge.

Design using free machine embroidery

It is in free machine embroidery that skill and imagination can come fully into play. The sewing machine is a very sensitive drawing instrument and while mastery of this craft takes practice it can be very rewarding. Even a beginner can soon produce spontaneous designs of great freshness and originality.

Consult your machine manual to find out how to convert your machine. If it is an old model the instructions may come under the heading of darning. The feed will either be covered with a special plate or will be retractable (see the opening chapter on Machine Embroidery).

Frame your work carefully. To do this lay the outer ring on a flat, level surface, lay your fabric right side up across it and press the inner into the outer ring. The screw should have been adjusted so that relatively heavy pressure is required to achieve this. Tighten the fabric by pulling it upwards and inwards to prevent the rings dislodging and taking care not to distort the threads. If there is any tendency for the fabric to slip back when pulled, the screw on the frame should be tightened and the pulling up process repeated until the fabric is stretched to its limit. It cannot be overstressed that the success of all kinds of free stitching depends on careful framing. If the work is loose it will tend to lift when the needle passes through it and the machine will miss stitches which may cause the thread to break. The tautness of the work is the only way in which the tension on the machine cotton is counteracted. Badly stretched work will not lie flat when removed from the frame and no amount of steam pressing will flatten it. Remove the presser foot and with the needle at its highest point slide the frame under. Draw the lower thread up through the fabric and lower the presser foot bar to re-set the tension on the upper thread. The stitch length lever should be set at 0. The size of the stitch is decided by the combination of the speed of the motor in conjunction with the speed at which you move the frame. Turn the stitch width

lever to 0. Hold the frame to guide the fabric under the needle. With practice you will find the most comfortable position for your hands. The work is done mainly by the right hand which should swing from the shoulder to move the frame. Control will be greater if thumb and little finger are outside the frame and the remainder inside, being careful not to get them too close to the needle. The left hand should be flat on the work to hold the work down while steadying it. The little finger braced against the edge gives greater control. If the frame is 20.5cm (8 inches) or less it is probably safer to have both hands positioned on the frame. The left elbow should rest on the table. The fabric should not lift while stitching but the larger the frame the more likely it is to do so.

Hold both threads under your left forefinger while you start, to prevent them getting pulled down into the race and tangling. Run the machine fairly fast and move the frame smoothly. As a safety measure do not put your foot on to the foot control unit until you are ready to stitch and train yourself to remove it every time you stop. Aim to make 20 – 30 stitches to 2.5cm (1 inch) using a large sharp needle. Anything finer than a 14/90 needle is too flexible and may be broken on the edge of the plate. A 14/90 needle will take up to a 40 sewing cotton but anything thicker, such as buttonhole twist, will need the largest needle.

Although you may not have to alter your tension with some threads, if you use 50 machine embroidery cotton for instance, it is wise to loosen the tension by a couple of numbers. If the cotton snaps, loosen it until this no longer happens. If this results in a bad stitch, loosen the lower tension as well. However, the effect you get with a tighter top tension when your spool colour will show on top may be just the one you want. If you do loosen the lower tension be sure to memorize the normal pull and only adjust the screw by a quarter turn at a time.

When moving from one part of a frame to

another raise the needle to its highest point, lift the presser foot bar to release the tension from the needle, move the frame to the new position, dip the needle down, lower the presser foot bar and continue. If at the end of a line of stitching you move your frame slowly to make small stitches which won't unravel, your ends can be cut off close to the work. If the back is to be visible, trim after the front but not so closely.

Apart from meticulous drawing, interesting filling textures can be made by running the machine at top speed and moving the frame backwards and forwards or in a small continuous circular movement. If the machine is set for zig-zag a heavy line can be made by moving the frame slowly. When the frame is moved from side to side with the needle swinging, large stitches can be made up to 1.3cm ($\frac{1}{2}$ inch) in length. These long stitches catch the light giving a quite different effect to the same movement done with a straight stitch. Always begin and end satin stitch with a few straight stitches or take the ends through and tie them.

The embroidered cloth

The circular, linen tablecloth illustrated is 122cm (48 inches) in diameter and divided into 8 sections. The motifs are worked using appliquéd fabric and eyelets (to be described in a later chapter) and free running stitch.

The design for each section was drawn on paper and tacked to the wrong side of the tablecloth. The fabric to be appliquéd was tacked to the right side and stitched in position from the wrong side using straight stitch and the presser foot. The excess appliquéd fabric was then cut away and satin stitch was used round the edges of the shapes. The paper was then torn away and the eyelets and free machining were worked from the right side in the frame.

The edges should be neatened with zigzag stitch, turned to the wrong side and slip-stitched. Decorative stitching may then be used on the right side to conceal the hem.

Whip stitch

When embroidering by machine you can forget all the rules for normal sewing. For it is by using different colours and thicknesses of thread through the needle and through the spool and experimenting with different tensions that varied and original effects will be discovered.

One of the most effective variations of free running stitch is whip stitch. This stitch lends itself well to small curving designs and looks particularily striking when shaded thread is used in the spool. Use 50 machine embroidery cotton in the spool for best results and a 40 cotton on top. Tighten the upper tension 2 or 3 numbers above normal, run the machine fast and move the frame slowly. If the top thread breaks it may be necessary to loosen both tensions.

The top thread should be flat on the fabric pulling the spool thread up. The stitches should be close enough together to enclose the top thread, giving a raised, corded appearance. If the frame is moved quickly so that the stitches are separated the top thread is visible. Different coloured upper and lower threads produce a speckled line, but if you move the frame slowly again a solid line will result. A most attractive graded line can be obtained by smoothly increasing and decreasing the speed at which you move the frame. If the upper tension is not tightened enough the top thread will appear at uneven intervals producing a pleasing textural line. Side to side and circular textures are very effective using whip stitch settings.

Whip stitch ends should be taken to the back of the work and fastened, so lines should be continuous wherever possible. If the upper tension is set to its tightest and the lower tension very loose or the spool spring completely removed, a feather stitch is obtained. This is because the tight upper tension causes a loop of the spool thread to be pulled through to the right side with each stitch. This stitch should be worked in a continuous clockwise or anti-clockwise movement. If it is worked in a straight line the result is merely a series of untidy loops.

Remember that whenever the upper tension is slightly tighter than the lower tension, the top colour will be affected by the

colour in the spool and can be purposely deepened or lightened. Experiment by using a range of different colours in the spool and by varying the length of stitch. Whenever you change the direction of the frame movement there will be a concentration of the spool colour at the point of change and if you run the machine at full speed and move the frame in a series of pauses and jerks a dotted texture is obtained. This effect can be used to give tinted edges to filled in shapes.

With a tighter upper tension and the needle swinging, a satin stitch with spool coloured edges is obtained. If the frame is moved from side to side (full speed essential) in a series of pauses and jerks, crisp satin stitch bars will occur. Do not move the frame until each bar is of the required density.

These bars can be used freely or more formally by stopping the machine after each one to position the frame accurately for the next. If the needle stops on the wrong side to lead on to the next bar, turn the balance wheel by hand.

These bars could be used to make an attractive decoration for the centre of a self covered button or the centre of an embroidered flower. Being raised they catch the light and give a rich beaded look but are best worked with a stitch width of 2 or more.

To avoid unravelling never cut the threads between the bars. You may if you wish, conceal the connecting threads with straight free machining round the bars.

The panel illustrated is worked entirely in whip stitch using shaded thread on the spool and moving the frame slowly so that the needle thread is concealed.

Cable stitch

Cable stitch is a useful means of introducing heavy lines and textures into a design. It is often used with the presser foot for decorative top stitching but can also be used freely in the frame. The design is worked from the wrong side. Cable stitch is hard wearing and as such is particularly appropriate for articles which will be in constant use.

With cable stitch the top thread passing round the thick thread with each stitch protects it from the chafing it may receive if the thread is applied by stitching along its length.

The thick thread must be wound on the spool either by hand or on the spool winder. You should create slight tension with your fingers to ensure the thread winds evenly. The thread should be smooth enough not to clog the tension spring. The tension should be loosened so that the pull of the thread feels the same as for normal sewing and the stitch appears even. If you are embroidering an article which will receive a lot of wear use 30 machine embroidery cotton or ordinary sewing cotton on top. Should you have difficulty getting the thick thread through

the fabric when you dip the needle, pierce a hole with a bodkin. Some machines have a separate spool case and the tension screw and spring may be completely removed. Without the tension spring, threads the thickness of soft hand embroidery cotton can be used. Textured yarns can be used provided they are fine enough to pass easily through the hole in the side of the spool case. Be sure when replacing the spring to insert the end into the slot in the spool case before replacing the screw.

It is a good idea to wind several spools at once if you are working a lot of cable stitch as the thick thread runs out quickly. If the spool colour is being changed frequently it is a good idea to change the top cotton as well so that the shape of each colour area can be seen on the wrong side (the side from which you are working). This is a good method of producing very rich and varied textures. If the lower tension is released completely and you are using a fairly fine thread it will tend to be released too quickly from the spool making a pleasing, textural looped line.

Unless you are completely familiar with the reactions of your machine always work a test sample. Set the upper tension just tight enough to grip the heavy thread firmly. If it is very tight it can pull a fine to medium thickness thread through a loosely woven fabric to the wrong side giving a moss-like texture which can be used on the right side by reversing your fabric.

With some machines it is possible to get an effect like heavy whip stitch by greatly increasing the lower tension and moving the frame slowly so that the spool thread is encased by the top thread. Even if you cannot manage to entirely conceal the thick thread it is a very interesting way of working the more solid areas of a design and looks particularly effective if shaded thread is used on top.

Cable stitching and its variations are especially useful for dress embroidery as the design may be marked on the wrong side. When the cable stitching is completed it should give enough guidance for free stitching or other work on the right side without further marking.

The sample shows a freely drawn motif worked in cable stitch and free running stitch. To achieve the bobbled effect on the cable stitch, the tension screw and spring on the spool are completely removed. Silky hand embroidery thread is used on the spool and sewing cotton through the needle. Machine embroidery cotton is used on the spool and through the needle for the free running stitch which is worked after the cable stitch from the right side.

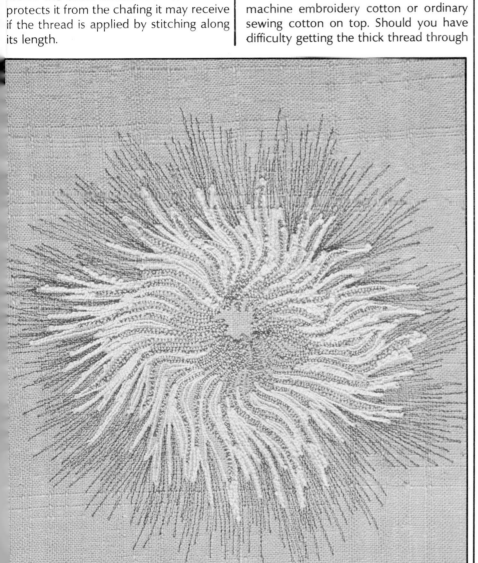

DECORATIVE EFFECTS
Shapes and appliqué

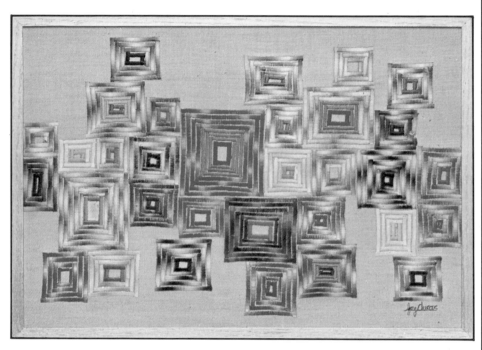

Decorative effects using the presser foot and satin stitch

With a little imagination decorative effects can be worked with the presser foot, without using a frame. Lines and sharp angles are easily incorporated. Sharp curves are more difficult to negotiate but are made easier by use of the quilting foot with its shorter length, rather than the presser foot, and a shorter than normal stitch length. Geometric designs should be marked out with a series of pencil dots which show on a dark or a light fabric. With more experience you will be able to machine straight between dots spaced further apart. Because the threads at each end of a line should be taken through to the back and tied, lines should be continuous wherever possible. Straight stitch effects can be worked on a reasonably firm fabric such as sailcloth without a backing.

Heavier effects can be achieved by working a zig-zag or satin stitch over an applied thread. There may be a special hole through

the embroidery foot to guide a fine thread under the needle. An Elna foot is designed to apply any number of threads the thickness of pearl cotton side by side which can be held down with the serpentine (multiple zig-zag) or other automatic stitch. This foot can be used on some other machines. On a straight stitch machine it is possible with practice to guide a thick thread under the needle so that it is stitched accurately down the centre. These suggestions can be used in conjunction with applied braids and ribbons for border patterns. Ends of ribbons and braids should have their edges turned in unless they go to the edge of the fabric or are enclosed in a seam. Heavy threads must be passed to the back. When a shape rather than a line is to be worked it is wise to take the thread through the back of the fabric before starting to stitch. This will avoid the thread obscuring your work as you machine and also helps prevent tangling. Always work the heaviest stitching in a design first forming the main

structure to which finer straight stitching or free machine embroidery may be added. On a fully automatic machine the stretch stitch makes a heavy line which can be used decoratively on the right side of the fabric. The twin needle can be used to make freely shaped pin-tucks either on the background fabric or on fabric to be applied. If a transparent fabric is used a coloured wool or embroidery thread can be laid under the needle to give a shadowed effect. Buttonhole twist can be used through the needle (largest size for your machine) to give a thick line on the right side. Thicker threads must be used in the spool and the lower tension should be released until it feels the same as for normal sewing. The work must be wrong side uppermost. This is called cable stitch. This technique was described in the previous chapter.

Always work a sample on the fabric to be used to check tensions and stitch length. Only use closely woven fabric or the satin stitch will have irregular edges. Work with tensions as light as possible and take care there is no weight on the fabric passing under the foot which might distort the fabric. If any pulling up of fabric occurs either back the fabric with vanishing muslin or stretch the work in a frame. If a lengthening of the stitch is required as well as variation of width this is best achieved by pulling the work gently through the machine. It is not possible to alter both stitch width and length at the same time. Ends should be taken through to the back and tied.

The panel is worked in satin stitch using the presser foot. 50 machine embroidery cotton in shaded colours is used throughout. The area of each square in the design is marked on the background with light pencil dots and the shapes are filled in from the outside towards the centre.

Table mats

These table mats were illustrated in the first chapter on Machine Embroidery. They are made of washable linen/cotton furnishing fabric. The fish design is worked before the mats are cut out.

The heavy line, designed to be continuous wherever possible, is marked on paper, transferred to the fabric (also explained in the earlier chapter) and worked by applying a medium weight embroidery thread with a zig-zag stitch using the presser foot. 50 machine embroidery cotton is used on the spool and through the needle. The design is then framed and free machining is worked in different colours to build up areas of texture.

The fringed edges of the mats are finished with a machine hemming stitch.

Embroidered and applied shapes on fine fabrics

One of the greatest attractions of machine embroidery is that intricate and delicate designs may be completed in a comparatively short time.

With a little experience it is possible to frame and embroider very fine fabrics but the utmost care must be taken when stretching them in the frame, as the tension necessary for good results could easily cause the fabric to split. To avoid this adjust the screw on the frame until it is just tight enough to grip the fabric, alternatively tighten the screw and gently pull up the fabric making sure you grip it along the width of both palms, spreading the strain as evenly as possible. This needs great patience but if you pull up the fabric between thumb and forefingers the fabric will almost certainly split.

Cotton organdie is a particularly attractive fabric to embroider but as it creases easily it is best used in a design where it will be covered with embroidery. Subtle effects may be obtained by applying pieces of organdie to an organdie background or by placing coloured fabric on the wrong side of the background for a shadow effect. Embroidered tablemats can be

particularly successful when worked on cotton organdie as it looks well placed over most colours.

Fine fabrics such as organza, cotton organdie or chiffon can be applied to net for evening dresses, or wedding dresses and veils. The fabric to be applied can be mounted on the net and then framed together and tightened securely.

Using free running stitch, outline the edges of all the shapes two or three times. Pull the work clear of the machine, cut away the excess applied fabric and finish the raw edges with further lines of machining or some fine texture. The shapes should be worked far enough apart to be able to insert the points of the scissors between them.

If the shapes to be applied are very small they may be cut out separately, laid in position and held with the fingers whilst they are stitched. With more experience you will not be afraid of putting your fingers close to the needle and it is a great advantage to be able to do so. This method is easier to work and there is no danger of damaging the net during the cutting away process. If you are applying pieces of net to net use the second method whatever the size but if the shapes are

very large use a presser foot.

Do not attempt to do anything other than straight stitch techniques on fragile fabrics. Satin stitch may pull up the fabric so that it is not possible to press your work flat and also fine threads may get dislodged spoiling the effect of the stitch unless its purpose is purely textural.

Embroidery worked on an open fabric gives a completely different effect to that worked on a closely woven fabric as with an open fabric both upper and lower threads are visible so the stitching appears heavier. All weights of net can be embroidered from the heavy net used for ballet tutus to a fine dress net. Shapes may be embroidered on net then cut out and applied to, or inserted into, another fabric. If you are applying net shapes to a solid background either turn the edges under, making a clearly defined edge which can be secured with hemming or zig-zag stitch. Alternatively leave 1.3cm ($\frac{1}{2}$ inch) outside the stitching on each shape and attach it with free machine embroidery which will soften the edge and blend it into the background.

This method of machine embroidery is very good for decorating clothes as the minimal amount of stitching on the background will not impair its draping qualities. Use soft dress net for the embroidered shapes which may be applied with some shapes in a more closely woven fabric for contrast, overlapping the net shapes on the others for even greater variety.

Use your imagination when choosing your background fabric. Plastic mesh vegetable bags can make interesting backgrounds for panels. Satin stitch can be used but generally straight running stitch is most effective used in a very textural way with contrasting spool colours to build up subtle shaded areas. Some cotton vegetable bags have a very open weave and, once washed, are very rewarding to use. The threads can be dislodged to make large holes and spaces contrasting with heavily worked areas. They are ideal for lampshades mounted over a fabric fine enough to allow the light to pass through.

The motif illustrated is worked in the frame. The organdie shapes are applied to the background with free running stitch using 50 machine embroidery cotton on the spool and through the needle. The edges of each shape are trimmed after stitching and emphasised with more running stitch. An eyelet is worked in the centre of the motif (see the following chapter in this section) and a free running texture worked round it. The leaves are then worked in free running stitch using sewing cotton.

The delicate art of eyelet embroidery and openwork

Eyelets are simple to work and extremely effective used on their own, or in combination with other free stitching effects and they make an interesting focal point in a design.

The attachments for eyelets are not sup-plied with the machine but can be bought in two or three sizes. When working eyelets the smaller you make your central hole, the wider your stitching can be and vice versa.

The work must be framed using a frame small enough to completely revolve around the needle and the eyelets should be positioned within the frame so that they do not hamper this movement.

Follow the machine manufacturers in-structions for fitting the eyelet plate. For best results use 50 machine embroidery cotton. When piercing the hole using the awl supplied with the attachment, be careful not to make the hole too large. Set your machine for satin stitch, place the work in position on the eyelet plate, (you may have to remove and replace the needle), position the needle to the left and draw the thread up through the hole. Hold both thread ends when starting and run the machine fast revolving the frame evenly. It is better to turn the frame twice quickly rather than once slowly, although a delicate effect can be achieved by spacing the stitches so that the fabric remains visible between them.

When the eyelet is complete the ends of the stitching should be tied on the wrong side of the fabric. If a number of eyelets are to be worked this can be avoided by making the eyelets touch each other or else designing the work so that the linking threads may be concealed by further textural stitching. Another way of finishing is to position the needle to the right and work another row of small straight stitching round the circumference of the eyelet. The threads can then be cut close to the work and the stitching gives an added finish.

A further textural variation can be given to eyelets by working with a different colour through the needle to that on the spool and with the upper tension tighter than the lower so that the bobbin colour shows round the edges. Loosen the lower tension as well if necessary.

Openwork may be described as a decorative version of darning. It is the technique either of inserting a delicate web-like pattern of machine stitching into specially prepared holes and spaces, or, working over the spaces so solidly that they become as heavy as the background fabric. If this technique is to be used for dress embroidery the shapes should be well filled if they are large. If the shapes are small they may be left more open but are best worked where there is no likelihood of damage from such things as buckles, handbags or bracelets.

Generally with openwork the same thickness of thread is used through the needle and on the spool. It is important to use a thread which will stand up to wear and washing so choose a thread thicker than 50 machine embroidery cotton. Cable stitch is a good choice of stitch to work as it fills in the space quickly. The tensions should always be set as for normal sewing. For best results use a closely woven fabric of any weight such as linen sailcloth, cotton lawn or organdie. Frame the work and outline the shapes with three or four lines of free running stitch which lie either on top of each other or touching. This will prevent the edges of the shape from stretching. Remove the work from the machine and cut out the shapes close to the stitching. Work a few stitches round the edge to secure the threads, then machine backwards and forwards across the space carrying the stitching round the edge to the next line if necessary until a framework has been made. The focal points may then be built up by machining continuously round any area where lines intersect without necessarily continuing the stitching to the edge. If you change colours during your design either secure the ends by close stitching or else take them through to the wrong side and tie them.

The edges of the hole may be finished with satin stitch, either freely if you are sufficiently skilled or else using the presser foot. Whichever method you use the work should remain stretched in a frame small enough to pass easily round the needle. A softer edge is obtained by working a whipstitch or free running texture over the edge of the hole which blends it into the background. It is a good idea on a swing needle machine to use a throat plate with a needle hole rather than a slit. If it is necessary to reframe the work to complete your design avoid the edge of the frame crossing the stitching if possible. If this cannot be avoided see that the main bulk of stitching is at right angles to the edge of the frame to minimise the risk of damage and tighten the work from the opposite side.

For purely decorative designs, such as wall hangings and panels, holes of any size up to the size of the frame can be filled. The holes should be rounded rather than crescent shaped as the lack of edge tension on the latter causes too many difficulties in working.

Openwork can look particularly exciting if different fabrics are laid underneath the shapes such as leather, foil or metallic fabrics but you should bear in mind the function of the finished article.

For permanent objects such as mobiles, lampshade rings or millinery wire may be used to give the edges of the shape support. Millinery wire should be cut long enough to go round the circumference twice with the ends touching each other. Conceal the join with thread tied over it. To secure each line of stitching as you work wired shapes, you should stop your machine each time you reach the wire and work four stitches backwards and forwards over it, (finishing the fourth stitch inside), turning the balance wheel by hand. You should also try to make the basic structure of wide angles to prevent the threads of your embroidery slipping. To also help avoid this, it is a good idea, having completed a horizontal line of stitching in your shape, to work the fourth stitch over the wire so that the stitch finishes inside the wire and above that line of embroidery. This means that when you work the vertical line, the first stitch is worked over the horizontal line so pulling the stitches over the wire close together helping to anchor them. Satin stitch can be worked over the wire or ring to conceal it using the widest needle throw to lessen the risk of the needle catching on the wire and breaking. Shapes may be worked on stiff wire, which can be bent into more complex shapes. To join the wire, cross the ends and wind an elastic band round them. When the shape is complete, it can be laid in position on a background and fastened with a few running stitches inside the wire at each point. Then cut the wire at intervals, carefully remove each section, and further strengthen the points of the shape with stitching or conceal them with satin stitch or applied thread. Never cut the loops which result when the wire is removed.

Several of these shapes can make a pleasing arrangement for a panel but should only be used when the completed work will be stretched, or the effect will be lost. This particular aspect of openwork therefore is unsuitable for dress embroidery.

The sample shows a motif worked with eyelets and a variation of whip stitch. 40 sewing cotton is used through the needle and 50 machine embroidery cotton on the spool throughout.

Embroidered At Home Dress

This embroidery can be used on any dress with a plain yoke, such as the one illustrated. It is worked on the front bodice before the dress is made up. When you cut out the front bodice piece make sure you allow extra fabric all round to enable you to frame your work.

The free shapes are worked in the frame using running stitch and cable stitch. Because you are working across spaces the cable stitch can be worked from the right side. Pure silk thread is used through the needle throughout and silky hand embroidery thread is wound on the spool. A free running texture is used round the edge of the shape to conceal the raw edges and soften them into the background.

The front bodice is cut out in lining tacked in position on the wrong side of the front bodice matching notches. The pattern piece is then treated as one layer during making up.

QUILTING
Basic techniques

From the small fragments found in early Egyptian tombs, quilting is known to have been used as a means of padding garments and bed covers for warmth and as decoration from the very earliest times. Later, quilting was worn instead of armour in battle and it was also worn under metal armour to prevent chafing.

As well as bed covers and household furnishings, quilting of garments of all kinds for warmth and decoration was universal during the 16th to mid 19th centuries. In the 19th century, which was the heyday of decorative sewing, quilting was practised on a scale similar to patchwork and the two crafts became closely allied. In America, where patchwork was an economy measure with the early settlers, it was customary to make the patchwork quilt tops during the winter and hold a neighbourhood quilting party in the spring to complete the quilts, so the two crafts progressed together to an equal degree of technical expertise.

Types of quilting

Nowadays five different types of quilting are practised in embroidery. These are English quilting, Italian quilting, Trapunto quilting, and the delicate shadow quilting.

Of these, English quilting is the most popular and is the only one which provides real extra warmth because it incorporates all-over padding, although the other methods can give added weight and substance to fabrics as well as decoration. All five methods can be used for bedcovers, quilts, cushions, tea and coffee pot covers, jackets, housecoats and other similar garments.

English quilting

This is the method of sandwiching padding between a top cover and muslin backing or fabric lining and then securing the three layers together by over-all running stitching. The decoration comes from the patterns worked by the stitching and the attractive texture produced.

Quilting in Britain is particularly associated with North West England and South Wales, and many of the designs have local names, such as the Welsh heart and Weardale chain. Most of them are based on simple shapes of leaves, feathers, circles, scissors, spectacles, etc., and it is worth obtaining templates of these basic shapes which can be increased or reduced in size according to the size of the article being made.

Alternatively, some designs used on Continental ceramic tiles might give ideas for patterns. When planning the design for a piece of English quilting, the pattern should traditionally consist of principal motifs and a background filling pattern which throws into relief the main areas of the design. The filling pattern can be a lattice of squares or diamonds or a series of lozenge shapes.

Italian quilting

This is worked through two thicknesses of fabric only, a top cover and a muslin or lawn backing. The stitching is worked in double lines, 0.6cm – 1cm ($\frac{1}{4}$ inch – $\frac{3}{8}$ inch) apart to form channels which are threaded with soft wool, known as quilting wool, to give a raised design on the front of the work.

The designs for Italian quilting should be linear and preferably continuous. The scroll patterns on wrought-iron work and the interlaced forms of Celtic decorative lettering are often suitable as the basis for designs.

Trapunto quilting

This is also worked on a top fabric and muslin backing but differs from Italian quilting in that the stitching is worked in single lines which completely encircle shapes which are then raised by padding them with a stuffing of soft wool or wadding.

Shadow quilting

This is a variation of both Italian and Trapunto quilting. The stitching is worked on a transparent fabric such as organdie or organza with a backing of a similar fabric

or muslin. The areas to be raised are stuffed and threaded with a coloured quilting wool or soft thick knitting wool.

Fabrics for all quilting

Because it is the design which is all-important in quilting rather than the stitches which are worked in a colour to match the fabric, the top cover fabric should be one which really shows the texture formed. For this reason if you are using satin, it should be the dull sort rather than the shiny surfaced one. Other suitable fabrics are fine silk, shantung, rayon, glazed cotton, fine wool, Viyellas, cotton poplin and closely woven linen.

Thread and needles

Pure silk thread in a colour to match the fabric is the most satisfactory, although cotton or fine linen thread can be used. For stitching use a No.7, 8, or 9 betweens needle, according to the weight of the fabric. For marking the design for English quilting, you will also need a yarn or rug needle. For threading the quilting wool in Italian quilting, you will need a large blunt needle, such as a tapestry needle.

The stitches

Running stitch is used for all methods of quilting except for English which is sewn in either back, running or chain stitch.

Working English quilting

In the past carded sheep's wool or cotton wadding was used for padding, but nowadays it is best to use nylon or Terylene wadding as these can be washed easily (cotton wadding tends to become lumpy

with wear and washing). The backing fabric can be muslin or soft cotton if you are lining the article separately, or a toning rayon lining fabric if a separate lining is not required.

1 Tack the layers together, sandwiching the padding between the top fabric and backing. Work a line of tacking across the centre of the fabric in both directions.

2 Mount the triple layer of fabric on to a traditional frame, with top fabric facing up.

3 Cut a template of the principal motif, keeping its size in proportion to the article. Place in position on the fabric, using the centre tacking lines as a guide.

4 To transfer the design to the fabric, mark round the edge of the template with a large needle held at an angle to the work. The point of the needle will leave an impression on the fabric which is easy to follow with running stitch.

5 Work the main areas of the design first in even running stitch. Start stitching with a small knot on the back of the work which buries itself in the wadding and finish with a small back stitch.

6 When the main areas have been worked, mark the filling background pattern with a flat ruler and yarn needle. Work along the lines in running stitch.

7 When all the quilting has been worked, take the work off the frame and finish the article as required. If you are making something like a bed cover or quilt, one of the best finishes is a piping in the same fabric as the top cover.

8 To attach the piping, make up the casing and enclose the cord in the standard way.

9 If you are having a separate lining, attach

the piping round the edges of the article on the right side and stitch through all layers. Cut the lining fabric to the required size and place it on the quilting with right sides together and edges matching. Stitch on the piping line, leaving an opening in one side. Turn right side out and close the opening with neat hemming.

10 If the lining is not separate, un-do the tacking joining the layers together and stitch the piping to the top cover and wadding only. Turn under the edges of the lining and slip-stitch neatly to the piping line.

Working Italian quilting

Traditionally the design was marked on the muslin backing and the stitching worked on this side. However, you may find it easier to keep the running stitches even if you work on the top fabric, in which case the design should be marked by the prick and pounce method (see Transferring designs earlier) and not by tracing or drawing which would still show when the work is finished.

1 Tack the fabric and backing round the edges and mount them as one on to a frame, with the working side facing up.

2 Trace your design on to the fabric and work along the double lines in running stitch. If you like, some parts of the design can be emphasised by working in chain or back stitch on the right side of the fabric instead of running stitch.

3 Thread a large blunt needle with the quilting wool and insert it along the channels formed by the double lines of stitching. Where there is an angle, break or intersection in the design, bring the wool to the surface on the muslin and reinsert the needle leaving a small loop. This allows for even tension and a small amount of shrinkage if the quilting is washed or dry cleaned.

Working Trapunto quilting

This is worked in a similar way to Italian quilting, with the main exception that the design is marked in single lines which enclose the area to be raised or padded. The method of padding, however, is different and also applies to shadow quilting.

1 When the stitching is complete, make an incision through the muslin into the areas to be stuffed, with a blunt needle, or knitting needle if the area is large.

2 Remove the top skin of wadding and tease the wadding into small amounts which can easily be inserted through the incision. The amount of stuffing you use depends on the effect your require.

3 When enough padding is inserted, close the opening with overcasting stitches before moving on to the next area.

Quilted cushion

This simple design for quilting can be modified and used to decorate various objects of home furnishings.

The directions are given for a pillow 40.5cm (16 inches) × 30.5cm (12 inches), but the quilting can be adapted for a larger pillow by spacing out the motifs or for a small square pillow by omitting the small leaf shapes.

Fabric required

0.70 metre (¾ yard) rayon kafka, or a not too shiny pure silk, or a dull satin, 91cm (36 inches) wide

You will also need

- ☐ 0.45 metre (½ yard) thin cotton fabric, 91cm (36 inches) wide for backing the quilting
- ☐ 0.45 metre (½ yard) synthetic wadding
- ☐ 1.60 metres (1¾ yards) cotton piping cord, no. 2 size
- ☐ 1 reel pure sewing silk to match the fabric
- ☐ 1 reel mercerized sewing cotton
- ☐ Tracing paper
- ☐ Thin white card for the templates
- ☐ 1 large fine-pointed darning needle
- ☐ Sewing needles (fine crewels or betweens) for quilting
- ☐ Cushion pad to fit pillowcase

Making the templates

1 Trace the heart and leaf motifs for the quilting on to the quilting paper.
2 Place the tracing on to the card, pin or stick in position and cut round.

Working the quilting

1 Cut the quilting fabric to the size of the finished pillow, plus 1.3cm (½ inch) all round for turnings. Cut the wadding and the cotton backing fabric to the same size.
2 Tack the three layers together, sandwiching the wadding between the fabrics.
3 Mark the centre lines of the fabric with tacking diagonally from corner to corner.
4 Mount the fabric into the embroidery frame (see Embroidery frames, earlier).
5 Lay the mounted fabric (in the frame) right side up on a folded blanket on a firm surface.
6 Position the heart template in the four positions as shown in the diagram. Holding the large needle at an angle, trace round the card shape firmly to leave a sharp impression on the fabric. Take care not to cut the fabric with the needle point if your fabric is thin. Trace round the leaf shape at each end of the cushion. Place the smaller shape inside the heart and trace round.
7 Start to quilt the fabric, using the matching silk and working in small even running stitch.
8 When the main motifs are complete, draw in the background diamond shapes using a ruler and large needle. Draw in the lines, working from each corner and keeping them 2cm (¾ inch) apart. Quilt along the lines.
9 When all the quilting is complete,

remove it from the frame and fasten off all ends neatly.

Making up the pillow case

1 From the surplus fabric, cut a piece the same size as the quilting for the back of the pillowcase and then cut bias strips 4cm (1½ *inches*) wide for the piping casing. Make up the piping casing.

2 Pin the piping in position round the edge of the quilting and tack. Place the two sides of the pillowcase together with right sides facing. Tack and machine stitch using the mercerized sewing cotton along the piping line. Leave one side of the pillowcase open and turn it right side out.

3 Insert a zip fastener into the open side and then insert the cushion pad, or insert the pad first and slip-stitch the sides of the opening together.

Travelling slippers and case
Fabric required

0.45 metre (½ *yard*) fabric for quilting, 91cm (36 *inches*) wide

0.45 metre (½ *yard*) cotton fabric, 91cm (36 *inches*) wide, for the backing

0.45 metre (½ *yard*) rayon lining fabric, 91cm (36 *inches*) wide

You will also need

☐ 0.45 metre (½ *yard*) synthetic wadding
☐ One pair of foam rubber inner soles in required size
☐ Felt, to cover foam soles
☐ PVC, to cover bottom of slippers
☐ Adhesive
☐ Quilting equipment as for pillowcase

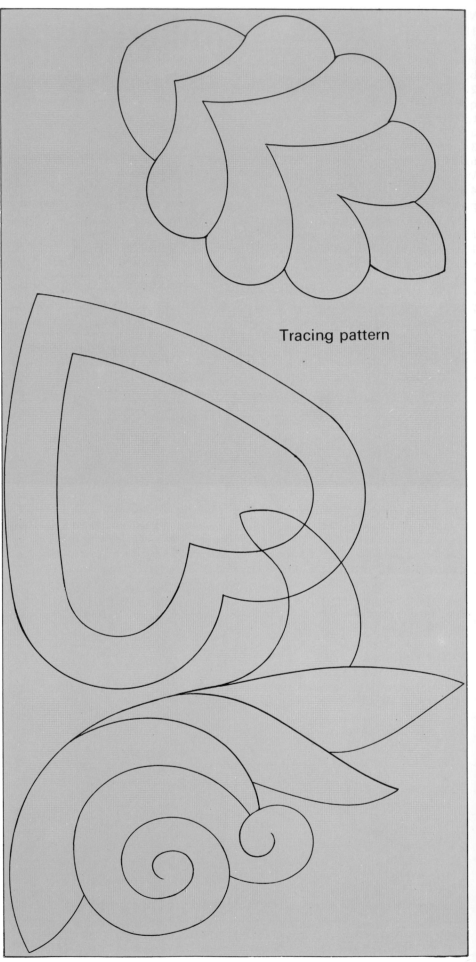

Tracing pattern

Working the quilting

1 Trace the shapes for the slipper fronts and case and tack the shapes on to the quilting fabric, allowing at least 2.5cm (1 inch) between each one.

2 Sandwich the wadding between the quilting fabric and cotton backing and tack the layers together. Mount them into an embroidery frame.

3 Mark the quilting shapes, using the leaf for the slippers and the scroll for the case. Work the quilting.

4 Mark the background diamond pattern, placing the lines 1.3cm ($\frac{1}{2}$ inch) apart.

Making up the slippers

1 Cut round the tacked shapes of the slippers, leaving 2.5cm (1 inch) for turnings. Cut out linings for the slippers to the same size.

2 Cut bias strips and make up piping about 12.5cm (5 inches) long for each slipper. Tack in place along each top edge. Place the lining on to the slipper front with right sides together and stitch close to the piping. Turn right side out and tack the lining and quilting together round the remaining edge.

3 Place the foam inner soles on to the felt and draw round, leaving 1.3cm ($\frac{1}{2}$ inch) turnings.

4 Clip into the turnings of the felt, place on to the foam inner soles and stick the turnings down on the underside.

5 Place the slipper fronts right side up on to the felt side of the soles, fold the turnings on to the underside and pin in position. Try on the slippers and adjust the size of the turnings if necessary. Stick in position with adhesive.

6 Cut out two shapes of the soles from the PVC and stick in position on the under-side to cover the raw edges of the quilting and felt.

Making up the slipper case

1 Cut out the lining to the same size as the quilting.

2 Place the quilting and lining together with right sides facing and tack and machine stitch along the top curved edge, taking 0.6cm ($\frac{1}{4}$ inch) turnings. Clip into the angle and turn right side out.

3 Tack along the top seam so that no lining shows on the quilted side of the case. Press.

4 Fold the case in half so that the curved edges match and the quilted side is inside. Tack and machine stitch down the side and bottom edge, taking 0.6cm ($\frac{1}{4}$ inch) turnings. Neaten the edges by overcasting or zig-zag stitching. Turn the finished case right side out.

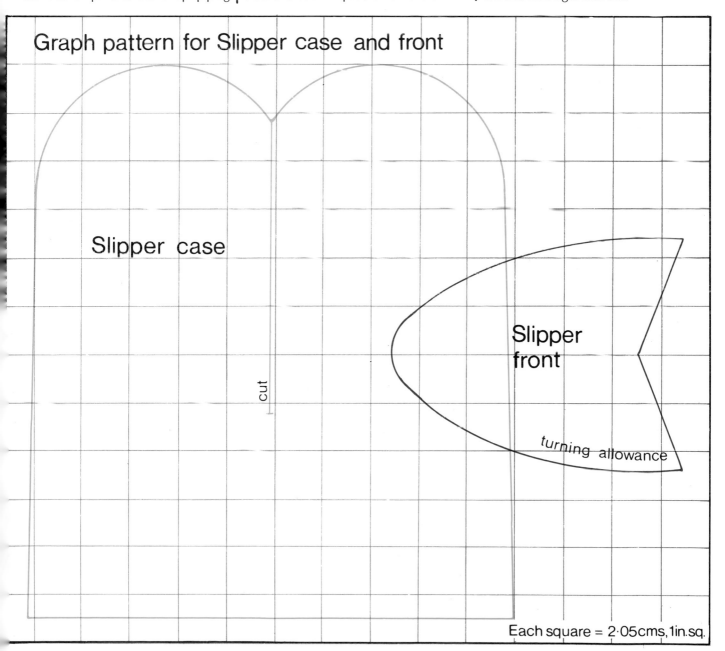

Graph pattern for Slipper case and front

Slipper case

cut

Slipper front

turning allowance

Each square = 2·05cms, 1in.sq.

QUILTING BY MACHINE

The cording foot and quilting

Most machines have a cording or braiding foot as an extra attachment. This foot guides a thick thread or cord under the needle. It can be straight stitched down the centre, zig-zagged or enclosed with satin stitch. This is an effective way of working solid shapes.

The shapes can be worked directly on to the article or on separate pieces of fabric which are then applied to give a more raised effect. The edges of the applied shapes can then be turned under and hem stitched so they are not visible or the application may become part of the design and can be satin stitched for instance, or concealed with free embroidery. Whichever of these methods you choose the shapes should be worked from the outside towards the centre or the shape may become distorted.

If the fabric is a fine one it will be necessary to back the shape with paper. Iron-on interfacing is excellent for dress embroidery providing the work does not have to drape.

A test sample should always be worked to make sure that the cord used is fine enough to be gripped firmly by the foot. A thicker cord might cause subsequent lines to be uneven and the groove on the underside of the foot, which allows for the passage of the thick thread, may catch on an adjacent line dislodging the work. However, if you wish to use a thicker cord, this difficulty can be overcome by changing to the presser foot after the first round has been completed. To make stitching easier use soft yarns which flatten under the presser foot. Textured yarns may be used and generally look best if a matching thread is used to attach them. In the absence of a good match use transparent thread on top and the nearest colour match in the spool.

Quilting can be used on its own or combined with areas of free embroidery or any other stitch effects already described. It can be worked in the usual way using the quilting foot and guide, and also in the frame making it possible to sew smaller and more intricate shapes. For the best effect the work should not be too tightly stretched in the frame and only a limited amount of wadding can be used to allow it to fit into the frame at all. For this reason it is better not to use a frame with the inner ring bound. If, with the thickness of the work, the machine tends to miss stitches, use the darning foot and work with looser tensions. Quilting by this method could provide a decorative yoke and hem, or collar and cuffs for a dress.

Cotton, Terylene or thin foam make good

fillers for quilting and the latter two have the advantage of being washable. Fine soft fabric should be used for the backing. Cotton lawn is excellent. Italian quilting is particularly attractive for garment embroidery. Two parallel lines of stitching are worked holding two fabrics together and thick wool is inserted by hand from the back between the fabrics. The distance between the two lines is governed by the thickness of the wool. If a fine fabric is used on top an attractive shadow effect is achieved. An openweave fabric should be used for the backing to facilitate the wool insertion.

Quilting may be worked in cable stitch in which case the design can be marked on tissue paper, tacked to and worked from the wrong side, then torn away. Alternatively, the design may be drawn with tailors chalk and worked from the right side by applying a fine embroidery thread with a zig-zag stitch.

Work from the centre of a design outwards allowing plenty of extra fabric for the seam allowances. Do not trim the edges of cut-out pattern sections until the quilting has been completed.

The flower-shaped motif shown is worked freely in the frame and the geometric motif is worked with the quilting foot. The design for the floral motif is marked on paper first and tacked to the wrong side of the fabric. Cable stitch is worked from the wrong side using a silky hand embroidery thread on the spool and sewing cotton through the needle.

Pure silk thread is used for the straight machining which is worked from the right side. The upper and lower tensions are balanced.

The quilted waistcoat

The pattern for the waistcoat, illustrated opposite, is ideal for a geometric quilted pattern. Adapt a similar pattern to fasten edge to edge at the centre-front and omit the interfacing. This waistcoat is lined in self fabric. The pattern pieces are cut in 2oz. washable quilting, the dart shapes are cut out and the edges overstitched together by hand. The lining is made up and the darts are worked on each remaining pattern piece. The quilting is then tacked very firmly on the wrong side of those pieces.

The embroidery is worked using the quilting foot. The thread and tensions used are the same as those described for the motifs.

When the embroidery is complete the waistcoat is made up according to the instructions with the pattern. Hooks and eyes may be sewn at centre-front if required.

A GUIDE TO FABRICS AND THREADS

As more people experiment all the time with ever-increasing number of materials available, the days when a particular embroidery method was worked only on one specific type of fabric are past, but this chart endeavours to give both traditional methods and threads and suggestions for progressive embroidery.

| Type of Embroidery | Traditional Use | | Contemporary Use | |
	Fabrics	Threads	Fabrics	Threads
Basic stitchery	Linen (samplers) Cotton	Linen Silk	Any type of material from hessian to organdie	Threads of wool, silk, cotton, tricel, nylon, chenille, cords, nylon string
Quilting Traditional English padding – carded sheep's wool, cotton wadding, or flannel	Fine silk Fine linen Dull satin Fine wool	Pure silk Fine linen, silk, Sylko Silk	Shantung satin, nylon, tricel, glazed cotton, poplin, Viyella, fine wool	Pure silk Pure silk Molnlycke (similar to Sylko) Pure silk Pure silk
English Padding now synthetic wadding	As above	As above	As above	As above
Italian (soft quilting wool for padding – Traditional method, coloured wool and heavy cord for articles not requiring laundering	As above	As above	As above	As above
Trapunto Padding traditionally quilting wool and wadding, now is synthetic wadding	As above	As above	As above	As above

Counted thread Embroidery	Traditional Method Fabrics	Threads	Contemporary Method Fabrics	Threads
Drawn (or pulled) fabric	Linen of various weights with matching threads (even weave)		Cotton, wool, linen, synthetic even-weave fabrics	Coton perlé Coton à broder Wool and linen
Drawn thread	As above		As above	As above
Blackwork	As above		As above	As above
Hardanger Hedebo Assisi Cross stitch	Even-weave cotton and linen		As above, plus wool tweed, hessian, flannel, many linen, cotton and rayon dress fabrics	Variety of threads in cotton, silk, wool to contrast in weight and texture
Canvas work Florentine	Single and double canvas and linen worked with crewel wool		Hessian, single and double canvas and linen	Crewel wools, knitting wools, stranded cotton, silk and crochet threads
Shadow work	Traditionally worked in fine white threads on translucent white material, organdie and muslin		White and coloured organdie, organza, chiffon, nylon	Pure silk, sewing silk for applied areas. Silk, wool and stranded cotton for shadow embroidery
Smocking	Muslin, fine cotton, georgette, crepe de chine, silk, fine wool and chiffon, fine linen	Silk, cotton and linen threads (threads generally should be slightly heavier than fabric)	Chiffon, cotton, wool synthetics, some types P.V.C. needlecord, flannel and dress tweed	Crochet cotton, knitting wools, Raffene, silk, buttonhole twist, linen embroidery threads
Ayrshire work and Broderie Anglaise, (white work)	Fine linen, linen lawn fine cotton, muslin, organdie (always white)	Matching fine threads in cotton and linen (cotton floche and coton à broder)	Cotton, organdie, linen lawn, Swiss cotton and muslin organza	Matching threads in cotton, silk and linen
Cutwork Simple (stranded cotton is unsuitable for working threads)	White or natural linen with matching threads of linen, cotton or mercerised threads		Coloured linen, strong cotton, dress tweed, furnishing fabrics if firm woven	Matching threads (in linen and cotton)
Renaissance embroidery	As above		As above	As above
Richelieu embroidery	As above		As above	Also fine crochet threads
Reticella embroidery	As above		As above	As above
Needleweaving	Loosley woven linen, linen crash huckaback, furnishing fabrics	Threads should be slightly thicker than withdrawn thread	Hessian, canvas, heavy linens, linen scrim, dress tweeds	Linen thread of different sizes

A DICTIONARY OF STITCHES

This alphabet of free style embroidery stitches includes outline, flat, looped, chained, knotted, couching, filling and composite stitches. Diagrams and step-by-step instructions make the alphabet a useful source of reference material for both a beginner and the more experienced embroiderer.

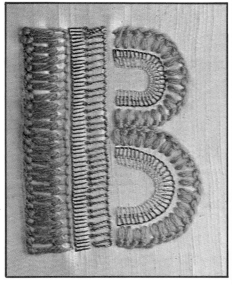

Back stitch

Bring the thread through on the stitch line, then take a small backward stitch through the fabric. Bring the needle through again a little in front of the first stitch and take another stitch, inserting the needle at the point where it first came through.

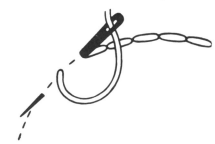

Blanket stitch and buttonhole stitch

These stitches are worked in the same way – the difference being that in buttonhole stitch the stitches are close together. Bring the thread out on the lower line, insert the needle in position in the upper line, taking a straight downward stitch with the thread under the needle point.
Pull up the stitch to form a loop and repeat.

This stitch may also be worked on even-weave fabric.

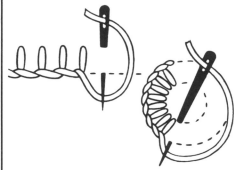

Bokhara couching

This stitch is useful and ornamental for filling in shapes of leaves and petals of flowers. It is worked in the same way as Roumanian stitch, but the small tying stitches are set at regular intervals over the laid thread to form pattern lines across the shape. The tying stitches should be pulled tight, leaving the laid thread slightly loose between.

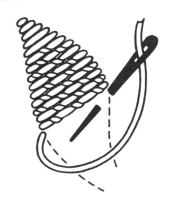

Bullion stitch

Pick up a back stitch, the size of the bullion stitch required, bring the needle point out where it first emerged. Do not pull the needle right through the fabric. Twist the thread round the needle point as many times as required to equal the space of the

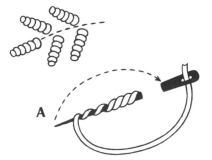

back stitch. Hold the left thumb on the coiled thread and pull the needle through; still holding the coiled thread, turn the needle back to where it was inserted (see arrow) and insert in the same place (A). Pull the thread through until the bullion stitch lies flat. Use a needle with a small eye to allow the thread to pass through the coils easily.

Buttonhole stitch bars and double buttonhole stitch bars

These bars are used in cut-work and Richelieu work. Make a row of running stitch between the double lines of the design as a padding for the buttonhole stitch. Where a single line bar occurs, take a thread across the space and back, securing with a small stitch and buttonhole stitch picking up any of the fabric (A). Buttonhole stitch round the shape, keeping the looped edge of the stitch to the inside, then cut away the fabric from behind the bar and round the inside of the shape. Where a double line or a broad bar is required between shapes or for stems of flowers, when the fabric is to be cut away on each side, make a row of running stitch along one side, spacing the stitches slightly. Buttonhole stitch along the other side into the spaces left by the first row. The fabric is then cut away close to the buttonhole stitch, leaving a strong, broad bar (B).

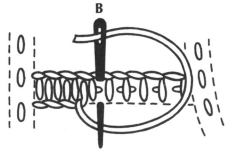

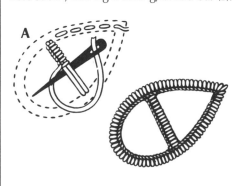

Buttonhole insertion stitch

This insertion stitch consists of groups of four buttonhole stitches worked alternately on each piece of fabric to be joined. The upper row is worked as in ordinary buttonhole stitch. The diagram shows the method of working the groups on the lower row.

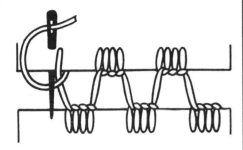

Buttonhole stitch and picot

Work as for ordinary buttonhole stitch until a picot is required, then hold the thread down with the left thumb and twist the needle three times round the thread (A). Still holding the thread securely, pull the working thread until the twisted threads are close to the buttonhole stitch, then make a buttonhole stitch into the last loop (B).

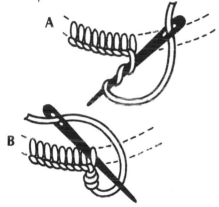

Cable stitch

This stitch is worked from left to right. Bring the thread through on the line of the design. Insert the needle a little to the right on the line and bring the needle out to the left midway between the length of the stitch, with the thread below the needle (Figure A). Work the next stitch in the same way but with the thread above the needle. Continue in this way, alternating the position of the thread. This stitch may also be worked on evenweave fabric (Figure B).

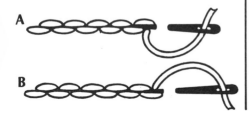

Cable chain stitch

Bring the thread through at A and hold it down with the left thumb. Pass the needle from right to left under the working thread, then twist the needle back over the working thread to the right and, still keeping the thread under the thumb, take a stitch of the required length. Pull the thread through.

Chain stitch

Bring the thread out at the top of the line and hold down with left thumb. Insert the needle where it last emerged and bring the point out a short distance away. Pull the thread through, keeping the working thread under the needle point.

Chained feather stitch

Working between two parallel lines, bring the thread through at A and make a slanting chain stitch, tying down the stitch at B. Take a second slanting chain stitch from the right at C, tying it down at D. The tying stitches must form a regular zig-zag pattern.

Chequered chain stitch

This stitch is worked in the same way as chain stitch, but with two contrasting threads in the needle at the same time. When making the loops, pass one colour under the needle point and let the other colour lie on top. Pull through both threads. Work the next loop with the other colour under the needle point.

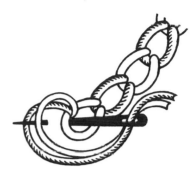

Chevron stitch

Bring the thread through on the lower line at the left side, insert the needle a little to the right on the same line and take a small stitch to the left, emerging halfway between the stitch being made. Next, insert the needle on the upper line a little to the right and take a small stitch to the left as at A. Insert the needle again on the same line a little to the right and take a small stitch to the left, emerging at the centre as at B. Work in this way alternately on the upper and lower lines. This stitch may also be worked on evenweave fabric.

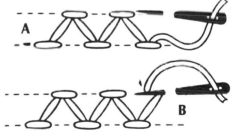

Closed buttonhole stitch

The stitches are made in pairs forming triangles. Bring the thread through at A, insert the needle at B and, with the thread under the needle, bring it through at C. Insert the needle again at B and bring it through at D. This stitch may also be worked on evenweave fabric.

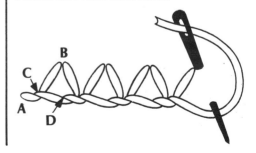

Closed feather stitch

This stitch is worked along two parallel lines. Bring the thread through at A and with the thread under the needle, take a stitch from B to C. Swing the thread over to the left and, with the thread under the needle, take a stitch from D to E. Repeat these two stitches.

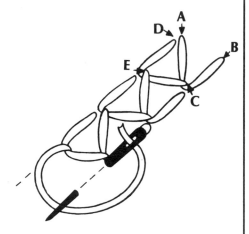

Coral stitch

Bring the thread out at the right end of the line, lay the thread along the line of the design and hold it down with the left thumb. Take a small stitch under the line and the thread and pull through, bringing the needle over the lower thread as in the diagram.

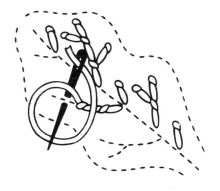

Couching

Lay a thread along the line of the design and, with another thread, tie it down at even intervals with a small stitch into the fabric. The tying stitch can be in a colour which contrasts with the laid thread if desired.

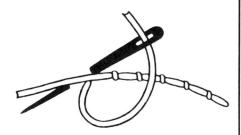

Cretan stitch

Bring the needle through centrally at the left-hand side, taking a small stitch on the lower line, needle pointing inwards and with thread under the needle point, as shown at A. Take a stitch on the upper line and thread under the needle as shown at B. Continue in this way until shape is filled.

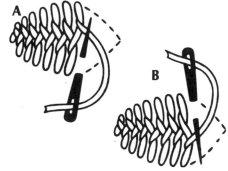

Cross stitch

Bring the needle through on the lower right line of the cross and insert at the top of the same line, taking a stitch through the fabric to the lower left line (Figure A). Con-

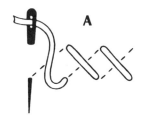

tinue to the end of the row in this way. Complete the other half of the cross (Figure B). It is important that the upper half of each stitch lies in the same direction.

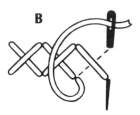

Double back stitch or closed herringbone stitch

This stitch is used for shadow work on fine, transparent fabric and can be worked on the right side of the fabric as at A – a small back stitch worked alternatively on each side of the traced double lines (the dotted lines on the diagram show the formation of the thread on the wrong side of the

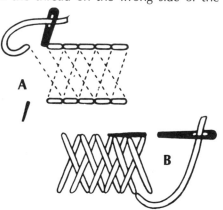

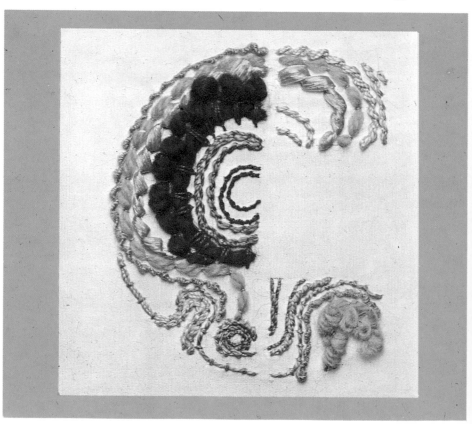

fabric). The colour of the thread appears delicately through the fabric. Figure B shows the stitch worked on the wrong side of the fabric as a closed herringbone stitch with no spaces left between the stitches. Both methods achieve the same result.

Daisy or detached chain stitch

Work in the same way as chain stitch (A), but fasten each loop at the foot with a small stitch (B). Daisy stitch may be worked singly or in groups to form flower petals.

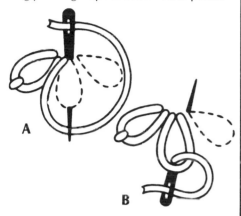

Double knot stitch

Bring the thread through at A. Take a small stitch across the line at B. Pass the needle downwards under the surface stitch just made, without piercing the fabric, as at C. With the thread under the needle, pass the needle again under the first stitch at D. Pull the thread through to

form a knot. The knots should be spaced evenly and closely to obtain a beaded effect.

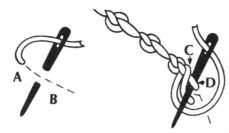

Eyelet holes

Figure A. Work a row of small running stitches round the circle. Pierce the centre with a stiletto and fold back the ragged edge. Closely overcast the folded edge with running stitch. Trim away any ragged edges at the back. Figure B shows the appearance of the finished eyelet hole. Instead of piercing with a stiletto, larger circles or longer eyelet holes may be cut across the centre both ways and the cut ends folded back.

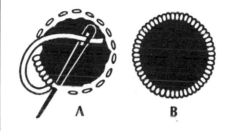

Feather stitch

Figure A. Bring the needle out at the top centre, hold the thread down with the left thumb, insert the needle a little to the right on the same level and take a small stitch down to the centre, keeping the thread under the needle point. Next, insert the needle a little to the left on the same level and take a stitch to centre, keeping the thread under the needle point. Work these two movements alternately. Figure B shows double feather stitch, in which two stitches are taken to the right and left alternately.

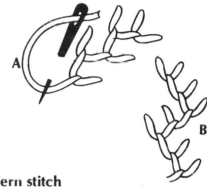

Fern stitch

This stitch consists of three straight stitches of equal length radiating from the same central point, A. Bring the thread through at A and make a straight stitch to B. Bring the thread through again at A and make another straight stitch to C. Repeat once more to D and bring the thread through at E to commence the next three radiating stitches. The central stitch follows the line of the design. This stitch may also be worked on evenweave fabric.

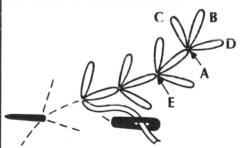

Fishbone stitch

This stitch is useful for filling small shapes. Bring the thread through at A and make a small straight stitch along the centre line of the shape. Bring the thread through

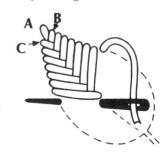

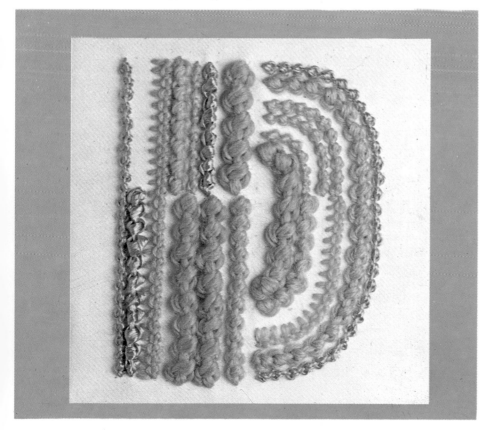

again at B and make a sloping stitch across the central line at the base of the first stitch. Bring the thread through at C and make a similar sloping stitch to overlap the previous stitch. Continue working alternately on each side until the shape is filled.

Flat stitch
Take a small stitch alternately on each side of the shape to be filled, with the point of the needle always emerging on the outside line of the shape. Two lines may be drawn down the centre of the shape as a guide for the size of the stitch. The stitches should be close together and fold into one another.

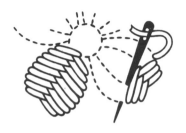

Fly stitch
Bring the thread through at the top left, hold it down with the left thumb, insert the needle to the right on the same level, a little distance from where the thread first emerged and take a small stitch downwards to the centre with the thread below the needle. Pull through and insert the needle again below the stitch at the centre (A) and bring it through in position for the next stitch. This stitch may be worked singly or in horizontal rows (A) or vertically (B).

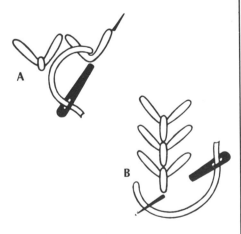

French knots
Bring the thread out at the required position, hold it down with the left thumb and encircle the thread twice with the needle as at A. Still holding the thread firmly, twist the needle back to the starting point and insert it close to where the thread first emerged (see arrow). Pull the

thread through to the back and secure for a single French knot or pass on to the position of the next stitch as at B.

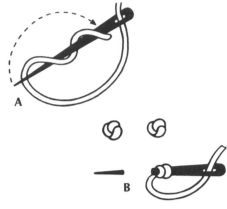

Heavy chain stitch
Bring the thread through at A and make a small vertical stitch. Bring the thread through again at B and pass the needle under the vertical stitch, without piercing the fabric, and insert it again at B. Bring the thread through at C and again pass the needle under the vertical stitch and insert

it at C. The third and all following stitches are made in exactly the same way, except that the needle always passes under the two preceding loops.

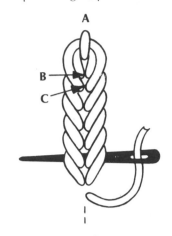

Herringbone stitch
Bring the needle out on the lower line at the left side and insert on the upper line a little to the right, taking a small stitch to the left with the thread below the needle. Next, insert the needle on the lower line

a little to the right and take a small stitch to the left with the thread above the needle. These two movements are worked throughout. For the best effect, the fabric lifted by the needle and the space between the stitches should be of equal size. This stitch can be laced with a matching or contrasting thread. Use a round pointed needle for lacing and do not pick up any of the fabric. Herringbone stitch may also be worked on evenweave fabric.

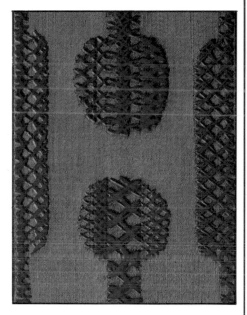

Interlaced band

This stitch is composed of two rows of back stitch with an interlacing. Work two parallel rows of back stitch (as shown at the top of the diagram) having the rows approximately 1.5–2.0cm ($\frac{1}{2}$–$\frac{3}{4}$ inch) apart, with the stitches worked as on the diagram, i.e., the end of one stitch is directly in line with the centre of the opposite stitch. Bring a matching or contrasting thread through at A and, follow the diagram, interlace it through every stitch.

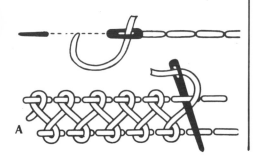

Interlacing stitch

The foundation of the border stitch is a double row of herringbone stitch worked in two journeys, with the stitches intertwined in a certain way. The first row of herringbone stitch is shown in medium tone on the diagram. In working the rows of herringbone stitch for the interlacing, there is a slight change in the usual method. In the top stitch the needle is passed under the working thread in each case instead of over it, and attention should be paid to the alternate crossing of the threads when working the second row. Do not work this foundation tightly, as the interlacing thread tends to draw the stitches together. When the rows of herringbone stitch are worked, bring the thread for the surface interlacing through at A and follow the diagram closely. When the end of the row is reached, lace the thread round the last cross in the centre and work back in a similar fashion along the lower half of the foundation. The last two crosses on the diagram have been left unlaced so that the construction of the herringbone stitch may be seen clearly.

Jacobean couching or trellis

This stitch makes an attractive filling stitch for the centres of flowers or shapes where an open effect is required. It consists of long evenly spaced stitches (laid threads) taken across the space horizontally and vertically (A) or diagonally (B). The crossed threads are then tied down at all intersecting points. The tying or couching stitch can be a small slanting stitch or cross stitch.

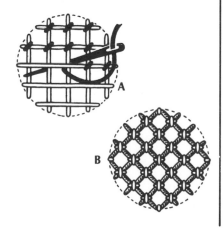

Knot stitch edging or Antwerp edging

Bring the thread through from the back of the fabric and work a single buttonhole stitch. Pass the needle behind the loop of the stitch and over the working thread as shown in the diagram. Space the stitches about 0.5cm ($\frac{1}{4}$ inch) apart. This edging is very useful for handkerchiefs or lingerie. Several rows, using a different colour for each row, make a lacy edging. The stitches of the second and following rows are worked over the loops between the stitches of the previous row.

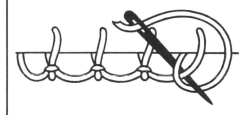

Knotted buttonhole stitch

Make a loop from right to left over the left thumb. Insert the needle, point upwards, under the loop as at A. Slip the loop onto the needle and, with the loop still round the needle, take a stitch into the fabric as at B. Before drawing the needle through, tighten the loop round the head of the needle by pulling the working thread.

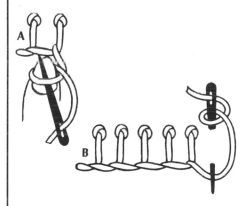

Knotted buttonhole filling stitch

Make an outline of back stitch or close running stitches, then work the detached filling as shown in the diagram. The link with the edging stitches is exaggeratedly large for clarity.

Knotted cable chain stitch

This stitch is worked from right to left. Bring the thread through at A and place it along the line of the design; then, with the thread under the needle, take a stitch at B, which is a coral knot. Then pass the needle under the stitch between A and B without piercing the fabric, as shown at C. With the thread under the needle, take a slanting stitch across the line at D, close to the coral knot. Pull the thread through to form a chain stitch.

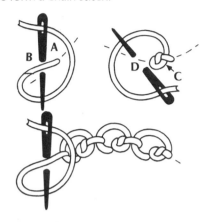

Knotted insertion stitch

This stitch is similar to knot stitch (or Antwerp stitch) edging, except that the stitches are made alternately on each piece of fabric to the joined. A small buttonhole stitch is worked into the edge of the fabric and a second stitch worked over the loops as shown in the figure.

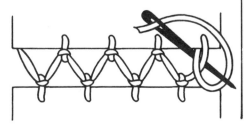

Laced running stitch

Running stitch can be laced with a contrasting colour to form a decorative border. Use a round pointed needle for lacing and do not pick up any of the fabric.

Ladder stitch

This stitch may be used to fill shapes of varying widths, but it is shown worked between parallel lines. Bring the thread through at A, insert the needle at B and bring it out at C. Insert the needle again at D and bring out at E. Pass the needle under the first stitch at F and through the double stitch at G. Continue in this way, the needle passing under two stitches at each side to form the plaited edge.

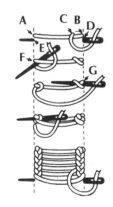

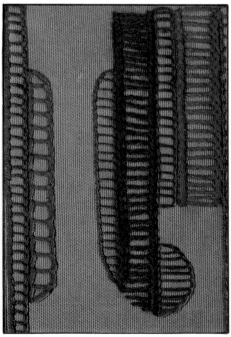

Leaf stitch

Bring the thread through at A and make a sloping stitch to B. Bring the thread through at C and make a sloping stitch to D. Bring the thread through at E, then continue working alternate stitches on each side in this way until the shape is lightly filled. This stitch is generally finished with an outline worked in stem stitch or chain stitch.

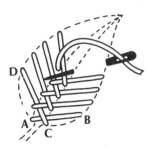

Long and short stitch

This form of satin stitch is so named because all the stitches are of varying lengths. It is often used to fill a shape which is too large or too irregular to be covered by ordinary satin stitch. It is also used to achieve a shaded effect. In the first row the stitches are alternately long and short and closely follow the outline of the shape. The stitches in the following rows are worked to achieve a smooth appearance. The figure shows how a shaded effect may be obtained.

Loop stitch

This stitch is worked from right to left. Bring the thread through at A and insert the needle at B. Bring it though again at C immediately below B. With the thread to the left and under the needle, pass the needle under the first stitch without piercing the fabric.

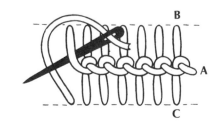

Maltese cross

This decorative motif is worked in a similar way to interlacing stitch. The intertwining of the herringbone stitch must be worked accurately, otherwise the interlacing cannot be achieved. Bring the thread through at A and take a stitch from B to C. Carry the thread from C to D and take a stitch from D to E. Continue in this way following Figure 1 until the foundation is complete. Figure 2 shows the method of interlacing, which commences at F. Figure 3 shows the complete motif.

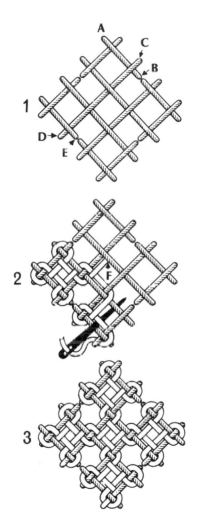

Open chain stitch

This stitch is shown worked on two parallel lines, but it may be used for shapes which vary in width. Bring the thread through at A and, holding the thread down with the

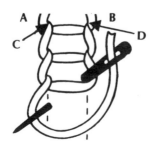

left thumb, insert the needle at B. Bring the needle through at C, the required depth of the stitch. Leave the loop thus formed slightly loose. Insert the needle at D and, with the thread under the needle point, bring it through in readiness for the next stitch. Secure the last loop with a small stitch at each side.

Open Cretan stitch

Bring the thread through at A and, with the thread above the needle, insert the needle at B and bring it through at C. With the thread below the needle, insert the needle at D and bring it through at E. All stitches lie at right angles to the guiding lines as shown in the diagram and are spaced at regular intervals. This is a useful stitch for borders.

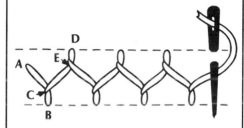

Open fishbone stitch

Bring the thread through at A and make a sloping stitch to B. Bring the thread through again at C and make another sloping stitch to D. Bring the thread through at F, continue in this way until the shape is filled.

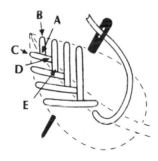

Overcast stitch (or trailing)

Bring the laid threads through at A and hold with the left thumb, then bring through the working thread at A and work small satin stitches closely over the laid threads, following the line of the design.

The laid threads are taken through to the back of the fabric to finish. This stitch resembles a fine cord and is useful for embroidering delicate stems and outlines.

Pekinese stitch

Work back stitch in the usual way, then interlace with a thread to tone or a thread of a different colour. The stitch is shown open in the diagram but the loops should be pulled slightly tighter when working.

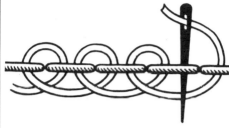

Portuguese border stitch

Work the required number of foundation bars, which are evenly spaced horizontal straight stitches. Bring the thread through at A, with the working thread to the left of the needle. Carry it over and under the first two bars and under the second bar only without piercing the fabric. The thread is now in position at B to commence the second pair of stitches. Continue working in the same way to the top of the row. Bring a new thread through at C and proceed in exactly the same way, but with the working thread to the right of the needle. Do not pull the surface stitches tightly.

Portuguese stem stitch

Figure A, begin as for ordinary stem stitch. Figure B, pull the thread through and pass the needle under the stitch just made, without entering the fabric. Figure C, pass the needle under the same stitch below the first coil. Figure D, make another stem stitch. Figure E, pass the needle twice under the stitch just made and under the previous stitch. Figure F, a section showing the formation of the stitch.

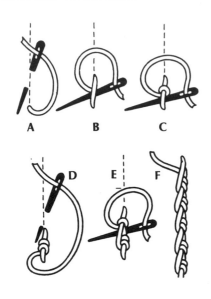

Punch stitch

This stitch can be used as a filling stitch in free embroidery – that is, over a tracing of squares or spots. A punch needle is used for the traced design to make the holes. The stitches are pulled firmly. Bring the thread through and take a stitch directly above, bringing the needle out where the thread first emerged (A). Insert the needle into the same hole above and bring out the same distance to the left on the lower line (B). Work along the row in this way, two stitches into the same place in each case (C). Turn the work upside down for each following row and continue in the same way until all vertical rows are complete (D). Turn the work sideways and repeat the process to complete the squares (E).

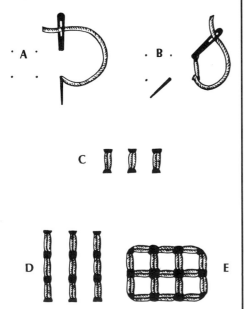

Raised chain band

Work the required number of foundation bars, which are fairly closely spaced horizontal straight stitches. Bring the thread through at A, then pass the needle upwards under the centre of the first bar and to the left of A. With the thread under the needle, pass the needle downwards to the right of A and pull up the chain loop thus formed.

Rosette chain stitch

Bring the thread through at the right end of the upper line, pass the thread across to the left side and hold down with the left thumb. Insert the needle into the upper line a short distance from where the thread emerged and bring it out just above the lower line, passing the thread under the needle point (A). Draw the needle through and then pass the needle under the top thread (B) without picking up any of the fabric. This stitch can be used for small flowers if worked round in a circle or for borders when worked straight.

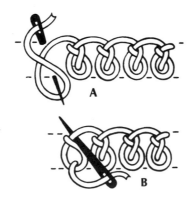

Roumanian couching

This form of couching is useful for filling in large spaces in which a flat, indefinate background is required. Bring the thread through on the left, carry the thread across the space to be filled and take a

small stitch on the right with the thread above the needle (A). Take small stitches along the line at intervals, as in B and C, to the end of the laid thread, emerging in position for the next stitch (D).

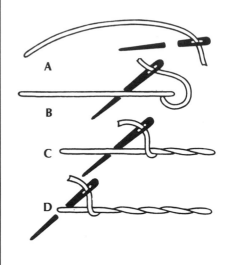

Roumanian stitch

Figure A, bring the thread through at the top left of the shape, carry the thread across and take a stitch on the right side of the shape with the thread below the needle. Figure B, take a stitch at the left side, thread above the needle. These two movements are worked until the shape is filled. Keep the stitches close together. The size of the centre crossing stitch can be varied to make a longer oblique stitch or a small straight stitch.

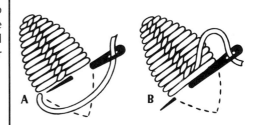

Running stitch

Pass the needle over and under the fabric, making the upper stitches of equal length. The under stitches should also be of equal length, but half the size or less of the upper stitches.

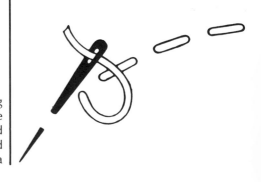

Satin stitch

Proceed with straight stitches worked closely together across the shape, as shown in the diagram. If desired, running stitch or chain stitch may be worked first to form a padding underneath; this gives a raised effect. Care must be taken to keep a good edge. Do not make the stitches too long, as this makes them liable to be pulled out of position. To keep a neat edge outline the shape first in chain or split stitch.

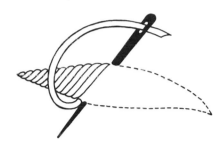

Scroll stitch

This stitch is worked from left to right. The working thread is looped to the right then back to the left on the fabric. Inside this loop the needle takes a small slanting stitch to the left under the line of the design, with the thread of the loop under the needle point. The thread is then pulled through. The stitches should be evenly spaced. This stitch forms an attractive border.

Seeding

This simple filling stitch is composed of small straight stitches of equal length placed at random over the surface, as shown in the figure.

Sheaf stitch

This is an attractive filling stitch consisting of three vertical satin stitches tied across the centre with two horizontal overcasting stitches. The overcasting stitches are worked round the satin stitches; the needle only enters the fabric to pass on to the next sheaf. The sheaves may be worked in alternate rows as shown, or in close horizontal rows directly below each other.

Spanish knotted feather stitch

Bring the thread through and hold down to the left with the left thumb. Take a slanting stitch to the left through the fabric under the laid thread and pull through with the needle point over the working thread as shown at A. Pass the thread over to the right and back to the left to form a loop and hold down, then take a slanting stitch to the right under the laid thread and pull through with the needle over the working thread B. Take a stitch in the same way to the left C. Repeat B and C to the end of the line, then fasten off with a small stitch as shown at D.

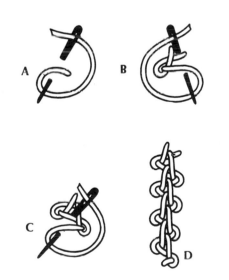

Spider's web filling

Commence with a fly stitch to the centre of the circle as shown in A. Then work two straight stitches, one on each side of the fly stitch tail, into the centre of the circle. This divides the circle into five equal sections and the 'spokes' form the foundation of the web. Weave over and under the 'spokes' until the circle is filled as at B. In drawn thread embroidery the 'spokes' are not completely covered by the weaving; only half the circle is filled, which gives the filling an open, lacy appearance.

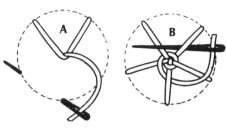

Split stitch

Bring the thread through at A and make a small stitch over the line of the design, piercing the working thread with the needle as shown in the figure. Split stitch may be used as a filling where a fine flat surface is required.

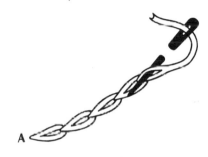

Stem stitch

Work from left to right, taking regular, slightly slanting, stitches along the line of the design. The thread always emerges on the left side of the previous stitch. This stitch is used for flower stems, outlines, etc. It can also be used as a filling, where rows of stem stitch are worked closely together within a shape until it is filled completely.

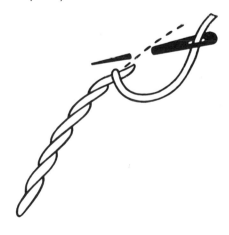

Straight stitch or single satin stitch

This is shown as single spaced stitches worked either in a regular or irregular manner. Sometimes the stitches are of varying size. The stitches should be neither too long nor too loose. This stitch may also be worked on evenweave fabric.

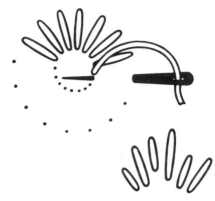

Striped woven band

Work the required number of foundation bars which are evenly spaced horizontal straight stitches. Thread two needles with contrasting threads and bring them through the fabric to lie side by side at A, the light thread on the left side. Pass the light thread under the first straight stitch and leave it lying. Take the dark thread over the first straight stitch and under the second straight stitch and also under the light thread. Leave the dark thread lying and pass the light thread over the second straight stitch, under the third straight stitch and also under the dark thread. Continue to the end of the border. Begin each following row from the top. By altering the sequence of the contrasting threads, various patterns may be achieved.

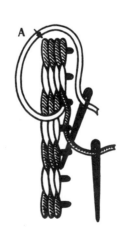

Twisted chain stitch

Commence as for ordinary chain stitch, but instead of inserting the needle into the place from where it emerged, insert it close to the last loop and take a small slanting stitch, coming out on the line of the design. Pull the thread through. The loops of this stitch should be worked closely together to give the correct effect.

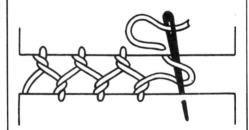

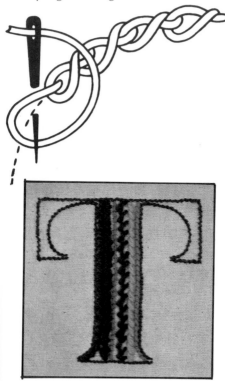

Twisted insertion stitch

A small stitch is taken alternately on each piece of fabric to be joined. The needle always enters the fabric from beneath and is twisted once round the thread before entering the fabric for the opposite stitch.

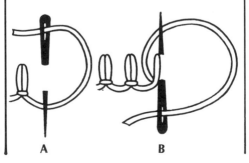

Up and down buttonhole stitch

Figure A. Commence as for ordinary buttonhole stitch and pull thread through. Figure B. Insert the needle on the bottom line and take a straight upward stitch with the thread under the needle point. Pull the thread through first in an upward move-

A   B

ment, then downwards to continue. This stitch may also be worked on evenweave fabric.

Vandyke stitch

Bring the thread through at A. Take a small horizontal stitch at B and insert the needle at C. Bring the thread through at D. Without piercing the fabric, pass the needle under the crossed threads at B and insert at E. Do not pull the stitches too tightly, otherwise the regularity of the centre plait will be lost.

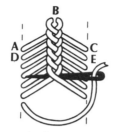

Wheatear stitch

Work two straight stitches at A and B. Bring the thread through below these stitches at C and pass the needle under the two straight stitches without entering the fabric. Insert the needle at C and bring it through at D.

Zigzag cable chain stitch

This stitch is a variation of ordinary cable chain stitch, each stitch being taken at a right angle to the previous stitch. Pull the twisted thread firmly round the needle before drawing the needle through the fabric.